French Verbs For Dummies®

Personal Pronouns

Subject Pronoun Classification	Singular	Plural
First Person	**je** (*I*)	**nous** (*we*)
Second Person	**tu** (*you*, informal)	**vous** (*you*, formal)
Third Person	**il** (*he/it*), **elle** (*she/it*), **on** (*one*)	**ils** (*they*, masculine), **elles** (*they*, feminine)

Conjugating the Five Simple Tenses of Regular Verbs

Check out the conjugations of three common regular verbs in the five simple tenses. **Parler** (*to speak*) serves as the **-er** verb example, **finir** (*to finish*) as the **-ir** verb example, and **vendre** (*to sell*) as the **-re** verb example. Just take the appropriate stem for each tense and add the desired ending.

Regular -er Verb Endings

Tense (stem)	je	tu	il/elle/on	nous	vous	ils/elles
Present (parl)	-e	-es	-e	-ons	-ez	-ent
Imperfect (parl)	-ais	-ais	-ait	-ions	-iez	-aient
Future (parler)	-ai	-as	-a	-ons	-ez	-ont
Conditional (parler)	-ais	-ais	-ait	-ions	-iez	-aient
Subjunctive (parl)	-e	-es	-e	-ions	-iez	-ent

Regular -ir Verb Endings

Tense (stem)	je	tu	il/elle/on	nous	vous	ils/elles
Present (fini)	-s	-s	-t	-ssons	-ssez	-ssent
Imperfect (finiss)	-ais	-ais	-ait	-ions	-iez	-aient
Future (finir)	-ai	-as	-a	-ons	-ez	-ont
Conditional (finir)	-ais	-ais	-ait	-ions	-iez	-aient
Subjunctive (finiss)	-e	-es	-e	-ions	-iez	-ent

Regular -re Verb Endings

Tense (stem)	je	tu	il/elle/on	nous	vous	ils/elles
Present (vend)	-s	-s	(nothing)	-ons	-ez	-ent
Imperfect (vend)	-ais	-ais	-ait	-ions	-iez	-aient
Future (vendr)	-ai	-as	-a	-ons	-ez	-ont
Conditional (vendr)	-ais	-ais	-ait	-ions	-iez	-aient
Subjunctive (vend)	-e	-es	-e	-ions	-iez	-ent

French Verbs For Dummies®

Cheat Sheet

Conjugating Five Compound Tenses of Regular Verbs

In French compound tenses, most verbs take the auxiliary verb **avoir,** and some verbs take the auxiliary verb **être.** These auxiliary verbs accompany the past participle of the verb in question. In the tables below, I use the past participles of **parler** (*to speak*), which takes the auxiliary **avoir,** and **arriver** (*to arrive*), which takes the auxiliary **être** as examples. You can substitute the past participle of other verbs as necessary.

Creating Compound Tenses with the Auxiliary Avoir (Parler)

Tense	je	tu	il/elle/on	nous	vous	ils/elles
Passé Composé	ai parlé	as parlé	a parlé	avons parlé	avez parlé	ont parlé
Pluperfect	avais parlé	avais parlé	avait parlé	avions parlé	aviez parlé	avaient parlé
Future Perfect	aurai parlé	auras parlé	aura parlé	aurons parlé	aurez parlé	auront parlé
Past Conditional	aurais parlé	aurais parlé	aurait parlé	aurions parlé	auriez parlé	auraient parlé
Past Subjunctive	aie parlé	aies parlé	ait parlé	ayons parlé	ayez parlé	aient parlé

Creating Compound Tenses with the Auxiliary Être (Arriver)

Tense	je	tu	il/elle/on	nous	vous	ils/elles
Passé Composé	suis arrivé (e)	es arrivé (e)	est arrivé (e)	sommes arrivés (es)	êtes arrivé (e) (s) (es)	sont arrivés (es)
Pluperfect	étais arrivé (e)	étais arrivé (e)	était arrivé (e)	étions arrivés (es)	étiez arrivé (e) (s) (es)	étaient arrivés (es)
Future Perfect	serai arrivé (e)	seras arrivé (e)	sera arrivé (e)	serons arrivés (es)	serez arrivé (e) (s) (es)	seront arrivés (es)
Past Conditional	serais arrivé (e)	serais arrivé (e)	serait arrivé (e)	serions arrivés (es)	seriez arrivé (e) (s) (es)	seraient arrivés (es)
Past Subjunctive	sois arrivé (e)	sois arrivé (e)	soit arrivé (e)	soyons arrivés (es)	soyez arrivé (e) (s) (es)	soient arrivés (es)

Imperative Forms of Regular Verbs

Parler (to speak)	Finir (to finish)	Vendre (to sell)	Se laver (to wash)
Parle!	Finis!	Vends!	Lave-toi!
Parlons!	Finissons!	Vendons!	Lavons-nous!
Parlez!	Finissez!	Vendez!	Lavez-vous!

For Dummies: Bestselling Book Series for Beginners

French Verbs

FOR

DUMMIES®

French Verbs

FOR

DUMMIES®

by Zoe Erotopoulos, PhD
Professor of French at Fairfield University

WILEY

Wiley Publishing, Inc.

French Verbs For Dummies®

Published by
Wiley Publishing, Inc.
111 River St.
Hoboken, NJ 07030-5774
www.wiley.com

For general information on our other products and services, please contact our Customer Care Department within the U.S. at 800-762-2974, outside the U.S. at 317-572-3993, or fax 317-572-4002.

For technical support, please visit www.wiley.com/techsupport.

Wiley also publishes its books in a variety of electronic formats. Some content that appears in print may not be available in electronic books.

Library of Congress Control Number: 2006926467

ISBN-13: 978-0-471-77388-7

ISBN-10: 0-471-77388-3

Manufactured in the United States of America

10 9 8 7 6 5 4 3 2 1

1B/RW/QY/QW/IN

About the Author

Zoe Erotopoulos was born in Macedonia, Hellas (Greece) and immigrated to the United States with her parents and brother at a young age. Her love of the French language and literature inspired her to pursue her academic dream. She holds an MA, MPhil, and PhD in French and Romance Philology from Columbia University in New York City. She has also studied in Aix-en-Provence, at the Sorbonne, and at the Ecole Normale Supérieure in Paris.

Her teaching experience in French ranges from elementary to advanced level courses, including literature and theater. Dr. Erotopoulos' area of expertise is 17th century French Theater. She has taught at a number of institutions, including Columbia University, Reid Hall in Paris, and Trinity College in Hartford, Connecticut. For the past 15 years, she has been teaching in the Department of Modern Languages and Literatures at Fairfield University in Fairfield, Connecticut. She serves as coordinator and supervisor of a number of teacher assistants each year. Dr. Erotopoulos lives in Connecticut with her husband and three children.

Dedication

This book is dedicated to my family.

Author's Acknowledgments

There are a great number of people I must thank for this joyous endeavor. First, I would like to thank my parents, George and Olga Erotopoulos for their unwavering encouragement and support, their sacrifice for a better future for their children, and their unconditional love. To my brother Jim, my sister-in-law Alissa, and their beautiful twin daughters, I am so thankful that you are a constant part of my life. A special thank you to my mother- and father-in-law, to my husband Steve, and our beautiful children, Despina, Olga, and Stathi for their love and support.

In addition, I would like to thank my colleagues at the Department of Modern Languages and Literatures at Fairfield University for their encouragement, especially Dr. Marie-Agnès Sourieau for her belief in me. Since teaching is also learning, I owe a big thank you to all my students throughout my many years of teaching. A heartfelt thanks to Cynthia Nadal for her insightful comments and suggestions. Last, but certainly not least, a special thank you to the editorial staff at Wiley for their professionalism, insightfulness, and expertise, especially to my project editor, Chad Sievers, acquisitions editor Tracy Boggier, and copy editor Sarah Faulkner. A special thanks to this book's technical editor, Joyce Roush, a French teacher at Culver Academies in Culver, Indiana.

Publisher's Acknowledgments

We're proud of this book; please send us your comments through our Dummies online registration form located at www.dummies.com/register/.

Some of the people who helped bring this book to market include the following:

Acquisitions, Editorial, and Media Development

Project Editor: Chad R. Sievers

Acquisitions Editor: Tracy Boggier

Copy Editor: Sarah Faulkner

Editorial Program Coordinator: Hanna K. Scott

Technical Editor: Joyce A. Roush

Editorial Manager: Michelle Hacker

Editorial Assistants: Erin Calligan, David Lutton

Cartoons: Rich Tennant (www.the5thwave.com)

Composition Services

Project Coordinator: Tera Knapp

Layout and Graphics: Denny Hager, LeAndra Hosier, Melanee Prendergast, Heather Ryan

Proofreaders: Leeann Harney, Henry Lazarek

Indexer: Anne Leach

Special Help
Sarah Westfall

Publishing and Editorial for Consumer Dummies

Diane Graves Steele, Vice President and Publisher, Consumer Dummies

Joyce Pepple, Acquisitions Director, Consumer Dummies

Kristin A. Cocks, Product Development Director, Consumer Dummies

Michael Spring, Vice President and Publisher, Travel

Kelly Regan, Editorial Director, Travel

Publishing for Technology Dummies

Andy Cummings, Vice President and Publisher, Dummies Technology/General User

Composition Services

Gerry Fahey, Vice President of Production Services

Debbie Stailey, Director of Composition Services

Contents at a Glance

Introduction 1

Part I: Living in the Here and Now: The Present Indicative 5

Chapter 1: Verbs 101: The Lowdown on Verbs 7
Chapter 2: Conjugating Regular Verbs in the Present Tense 17
Chapter 3: Knowing How to Handle Spelling-Change Verbs 29
Chapter 4: Wrestling with Some Irregular Conjugations 43
Chapter 5: Reflecting on Pronominal Verbs (Reflexive, Reciprocal, and Idiomatic) 61
Chapter 6: Forming the Present Participle and the Gerund 69

Part II: Using Verbs Correctly with Questions,
Commands, and Such 77

Chapter 7: Inquisitive Minds Want to Know: Asking and Answering Questions 79
Chapter 8: Telling People What to Do: The Regular, Irregular, and Pronominal Commands 89
Chapter 9: Looking Forward and Back: The Immediate Future and Past 101
Chapter 10: Correctly Using Often Misused Verbs in Daily Conversation 109

Part III: Taking a Look Back: The Past Tenses 119

Chapter 11: No Tense Is Perfect: The Imperfect Tense 121
Chapter 12: Comprehending the Passé Composé and the Pluperfect Tenses ...133
Chapter 13: Contrasting the Imperfect with the Passé Composé 153
Chapter 14: Deciphering the Literary Tenses: The Passé Simple and Passé Antérieur 163

Part IV: Looking Ahead: The Future and the Conditional Tenses ...171

Chapter 15: Moving Forward with the Future Tense 173
Chapter 16: Completing a Future Action with the Future Perfect 183
Chapter 17: Could-ing and Would-ing with the Present Conditional Tense 191
Chapter 18: Trying the Past Conditional Tense: Could Have and Would Have ...201

Part V: Considering Your Mood: Subjunctive or Not 209

Chapter 19: Creating the Present Subjunctive 211
Chapter 20: Knowing How to Use the Present Subjunctive 223
Chapter 21: Forming and Using the Past Subjunctive 237

Part VI: The Part of Tens 243

Chapter 22: Ten Verbs Used the French Way 245
Chapter 23: Ten Most Frequently Mixed-Up Verbs 249

Part VII: Appendixes 255

Appendix A: French-to-English Verb Glossary 257
Appendix B: English-to-French Verb Glossary 263
Appendix C: Conjugating Common Irregular Verbs 269

Index 283

Table of Contents

Introduction *1*

About This Book 1
Conventions Used in This Book 2
Foolish Assumptions 2
How This Book Is Organized 2
    Part I: Living in the Here and Now: The Present Indicative 3
    Part II: Using Verbs Correctly with Questions, Commands, and Such 3
    Part III: Taking a Look Back: The Past Tenses 3
    Part IV: Looking Ahead: The Future and the Conditional Tenses 3
    Part V: Considering Your Mood: Subjunctive or Not 3
    Part VI: The Part of Tens 3
    Part VII: Appendixes 4
Icons Used in This Book 4
Where to Go from Here 4

Part 1: Living in the Here and Now: The Present Indicative *5*

Chapter 1: Verbs 101: The Lowdown on Verbs 7

Identifying the Four Main Verb Types 7
Classifying Verbs 8
    Contrasting transitive and intransitive verbs 8
    Following up with a preposition 9
Linking, Auxiliary, Impersonal, and Helping Verbs, Oh My! 11
    Linking everything together 11
    Focusing on the auxiliaries 11
    Eyeing the impersonals 11
    Lending a helping hand 12
Watching Your Mood 12
    Making it personal 12
    Don't take it so personally: The impersonal mood 12
Categorizing the Tenses 13
Poring Over Pronouns 13
Answer Key 15

Chapter 2: Conjugating Regular Verbs in the Present Tense 17

Classifying Regular Present-Tense Verbs 17
Looking At -er Verbs 18
Focusing On -ir Verbs 20
Trying -re Verbs 21
Modifying Actions with Adverbs 23
Forming Sentences: Word by Word 24
Answer Key 26

Chapter 3: Knowing How to Handle Spelling-Change Verbs 29

Taking a Stab at Spelling-Change Verbs 29
    Managing -ger verbs 29
    Working with -cer verbs 31
    Keeping an eye on the silent types 32

           Handling é verbs..34
           Figuring out -eter and -eler verbs...35
           Dotting the i in -yer verbs...36
      Building Sentences: Word by Word..38
      Answer Key..40

Chapter 4: Wrestling with Some Irregular Conjugations.............................43

      Conjugating Irregular Verbs..43
           Focusing on the four most common irregular verbs 43
           Working through other "helpful" irregular verbs 45
      Grouping Irregular Verbs...47
           Looking at the "pseudo" -ir verbs 47
           The "wannabes": -ir verbs acting like -er verbs 49
           "Deceptive" -ir verbs: Same endings, different stem 50
           Comprehending irregular -re verbs...51
           Remembering the "mets"..53
           Continuing with irregular -re verbs..54
           Looking at other odd irregular verbs 55
      Answer Key..58

**Chapter 5: Reflecting on Pronominal Verbs
(Reflexive, Reciprocal, and Idiomatic)..61**

      Understanding Reflexive Verbs 61
      Looking At Reciprocal Verbs 64
      Attempting Idiomatic Verbs 65
      Answer Key..68

Chapter 6: Forming the Present Participle and the Gerund 69

      Introducing the Present Participle...69
      Using the Present Participle 70
      Forming the Gerund...71
           Using the gerund 71
           Pronominal verbs: Corresponding to the subject............................72
      Forming and Using the Past Present Participle...73
      Answer Key..75

*Part II: Using Verbs Correctly with Questions,
Commands, and Such* **77**

**Chapter 7: Inquisitive Minds Want to Know:
Asking and Answering Questions...79**

      Using Inversion to Ask Questions 80
           Inversion with vowels...80
           Inversion with a noun 81
           Inversion with pronominal verbs 81
           Inversion with two verbs in a sentence..82
      Responding in the Negative 83
      Forming the Negative with Inversion 85
      Making the Infinitive Negative 85
      Answer Key..87

**Chapter 8: Telling People What to Do: The Regular,
Irregular, and Pronominal Commands** 89

    Forming Commands with Regular Verbs 89
        Making -er verbs into commands 89
        Making -ir verbs into commands 90
        Making -re verbs into commands 91
    Forming Commands with Irregular Verbs 92
    Creating the Negative Imperative 94
    Using Pronominal Verbs to Make Commands 95
    Adding Pronouns to Commands 96
    Answer Key 99

Chapter 9: Looking Forward and Back: The Immediate Future and Past 101

    Creating the Immediate Future Tense 101
    Creating the Immediate Past Tense 102
    Going and Coming with Aller and Venir 103
        Going to and coming back 103
        Going and coming from 105
    Answer Key 108

Chapter 10: Correctly Using Often Misused Verbs in Daily Conversation 109

    Knowing the Difference between Connaître and Savoir 109
    Identifying What to Play 111
    Keeping Avoir and Faire in Line 112
        Using avoir 113
        Trying faire 115
    Answer Key 118

Part III: Taking a Look Back: The Past Tenses *119*

Chapter 11: No Tense Is Perfect: The Imperfect Tense 121

    Making Regular Verbs Imperfect 121
    Forming the Imperfect with Irregular Verbs 123
        "Eyeing" verb stems 125
        Working with -cer and -ger verbs 125
        The one true irregular imperfect verb — être 126
    Using the Imperfect 126
        Expressing habitual and continuous actions 127
        Describing the past 128
        Interrupting actions in progress 129
        Using the imperfect with certain constructions 129
        Describing simultaneous actions 129
        Making suggestions and expressing wishes 130
        Hypothesizing with the imperfect 130
    Answer Key 131

Chapter 12: Comprehending the Passé Composé and the Pluperfect Tenses 133

    Forming the Passé Composé 133
        Regular verbs and the passé composé 134
        Irregular verbs and the passé composé 135
        Making sure the past participle agrees with the preceding direct object 138

Creating the Passé Composé with Être 140
Making sure the subject and participle agree 142
Forming the passé composé with pronominal verbs 143
Flexible Verbs: Using Either Avoir or Être 146
Making the Passé Composé Negative 147
Forming the Pluperfect 148
Answer Key 150

Chapter 13: Contrasting the Imperfect with the Passé Composé 153
Identifying the Main Differences between the Two Tenses 153
Selecting the Right Tense: Imperfect or Passé Composé? 155
Relying on helpful key words 155
Eyeing verbs usually used with the imperfect 156
Looking at verbs that have different meanings
in imperfect and passé composé 157
Understanding the context 159
Answer Key 160

**Chapter 14: Deciphering the Literary Tenses:
The Passé Simple and Passé Antérieur 163**
Creating the Passé Simple 163
Regular verbs 163
Most irregular verbs 164
Irregular stem verbs with regular endings 166
Completely irregular 167
Creating the Passé Antérieur 167
Answer Key 169

Part IV: Looking Ahead: The Future and the Conditional Tenses....171

Chapter 15: Moving Forward with the Future Tense 173
Forming the Future of Regular Verbs 173
Forming the Future of Spelling-Change Verbs 175
Forming the Future of Irregular Verbs 177
Identifying the Differences between English and
French when Using the Future Tense 178
Expressing Yourself and Using References: Future Style 179
Answer Key 181

Chapter 16: Completing a Future Action with the Future Perfect 183
Forming the Future Perfect 183
Using the Future Perfect Correctly 187
Answer Key 189

Chapter 17: Could-ing and Would-ing with the Present Conditional Tense 191
Forming the Conditional 191
Considering spelling-change -er verbs 193
Creating the conditional with irregular verbs 194
Using the Conditional 195
Being polite, expressing a wish, and offering suggestions 196
Wondering if: The hypothetical 196
Conditional with indirect discourse 197
Answer Key 198

Chapter 18: Trying the Past Conditional Tense: Could Have and Would Have **201**

Creating the Past Conditional 201
Correctly Using the Past Conditional 203
Answer Key 207

Part V: Considering Your Mood: Subjunctive or Not *209*

Chapter 19: Creating the Present Subjunctive **211**

Forming the Present Subjunctive with Regular Verbs 211
Typically Irregular, but Regular in the Subjunctive 213
Looking At Stem Changers 215
Eyeing the Irregulars 218
Answer Key 221

Chapter 20: Knowing How to Use the Present Subjunctive **223**

Expressing Wish, Will, Preference, and Command 224
Showing Emotion or Judgment 225
Expressing Doubt or Uncertainty 227
Showing Opinion, Necessity, and Possibility 228
Expressing Condition, Time, Concession, and Consequence 229
Considering Indefinite, Doubtful, and Subjective Antecedents 231
Looking at Idiomatic Expressions and Commands 232
Answer Key 234

Chapter 21: Forming and Using the Past Subjunctive **237**

Forming the Past Subjunctive 237
Using the Past Subjunctive 238
Distinguishing between the Present and Past Subjunctive 239
Answer Key 241

Part VI: The Part of Tens *243*

Chapter 22: Ten Verbs Used the French Way **245**

Attendre (To Wait For) 245
Chercher (To Look For) 245
Écouter (To Listen To) 246
Payer (To Pay) 246
Regarder (To Look At, To Watch) 246
Demander (To Ask) 246
Obéir (To Obey) 247
Permettre (To Allow) 247
Répondre (To Answer) 247
Téléphoner (To Telephone, To Call) 247

Chapter 23: Ten Most Frequently Mixed-Up Verbs **249**

Visiting a Place or Visiting a Person 249
Spending Time or Spending Money 250
Knowing People or Places or Knowing Something 250
Playing a Game or Playing an Instrument 251
Leaving or Leaving Something Behind 251

Returning Home, Returning Something, or Just Returning 252
Leading, Bringing, or Taking Someone 252
Carrying, Bringing, Taking, or Taking Back Something 253
Thinking or Thinking About..253
Waiting or Attending..254

Part VII: Appendixes *255*

Appendix A: French-to-English Verb Glossary..**257**

Appendix B: English-to-French Verb Glossary..**263**

Appendix C: Conjugating Common Irregular Verbs..**269**

Index *283*

Introduction

Every day when speaking your native language, you use verbs. When you want to *walk* to the store, *eat* a pickle, *run* away from a dog, or even just *be* in the same room as your pesky brother, you use verbs. You probably don't even think about how you select the correct verb and the correct tense. However, when you're studying a new language, these choices may not be quite as intuitive. You need to know how to select the right tense and how to conjugate verbs before you can correctly use them. That's where this book fits in.

Whether you took French in high school or college, are currently taking it, or just know enough to get you by, *French Verbs For Dummies* can guide you in using verb tenses correctly. (If you have very little familiarity with French, check out the "Foolish Assumptions" section later in this Introduction to see whether this is really the book for you.) The concise and clear explanations in addition to the multiple examples in this book can eliminate any guesswork and show you how to form the various tenses step by step. Furthermore, I clearly explain verb tenses and moods from the present indicative to the past subjunctive with ample examples. *French Verbs For Dummies* isn't a textbook, but a workbook where you have a chance to practice the material in small doses. At the end of each chapter, I provide an answer key so that you can check your answers as you go. These answers can provide you with the certainty and confidence that you're using all the verbs correctly.

So sit back and relax. This book is no boring grammar class. It's a fun and straightforward way to use French verbs in order to greet people, ask questions, give orders, provide explanations, and express your wishes. Ready? **Commençons!** (*Let's begin!*)

About This Book

I designed this book to make it as accessible as possible. You can scan the Table of Contents or the Index and choose the chapters that interest you the most. Each chapter is self-contained, with an introduction of the verb tense and/or the verb mood as well as clear explanations regarding the particular construction on which it focuses.

This book provides clear explanations and examples from the onset — from the subject pronouns and forming hypothetical sentences to using the subjunctive correctly and confidently. You're guided in distinguishing transitive from intransitive verbs, in recognizing and using the various verb moods, such as indicative, conditional, and subjunctive; and you become aware of the differences between using verbs in French and in English.

Furthermore, I divide each chapter into sections so that you can find the specific information you need, followed by exercises, which you can choose to do for practice. The practice sections usually include fill-in-the-blank problems, questions where I ask you to conjugate the verbs in parentheses, and translation sentences. Then, you can take a look at the answer key at the end of each chapter to check your answers. *French Verbs For Dummies* guides you every step of the way toward the successful use of the backbone of any complete sentence: the verb.

Conventions Used in This Book

In order to make this book easy to use, I use the following conventions:

- ✔ In order for you to easily identify the French, I **boldface** all French words, including the complete sentences in the examples, French verbs when they appear by themselves, and the French verb endings when I show you how to conjugate the verbs.

- ✔ I *italicize* all the English translations that follow the French terms.

- ✔ Verb conjugations appear in verb tables. I **boldface** each verb ending to emphasize it.

- ✔ In the Answer Key, I provide English translations for all the problems (even when I don't ask you to provide the translation) to help you better understand the sentence. These translations are in *italics*.

- ✔ In the Answer Key, some practice problems may have more than one correct answer. I provide the most common answer in those instances.

- ✔ Before each series of practice problems, I provide a sample question in a Q-and-A format so that you can see how to answer those questions.

Foolish Assumptions

When writing this book, I made the following assumptions about you, my dear reader:

- ✔ You took French classes way back when and you remember very little, but you want to get a refresher on your verbs.

- ✔ You want to gather the bits and pieces and assemble them and apply them to regular, normal, everyday conversation.

- ✔ You have taken quite a few years of French, but you're still having difficulty distinguishing between the imperfect and the passé composé (or some other verb tense that's giving you headaches).

- ✔ You finally want to demystify and master the subjunctive.

If any of these assumptions apply to you, then *French Verbs For Dummies* is for you.

However, if you've never taken a French course or know very little, I suggest that you first start with *French For Dummies* by Dodi-Katrin Schmidt, Michelle M. Williams, and Dominique Wenzel (Wiley) or consider enrolling in an introductory French class.

How This Book Is Organized

French Verbs For Dummies is divided into parts, starting with the very basic present indicative tense and ending with the Appendixes. Each part has multiple chapters that expand on the general topic of the specific part.

Part I: Living in the Here and Now: The Present Indicative

This part introduces the subject pronouns and gives some basic verb information. Furthermore, it introduces and conjugates the present tense of regular verbs, spelling-change verbs, irregular verbs, and pronominal verbs. This part also introduces the present participle and gerund.

Part II: Using Verbs Correctly with Questions, Commands, and Such

In this part, I show you how to ask and answer questions, give commands, and go anywhere in or out of town and then come back. I also cover some verbs that you can use in common expressions that have a different meaning in French.

Part III: Taking a Look Back: The Past Tenses

This part introduces, forms, and explains the uses of the imperfect, passé composé, and pluperfect tenses of regular, irregular, and pronominal verbs. It also explains the difference between the imperfect and the passé composé in order to describe past events and actions. Also included in this part are two literary past tenses: the passé simple and the passé antérieur.

Part IV: Looking Ahead: The Future and the Conditional Tenses

In this part, I show you how to form and use the future, the future perfect, the conditional, and past conditional tenses. I also explain how to make polite requests and form hypothetical sentences.

Part V: Considering Your Mood: Subjunctive or Not

This part looks at forming the present and past subjunctive of regular, irregular, and pronominal verbs. It also explains step by step when and how to use the subjunctive with certain verbs, verbal expressions, and conjunctions.

Part VI: The Part of Tens

Consisting of two chapters, this part gathers the top tens in French verbs: ten verbs used the French way and the ten most frequently mixed-up verbs.

Part VII: Appendixes

The appendixes enable you to see at a glance all the various verb conjugations together. It starts off with a French-to-English verb glossary (Appendix A), an English-to-French verb glossary (Appendix B), and finishes with Appendix C for irregular verbs.

Icons Used in This Book

As in every *For Dummies* book, I use icons to help you find specific information. I place them on the left-hand margin throughout the book. The icons are

When you see this bulls-eye, you know I'm pointing out tips to help you grasp a specific concept.

The Remember icon indicates that you need to put this little tidbit in the back of your mind. I'm telling you something important about the verb or verb conjugation.

I use the Example icon in front of an example that demonstrates the format of a concept.

The Practice icon tells you that it's time for you to start the practice exercises. Get your pencils and pens ready.

Where to Go from Here

The best thing about *French Verbs For Dummies* is that you can take a look at the Table of Contents and choose the chapter in which you're interested or you need more practice. Now take a chance and just give it a try. Only you know what you don't know. Just pick a chapter and go at your own pace. Remember, I'm with you every step of the way!

Part I
Living in the Here and Now: The Present Indicative

The 5th Wave
By Rich Tennant

@RICHTENNANT

"I just think if we're going to be in a foreign country, we should know their units of measurement better. By the way, how's your un litre de espresso?"

In this part . . .

The present indicative is a mood of fact, of something that is happening. It's a simple tense that tells you about something that exists in the present, in the here and now. In this part, I cover the present tense, including its three distinct meanings in English. For example **je parle** means *I speak, I am speaking,* and *I do speak.* All three meanings are possible for all verbs in the present indicative tense. In Chapter 2, I focus on regular present tense verbs. In Chapter 3, I delve into spelling-change verbs. Chapter 4 jumps into irregular (but still fun) present tense verbs. In Chapter 5, I explain pronominal verbs. Knowing the conjugation of verbs in the present indicative can help you form other tenses, such as the imperfect, the subjunctive, and the present participle. And finally, in Chapter 6, if you're having trouble with present participles or gerunds, this chapter can help.

Chapter 1

Verbs 101: The Lowdown on Verbs

In This Chapter

▶ Looking at and classifying verbs

▶ Identifying transitive and intransitive verbs

▶ Considering mood

▶ Recognizing the tenses

▶ Eyeing pronouns

*W*hether you're speaking English, German, Spanish, or French (just to mention a few languages), a *verb* is an important word that indicates an action (for example, **Je parle** means *I am speaking, I speak,* and *I do speak*) or a state of being (for example, **Je suis optimiste** means *I am optimistic*). The verb is an essential component in a sentence because the sentence is incomplete without it. Verbs are the only words that change their forms in order to indicate the present, the future, and the past. A verb can also have several complements or provide further information. It can be followed by a noun, an adverb, a preposition, or a clause. It can also be followed by another verb, which is always in the infinitive form.

This chapter looks at the verb basics. I classify verbs, show how those classifications affect the way you use a verb, explain how mood impacts verbs, and look at the different verb tenses. This chapter can answer any quick questions you have about verbs before I go into the specifics in each chapter.

Identifying the Four Main Verb Types

A good way to remember various verb conjugations is by classifying the verbs. For example, if a verb is regular, check to see whether its infinitive ends in **-er, -ir,** or **-re.** This ending can help you follow a set pattern in conjugating the verb. Remember, if you know how to conjugate one verb in each of the three groups of regular verbs, then you know how to conjugate hundreds of verbs. The following four classifications help you identify the type of verb and enable you to conjugate it correctly.

✔ **Regular verbs:** These verbs shouldn't cause any undue stress. They follow the regular conjugation rules for **-er, -ir,** and **-re** verbs, which are the three groups of regular verbs. (Check out Chapter 2 for the lowdown on present-tense regular verbs.)

✔ **Spelling-change verbs:** When studying French verbs, you encounter some verbs that undergo spelling changes. This spelling change happens for many reasons. One reason is to enable you to pronounce a mute **e,** as in the verbs **appeler** (*to call*) and **jeter** (*to throw*), which double their consonants (**l** or **t**) after the mute **e.** For other verbs, you add an accent grave to the **e** so it becomes **è,** as in the verb **acheter** (*to buy*). Other verbs are affected because of the pronunciation of the consonant — specifically **g** and **c.** (Flip to Chapter 3 for more on spelling-change verbs.)

✔ **Irregular verbs:** With these verbs you need to keep on your toes. They have an irregular conjugation and don't follow a specific pattern like regular verbs do. (See Chapter 4 for more on these irregular verbs.)

✔ **Pronominal verbs:** These include *reflexive verbs,* and you use these verbs when you do something to yourself. The action reflects back to the subject of the sentence. For example, **Je me brosse les dents** means *I brush my teeth.* Other pronominal verbs include reciprocal verbs where two or more people do the action onto themselves. For example, **Ils s'écrivent** means *They write to each other.* Some idiomatic expressions also use pronominal verbs. For example, **Nous nous entendons bien** means *We get along well.* The one thing that all these verbs have in common is the addition of pronominal pronouns that correspond to the subject pronouns. (Check out Chapter 5 for more on pronominal verbs.)

Classifying Verbs

Classifying a verb as a particular verb type can help you conjugate the verb correctly every time. Look at the ending of its infinitive form. Does the infinitive end in an **-er, -ir,** or **-re?** Does it end in a **-cer** or a **-ger?** Is the verb a spelling-change verb? Is the infinitive preceded by a pronominal pronoun? (The answers to all these questions are answered in Chapters 2, 3, and 4 where I give you specific examples of conjugation patterns followed by a list of verbs that follow that exact pattern.) Another important way to classify verbs is to determine whether they're transitive or intransitive. In order to do so, determine whether they're followed by a preposition or by a direct object.

This section looks a bit closer at how you classify verbs, specifically noting whether a verb is transitive or intransitive as well as the different ways they are used in English and in French.

Contrasting transitive and intransitive verbs

Knowing whether a verb is transitive or intransitive enables you to use the verb correctly every time. It guides you in using a preposition after the verb or in eliminating the preposition altogether. Furthermore, the identification between a transitive and an intransitive verb also facilitates the choice between the auxiliaries **avoir** (*to have*) or **être** (*to be*) in the compound past tenses. In this section, I show you how to tell transitive and intransitive verbs apart.

Transitive verbs are followed be a direct object rather than a preposition. They take **avoir** as their auxiliary in the compound past tenses.

Je regarde la télévision. (*I am watching television.*)

Ils aiment leurs enfants. (*They love their children.*)

An *intransitive verb* isn't followed by a direct object. Often it's followed by a preposition or nothing at all.

Je monte. (*I am going upstairs.*)

Nous passons devant la bibliothèque. (*We are passing in front of the library.*)

You must be aware of verbs that may be transitive in French but intransitive in English, and vice versa. For example, in French, the verb *to answer* is intransitive because it must be followed by the preposition **à,** as in **Je réponds à la question.** However, in English, you say *I answer the question,* and therefore *to answer* is transitive in English.

As another example, in English you say *I listen to the radio.* This sentence indicates that the verb *to listen to* is an intransitive verb in English because it isn't followed by a direct object but by the preposition *to.* In French, however, **J'écoute la radio** indicates that the verb **écouter** is a transitive verb because it's followed by a direct object. Keep an eye out for the potentially tricky verbs in Table 1-1 and Table 1-2.

Table 1-1	Comparing Transitive to Intransitive
Transitive in French	*Intransitive in English*
attendre J'attends le bus.	**to wait for** *I am waiting **for** the bus.*
chercher Je cherche le livre.	**to look for** *I am looking **for** the book.*
écouter J'écoute le professeur.	**to listen to** *I am listening **to** the professor.*
payer Je paie les provisions.	**to pay for something** *I am paying **for** the groceries.*

Table 1-2	Comparing Intransitive to Transitive
Intransitive in French	*Transitive in English*
demander à Je demande de l'argent **à** mon père.	**to ask someone** *I ask my dad for money.*
obéir à Les enfants obéissent **à** leurs parents.	**to obey someone** *The children obey their parents.*
renoncer à Tu renonces **à** la télévision.	**to give up something** *You are giving up television.*
ressembler à Il ressemble **à** sa mère.	**to resemble someone** *He resembles his mother.*
assister à Nous assistons **au** concert.	**to attend an event** *We are attending the concert.*

Following up with a preposition

Most French intransitive verbs are followed by the preposition **à,** which can mean *to, in,* or *at.* When the preposition **à** is followed by a definite article plus a noun (**le** for the masculine singular, **la** for the feminine singular, **l'** for masculine and feminine nouns that begin with a vowel or a mute **h,** and **les** for masculine and feminine plural nouns), two contractions are made. Table 1-3 explains these two contractions.

Table 1-3	Combining Definite Articles with the Preposition à	
Preposition + Article	*Combination*	*Example*
à + le	**au**	Je réponds au professeur. (*I'm answering the professor.*)
à + la	**à la**	Je réponds à la question. (*I'm answering the question.*)
à + l'	**à l'**	Je réponds à l'étudiant. (*I'm answering the student.*)
à + les	**aux**	Je réponds aux questions. (*I'm answering the questions.*)

Notice that the only combinations that contract are **à + le,** which becomes **au** and **à + les,** which becomes **aux.** The same types of transformations occur with the preposition **de,** which means *of, about,* or *from,* as Table 1-4 indicates.

Table 1-4	Combining Definite Articles with the Preposition de	
Preposition + Article	*Combination*	*Example*
de + le	**du**	Il vient du cinéma. (*He's coming [back] from the movies.*)
de + la	**de la**	Il vient de la librairie. (*He's coming [back] from the bookstore.*)
de + l'	**de l'**	Il vient de l'épicerie. (*He's coming [back] from the grocery store.*) Il vient de l'hôtel. (*He's coming [back] from the hotel.*)
de + les	**des**	Il vient des champs. (*He's coming [back] from the fields.*)

Identify the transitive and intransitive verbs in the following questions. If the verb is intransitive, add the preposition **à** and make any necessary contractions with the definite article. If it's transitive, leave it alone.

Q. Tu renonces _____ chocolat. (*You are giving up chocolate.*)

A. Tu renonces **au** chocolat.

1. Nous écoutons _____ la radio. (*We listen to the radio.*)

2. Ils ressemblent _____ leur mère. (*They resemble their mother.*)

3. J'obéis _____ mes grands-parents. (*I obey my grandparents.*)

4. Vous attendez _____ le train. (*You wait/are waiting for the train.*)

5. Tu cherches _____ tes clés. (*You are looking for your keys.*)

6. Nous assistons _____ match de football. (*We attend/are attending a soccer game.*)

7. Je réponds _____ mes amis. (*I answer my friends.*)

8. Tu paies _____ tes achats. (*You pay/are paying for your purchases.*)

9. Elle demande _____ ses amis de sortir. (*She asks her friends to go out.*)

10. Nous renoncons _____ la glace. (*We give up/are giving up ice cream.*)

Linking, Auxiliary, Impersonal, and Helping Verbs, Oh My!

Verbs have many different functions. Besides being the core of a sentence, verbs dictate what you need to bring a sentence to its conclusion. They can be followed by another verb, a noun, a pronoun, an adjective, a preposition, or a clause. Some verbs link the subject to nouns, pronouns, or adjectives. Auxiliary verbs help form all compound past tenses in French. Some verbs exist only in the impersonal **il** (*it*) form, and others help emphasize and support the infinitive. Oh, the versatility of verbs!

Linking everything together

Some verbs are *linking* verbs, which means that they link the subject to the noun, to the pronoun, or to the adjective. These verbs include **être** (*to be*), **paraître** (*to appear*), **sembler** or **avoir l'air** (*to seem*), **devenir** (*to become*), and **rester** (*to stay*).

> **Il a l'air fatiqué.** (*He seems tired.*)
>
> **Elle est avocate.** (*She is a lawyer.*)

Focusing on the auxiliaries

The French language has two main *auxiliary* verbs: **avoir** (*to have*) and **être** (*to be*). You use them along with past participles to form all compound past tenses in French. Check out Part III for more on the past tenses and how to use these auxiliaries.

Eyeing the impersonals

Impersonal verbs are the ones that exist only in the third person masculine singular (**il**) form. In this form, the subject pronoun is always translated as *it* in English. These verbs include expressions like **il faut** (*it is necessary*), **il s'agit de** (*it is about*), **il pleut** (*it is raining*), **il neige** (*it is snowing*), and **il fait** used for weather. Examples include **il fait beau** (*it is nice out*), **il fait froid** (*it is cold*), and **il fait chaud** (*it is hot*). Furthermore, French has many impersonal expressions, many of which use **être** (*to be*) and are followed by the subjunctive tense, like **il est important que** (*it is important that*), **il est possible que** (*it is possible that*), **il est nécessaire que** (*it is necessary that*), and so on. Look at Chapter 19 for a list of these expressions.

Lending a helping hand

Some verbs are *semi-auxiliaries*. That means that they are helping verbs to the main verb, which is in the infinitive form. These verbs include **pouvoir** (*to be able to*), **vouloir** (*to want to*), **devoir** (*to have to*), **aller** (*to go*), **faire** (*to do, to make*), and **laisser** (*to leave — as in leave it alone or let it be*).

Watching Your Mood

Verbs are divided into various moods. Linguistically, the mood of a verb is a way of expressing oneself, or a way of speaking. A mood shows the speaker's attitude toward an event. The French language has seven such moods that are divided into two categories: personal moods and impersonal moods.

Making it personal

The verbs in the personal moods are conjugated in order to correspond to the subject pronouns. These are divided into four groups:

✔ **The indicative mood** (which is the mood that's used most often) indicates that the speaker is talking about a fact, or something that's happening, will happen, or has happened. (See Parts I, II, and III for more on the conjugations of the various tenses of the indicative mood.)

✔ **The subjunctive mood** (which you use more often in French than in English) is the mood of doubt, uncertainty, emotion, will, and command. (See Chapters 19, 20, and 21 for more details on the present and past subjunctive.)

✔ **The imperative mood** expresses an order, a request, or a directive. The imperative mood uses the present tense of most verbs and the conjugations of the following three subject pronouns: **tu, nous,** and **vous.** However, you never use the subject pronouns in an imperative construction. (See Chapter 8 for the formations and use of the imperatives or commands.)

✔ **The conditional mood** appears in a hypothetical sentence where you place the conditional form of the verb in the result clause. For example, you may say **Si j'avais de l'argent, je *voyagerais*.** (*If I had money, I would travel.*) You may also use the conditional to make polite requests or suggestions. (See Chapters 17 and 18 for more on the present and past conditional tenses as well as the hypothetical sentences.)

Don't take it so personally: The impersonal mood

Unlike the personal moods, the impersonal mood verbs aren't conjugated because they don't correspond to any particular subject pronoun. These impersonal mood verbs include the infinitive, the gerund, and the participle. The infinitive mood is often used as a noun. An example is in the French saying **Vouloir, c'est pouvoir,** which translates to *Where there's a will, there's a way.* Literally, it means *To want to is to be able to.* The gerund can be used as an adverb, like it is in the sentence **On réussit à la vie en travaillant dur,** meaning *One succeeds in life by working hard.* The participle can be used as an adjective, as in the example **Les devoirs finis, ils ont joué au basket,** which means *Once the homework was finished, they played basketball.*

Categorizing the Tenses

Tense means *time,* and verbs change their forms in order to tell present, past, or future time. Verbs have two parts, the stem and the endings that specify time, mood, and person.

French has two types of verbs:

- **Simple verbs.** A simple verb is formed when a verb is conjugated by itself without an auxiliary. It's composed of a stem to which you add endings. The present, the imperfect, the passé simple, the future, the present conditional, and the present subjunctive are all simple tenses.

    Elle partira bientôt. (*She will leave soon.*)

- **Compound tenses.** You construct these verbs with an auxiliary, either **avoir** (*to have*) or **être** (*to be*), plus the past participle of any verb you wish. The passé composé, the pluperfect, the passé antérieur, the future perfect, the past conditional, and the past subjunctive are all compound tenses.

    Vous avez téléphoné hier. (*You called yesterday.*)

Poring Over Pronouns

Every conjugated verb corresponds to a subject that makes a sentence complete. The subject can be a person, a thing, or an idea. You can see the subject pronoun classifications in Table 1-5.

Table 1-5	Subject Pronoun Classifications	
Subject Pronoun Classification	*Singular Subject Pronouns*	*Plural Subject Pronouns*
First Person	**je** (*I*)	**nous** (*we*)
Second Person	**tu** (*you*)	**vous** (*you*)
Third Person	**il/elle/on** (*he/she/it* or *one*)	**ils/elles** (*they*)

When a verb begins with a vowel or a mute **h,** drop the **e** from **je** and add an apostrophe.

J'aime (*I like, I love*)

J'habite (*I live*)

Remember that you never drop the **u** in **tu** (*you*) or the **e** in **elle** (*she*) before a vowel or a mute **h.** Instead you say **Tu aimes** (*You like, You love*) and **Tu habites** (*You live*). **Tu** and **vous** both mean *you,* and as you can see from Table 1-5, **tu** is singular whereas **vous** is plural. But as you probably already know, **vous** can also refer to one person when it's formal. You use **tu** with people you know well, like family members, peers, and children. You use **vous** with someone you don't know well, with someone who is older, and with a superior, like your boss, your teacher, or your supervisor. Note that even when **vous** refers to one person, you always conjugate the verb in the plural. In other words, the conjugation of **vous** doesn't change even if it refers to one person. Grammatically, you always conjugate it in the second person plural.

On is a subject pronoun that has several meanings. In the sentence **On parle français au Canada,** the word **on** can mean *one, we,* or *they,* so you translate the sentence *One/We/They speak French in Canada.* Whatever the meaning, conjugate **on** in the third person singular.

Il is a masculine subject pronoun that can replace a person or a thing, and it means *he* or *it.* For example, **Pierre est heureux** means *Pierre is happy.* You can replace **Pierre** with **il,** and it means *He is happy.* The same concept applies with a thing. **Le vent souffle** means *The wind is blowing.* You can replace **le vent** with the subject pronoun **il,** which means *It is blowing.*

The same applies to **elle,** which replaces a feminine singular noun. For example, you can say **Anne est avocate** (*Anne is a lawyer*) or **Elle est avocate** (*She is a lawyer*). In the sentence **La voiture est sale** (*The car is dirty*), you can replace **voiture** with **elle** because it's feminine singular. **Elle est sale** means *It is dirty.*

Again, the same is true of the plurals **ils** and **elles.** They can refer to people or things.

Les invités sont arrivés (*The guests have arrived*), **Ils sont arrivés** (*They have arrived*)

Les livres sont chers (*The books are expensive*), **Ils sont chers** (*They are expensive*)

Les filles sont jeunes (*The girls are young*), **Elles sont jeunes** (*They are young*)

Les cathédrales sont impréssionantes (*The cathedrals are impressive*), **Elles sont impréssionantes** (*They are impressive*)

Change the following boldfaced subjects into their corresponding subject pronouns. Write your answer in the blank at the end of the sentence.

Q. **Céline** est charmante. (*Céline is charming.*)

A. **Elle** est charmante. (*She is charming.*)

11. **Eric et Mathieu** jouent au football. (*Eric and Mathieu play soccer.*) _____

12. **Anne et moi** aimons la cuisine française. (*Anne and I like French cuisine.*) _____

13. **Sylvie** chante bien. (*Sylvie sings well.*) _____

14. **Mélanie et Sarah** aiment le chocolat. (*Mélanie and Sarah like chocolate.*) _____

15. **Benjamin** parle japonais. (*Benjamin speaks Japanese.*) _____

16. **Alexandre et Sophie** invitent leurs amis. (*Alexandre and Sophie invite their friends.*) _____

17. **Olivier** travaille dans une banque. (*Olivier works in a bank.*) _____

18. **Hélène et Antoine** partent en vacances. (*Hélène and Antoine are leaving for vacation.*) _____

19. **Claire** habite à Bordeaux. (*Claire lives in Bordeaux.*) _____

20. **Suzanne et Margot** sont de bonnes amies. (*Suzanne and Margot are good friends.*) _____

Answer Key

This section includes the answers from the practice problems in this chapter. Look at the correct answers and compare your answers.

1 Nous écoutons la radio. (*We listen to the radio.*)

2 Ils ressemblent **à** leur mère. (*They resemble their mother.*)

3 J'obéis **à** mes grands-parents. (*I obey my grandparents.*)

4 Vous attendez le train. (*You wait/are waiting for the train.*)

5 Tu cherches tes clés. (*You are looking for your keys.*)

6 Nous assistons **au** match de football. (*We attend/are attending a soccer game.*)

7 Je réponds **à** mes amis. (*I answer my friends.*)

8 Tu paies tes achats. (*You pay/are paying for your purchases.*)

9 Elle demande **à** ses amis de sortir. (*She asks her friends to go out.*)

10 Nous renoncons **à** la glace. (*We give up/are giving up ice cream.*)

11 **Ils** jouent au football. (*They play soccer.*)

12 **Nous** aimons la cuisine française. (*We like French cuisine.*)

13 **Elle** chante bien. (*She sings well.*)

14 **Elles** aiment le chocolat. (*They like chocolate.*)

15 **Il** parle japonais. (*He speaks Japanese.*)

16 **Ils** invitent leurs amis. (*They invite their friends.*)

17 **Il** travaille dans une banque. (*He works in a bank.*)

18 **Ils** partent en vacances. (*They are leaving for vacation.*)

19 **Elle** habite à Bordeaux. (*She lives in Bordeaux.*)

20 **Elles** sont de bonnes amies. (*They are good friends.*)

Chapter 2

Conjugating Regular Verbs in the Present Tense

• •

In This Chapter

▶ Categorizing French verbs

▶ Creating present-tense -er, -ir, and -re verbs

▶ Including adverbs

▶ Making complete sentences

• •

In French, you use the present tense in everyday conversation. In fact, it's the building block in forming sentences and expressing thoughts. You use the present tense to communicate things that are happening in your life, your job, and the world around you in the here and now. You also use the present tense to express ongoing actions in the present and to emphasize actions.

The present tense in French has three different meanings in English. For example, **Je parle** means not only *I speak,* but also *I am speaking* and *I do speak.* You can also use the present tense to express actions that you repeat over and over again. For instance, **Nous travaillons le samedi** means *We work on Saturdays*, meaning that we work every Saturday and therefore it expresses habitual action in the present. In French, the present tense is important because the stem of other tenses, such as the imperfect and the subjunctive, are derived from it.

In this chapter, I focus on conjugating this basic building block — the present tense. I first briefly classify the three regular types of verbs, and then I show you how to conjugate each one. Finally, I throw in some adverbs to help you make complete (and interesting) sentences.

Classifying Regular Present-Tense Verbs

The French language classifies verbs into different categories to make them easier to conjugate. For example, if you know the conjugation of one verb, then you can conjugate many verbs of the same type effortlessly because they follow the same pattern. Verbs are classified according to the endings of their infinitive. All French verb infinitives end in **-er, -ir, -re,** or **-oir.** However, within those four categories are regular and irregular verbs. This chapter focuses on the regular ones.

French has three groups of regular verbs:

✔ Verbs whose infinitive ends in **-er**, like **parler** (*to speak*)

✔ Verbs whose infinitive ends in **-ir**, like **finir** (*to finish*)

✔ Verbs whose infinitive ends in **-re**, like **vendre** (*to sell*)

The next three sections focus on each individual group of regular verbs. If you can master the conjugation of regular verbs, you'll be able to express yourself in everyday situations. When you speak to your friends, when you wait for the train, when you buy groceries, or when you visit your relatives, you use common, regular present-tense verbs.

Looking At -er Verbs

The **-er** verbs are the most common group of French verbs. But knowing this interesting bit of trivia can't help you correctly conjugate these verbs. Don't worry — in this section, I show you how to conjugate the present tense of **-er** verbs. This information can help you conjugate hundreds of **-er** verbs.

The verb **parler** (*to speak*) serves as an example in this group. Take **parler** and drop the **-er,** which leaves you with the stem (**parl-**). Then add the appropriate ending (**-e, -es, -e, -ons, -ez,** or **-ent**) depending on the subject pronoun. For example, if you start a sentence with **je** (*I*), and you have an **-er** verb, you need the **-e** ending.

Use the following table to correctly conjugate a regular present tense **-er** verb.

Regular Present Tense -er Verb Endings	
je **-e**	nous **-ons**
tu **-es**	vous **-ez**
il/elle/on **-e**	ils/elles **-ent**

The present-tense conjugations for a regular **-er** verb such as **parler** (*to speak*) are as follows:

parler (to speak)	
je parl**e**	nous parl**ons**
tu parl**es**	vous parl**ez**
il/elle/on parl**e**	ils/elles parl**ent**
Je **parle** français. (*I speak French, I am speaking French,* or *I do speak French.*)	

This pattern applies to all regular **-er** verbs. Table 2-1 lists some common **-er** verbs that you may encounter in everyday life when speaking French. (You can also check out Appendix A for more regular **-er** verbs.)

Table 2-1	Common Regular -er Verbs
-er Verb	*Translation*
adorer	*to adore*
aimer	*to like, to love*
arriver	*to arrive*
chanter	*to sing*
chercher	*to look for*

-er Verb	Translation
danser	to dance
demander	to ask
écouter	to listen to
enseigner	to teach
étudier	to study
habiter	to live (somewhere)
jouer	to play
jouer à	to play a sport or game
jouer de	to play an instrument
marcher	to walk
regarder	to watch/look at
rencontrer	to meet
téléphoner	to call
tomber	to fall
travailler	to work
trouver	to find
visiter	to visit (a place, not people)

If the verb begins with a vowel or a mute **h,** drop the **e** of **je** and add an apostrophe. For example, **j'aime** (*I like/love*) or **j'habite** (*I live*). However, the **u** in **tu** is never dropped, so you still have **tu aimes** or **tu habites.** And don't forget that the present tense has three different meanings in English. **Je chante** means *I sing, I do sing,* and *I am singing.*

Now it's your turn. In each blank, provide the correct conjugation of the verbs in parentheses. In the example and the following questions, use the corresponding endings for each subject pronoun. (I provide an English translation in the answers.)

0. Tu _____ (aimer) le théâtre.

A. Tu **aimes** le théâtre. (*You like the theater.*)

1. Mon père _____ (travailler).

2. Nous _____ (jouer) au tennis.

3. Le chœur _____ (chanter).

4. Ils _____ (habiter) à Boston.

5. Tu _____ (chercher) les billets.

6. Les enfants _____ (regarder) la télévision.

7. J' _____ (adorer) le chocolat.

8. Ma mère _____ (écouter) la radio.

9. Nous _____ (étudier) le français.

10. Mes amis _____ (chercher) un appartement.

Focusing On -ir Verbs

The second group of French verbs, the **-ir** verbs, is just as easy to form in the present as the **-er** verbs. You don't have to be a native to figure out these conjugations. The **-ir** verbs can help you *choose* (**choisir**), *succeed* (**réussir**), and even *grow old gracefully* (**vieillir**).

To form the present tense for **-ir** verbs, simply drop the final **r** of the infinitive and add the following endings to the stem:

Regular Present Tense -ir Verb Endings	
je **-s**	nous **-ssons**
tu **-s**	vous **-ssez**
il/elle/on **-t**	ils/elles **-ssent**

The present-tense conjugations for a regular **-ir** verb such as **finir** (*to finish*) are as follows:

finir (*to finish*)	
je fini**s**	nous fini**ssons**
tu fini**s**	vous fini**ssez**
il/elle/on fini**t**	ils/elles fini**ssent**
Je **finis** mes devoirs. (*I finish my homework, I am finishing my homework, I do finish my homework.*)	

Table 2-2 lists some common **-ir** verbs you may encounter when speaking French. No matter what verb you choose from this list, take it and try out the present tense conjugation.

Table 2-2	Common Regular -ir Verbs
-ir Verb	*Translation*
applaudir	*to applaud*
bâtir	*to build*
choisir	*to choose*
établir	*to establish*
finir	*to finish*
grandir	*to grow (up)*

-ir Verb	Translation
grossir	to gain weight
maigrir	to lose weight
obéir à	to obey
pâlir	to turn pale
punir	to punish
réagir	to react
réfléchir à	to reflect, to think (about)
remplir	to fill
réunir	to unite, to gather, to assemble, to meet
réussir (à)	to succeed (in)/to pass a test
vieillir	to grow old

If you're ready to try for yourself, check out the example, and then move on to the questions that follow. In the first blank for each question, write the correct conjugated form of the verb in parentheses.

Q. Les enfants _____ (grandir).

A. Les enfants **grandissent.** (*Children grow up.*)

11. Il _____ (grossir).

12. Nous _____ (applaudir).

13. On _____ (obéir) aux lois (*the laws*).

14. Tu _____ (choisir) le champagne.

15. Les ingénieurs _____ (bâtir) un pont.

16. Je _____ (réfléchir).

17. Vous _____ (pâlir).

18. Nous _____ (réunir) les pièces du puzzle.

19. Les enfants _____ (finir) leurs devoirs.

20. Tu _____ (réussir).

Trying -re Verbs

The third and final group of regular verbs is the **-re** group. This verb form is also easy to conjugate. Just drop the **-re** from the infinitive and add the appropriate endings to the stem. The following conjugation chart shows what I mean.

Regular Present Tense -re Verb Endings	
je **-s**	nous **-ons**
tu **-s**	vous **-ez**
il/elle/on (nothing)	ils/elles **-ent**

You don't add any endings to the third person singular **il**, **elle**, or **on**. The stem is enough. For example, **il attend** means *he waits*, *he's waiting*, or *he does wait*.

The present tense conjugations for a regular **-re** verb such as **vendre** (*to sell*) are as follows:

vendre (*to sell*)	
je vend**s**	nous vend**ons**
tu vend**s**	vous vend**ez**
il/elle/on vend	ils/elles vend**ent**
Je **vends** la maison. (*I sell the house, I'm selling the house, I do sell the house.*)	

Table 2-3 provides some more examples of common **-re** verbs that are conjugated exactly like **vendre**.

Table 2-3	Common Regular -re Verbs
-re Verbs	*Translation*
attendre	*to wait for*
descendre	*to go down* (*the stairs*)
entendre	*to hear*
fondre	*to melt*
pendre	*to hang*
perdre	*to lose, to waste time*
rendre	*to give back, to return*
rendre visite à quelqu'un	*to pay a visit to someone* (*to visit someone*)
répondre à	*to answer*

Conjugate the **-re** verbs in parentheses. I show you how in the example. (I give you a translation in the answer to help you out.)

Q. Je _____ (attendre).

A. **J'attends.** (*I wait, I am waiting, I do wait.*)

21. Nous _____ (répondre) aux questions.

22. Tu _____ (pendre) les vêtements.

23. La neige _____ (fondre) lentement.

24. Je _____ (rendre) visite à ma tante.

25. Ils _____ (entendre) les cloches.

26. Françoise _____ (descendre).

27. Le professeur _____ (rendre) les compositions.

28. Tu _____ (perdre) ton temps.

29. Vous _____ (attendre) vos amis.

30. Les étudiants _____ (vendre) leur livre.

Modifying Actions with Adverbs

You can make all the verbs in this chapter more interesting by adding adverbs and placing them after the verb. To add an adverb to a sentence, just conjugate the verb and place an adverb after it. Think of how you can do something frequently, often, sometimes, rarely, and so on.

Il parle constamment. (*He is constantly talking* or *he talks constantly.*)

Table 2-4 provides some of the more commonly used adverbs with the present tense.

Table 2-4	Present-Tense Adverbs
Adverb	*Translation*
absolument	*absolutely*
assez	*enough*
attentivement	*attentively*
beaucoup	*a lot*
bien	*well*
constamment	*constantly*
facilement	*easily*
fréquemment	*frequently*
lentement	*slowly*
mal	*poorly, badly*
parfois	*at times*
peu	*little*
quelquefois	*sometimes*
rarement	*rarely*

(continued)

Table 2-4 *(continued)*	
Adverb	*Translation*
sérieusement	*seriously*
souvent	*often*
toujours	*always*
trop	*too much*
vite	*quickly*
vraiment	*truly*

It's your turn. Find and conjugate the French verb correctly and add the appropriate adverb after you consult the English translation, just like in the example.

Q. Federer _____ au tennis. (*Federer plays tennis well.*)

A. Federer **joue bien** au tennis.

31. L'étudiant _____. (*The student listens attentively.*)

32. Mon frère _____. (*My brother studies little.*)

33. Je _____. (*I go down the stairs quickly.*)

34. Nous _____ ce restaurant. (*We often choose this restaurant.*)

35. Les ouvriers _____. (*The workers work too much.*)

36. Ma sœur _____. (*My sister talks constantly.*)

37. Tu _____. (*You hear well.*)

38. Ma collègue _____ la radio. (*My colleague always listens to the radio.*)

39. Je _____ à mes messages. (*I sometimes answer my messages.*)

40. Ils _____ en retard. (*They rarely finish late.*)

Forming Sentences: Word by Word

When forming sentences, identifying the type of verb you're using is important. Look at the ending of the regular verb. Is it an **-er, -ir,** or **-re** verb? The answer is important because it allows you to follow a specific pattern. After you determine what type of verb you have, then you conjugate it the same way as one of the example verbs in this chapter. If it's an **-er** verb, conjugate it like **parler;** an **-ir** verb, conjugate it like **finir;** or an **-re** verb, conjugate it like **vendre.**

Make sure that the verb endings correspond to the subject that you choose. Remember that **nous** endings always end in **-ons, vous** in **-ez,** and **ils/elles** end in **-ent** for all regular verbs. After you check your subject and verb, add an adverb of your choice, and voilà, you've formed a sentence.

Put the following fragments into complete French sentences.

Q. Tu/réussir/toujours

_____

A. **Tu réussis toujours.** (*You always succeed.*)

41. Il/jouer/bien

_____

42. Nous/attendre/fréquemment

_____

43. Ils/perdre/rarement

_____

44. Elle/écouter/attentivement

_____

45. Tu/étudier/beaucoup

_____

46. Nous/manger/assez

_____

47. Je/choisir/bien

_____

48. Elles/réagir/mal

_____

49. Nous/répondre/sérieusement

_____

50. Tu/travailler/constamment

_____

Answer Key

In this section you can find the answers to all the practice problems in this chapter. (Remember that the present tense in French has three different meanings in English.) How did you do?

1 Mon père **travaille**. (*My father is working.*)

2 Nous **jouons** au tennis. (*We play tennis.*)

3 Le chœur **chante**. (*The choir is singing.*)

4 Ils **habitent** à Boston. (*They live in Boston.*)

5 Tu **cherches** les billets. (*You are looking for the tickets.*)

6 Les enfants **regardent** la télévision. (*The children are watching television.*)

7 J'**adore** le chocolat. (*I adore chocolate.*)

8 Ma mère **écoute** la radio. (*My mother listens to the radio.*)

9 Nous **étudions** le français. (*We study French.*)

10 Mes amis **cherchent** un appartement. (*My friends are looking for an apartment.*)

11 Il **grossit**. (*He is gaining weight.*)

12 Nous **applaudissons**. (*We are applauding.*)

13 On **obéit** aux lois. (*One/We obeys/obey the laws.*)

14 Tu **choisis** le champagne. (*You choose/are choosing the champagne.*)

15 Les ingénieurs **bâtissent** un pont. (*The engineers are building a bridge.*)

16 Je **réfléchis**. (*I am thinking.*)

17 Vous **pâlissez**. (*You are turning pale.*)

18 Nous **réunissons** les pièces du puzzle. (*We are gathering the pieces of the puzzle.*)

19 Les enfants **finissent** leurs devoirs. (*The children are finishing their homework.*)

20 Tu **réussis**. (*You are succeeding.*)

21 Nous **répondons** aux questions. (*We answer the questions;* Literally: *We respond to the questions.*)

22 Tu **pends** les vêtements. (*You hang up the clothes.*)

23 La neige **fond** lentement. (*The snow melts slowly.*)

24 Je **rends** visite à ma tante. (*I am visiting my aunt.*)

25 Ils **entendent** les cloches. (*They hear the bells.*)

26 Françoise **descend**. (*Françoise goes down [the stairs].*)

27   Le professeur **rend** les compositions. (*The professor is handing back the compositions.*)

28   Tu **perds** ton temps. (*You are wasting your time.*)

29   Vous **attendez** vos amis. (*You are waiting for your friends.*)

30   Les étudiants **vendent** leur livre. (*The students sell their books.*)

31   L'étudiant **écoute attentivement.** (*The student listens attentively.*)

32   Mon frère **étudie peu.** (*My brother studies little.*)

33   Je **descends vite.** (*I go down the stairs quickly.*)

34   Nous **choisissons souvent** ce restaurant. (*We often choose this restaurant.*)

35   Les ouvriers **travaillent trop.** (*The workers work too much.*)

36   Ma sœur **parle constamment.** (*My sister talks constantly.*)

37   Tu **entends bien.** (*You hear well.*)

38   Ma collègue **écoute toujours** la radio. (*My colleague always listens to the radio.*)

39   Je **réponds quelquefois** à mes messages. (*I sometimes answer my messages.*)

40   Ils **finissent rarement** en retard. (*They rarely finish late.*)

41   **Il joue bien.** (*He plays well.*)

42   **Nous attendons fréquemment.** (*We frequently wait.*)

43   **Ils perdent rarement.** (*They rarely lose.*)

44   **Elle écoute attentivement.** (*She listens attentively.*)

45   **Tu étudies beaucoup.** (*You study a lot.*)

46   **Nous mangeons assez.** (*We eat enough.*)

47   **Je choisis bien.** (*I choose well.*)

48   **Elles réagissent mal.** (*They react badly.*)

49   **Nous répondons sérieusement.** (*We respond seriously.*)

50   **Tu travailles constamment.** (*You are constantly working.*)

Chapter 3

Knowing How to Handle Spelling-Change Verbs

In This Chapter
▶ Trying out different spelling-change verbs
▶ Making sentences with these verbs

Spelling-change verbs are common verbs that you use every day. For instance, when you buy (**acheter**) groceries, when you call (**appeler**) someone, or when you travel (**voyager**) somewhere, you use this type of verb. Spelling-change verbs are similar to regular **-er** verbs but with a slight change in the stem. For example, verbs whose infinitives end in **-ger** or **-cer** require changes only in the first person plural (the **nous** form). Everything else is regular. Other verbs require an accent grave on the mute **e** or a double consonant after the mute **e.** Don't worry though, in this chapter I show you these changes step by step. Keep in mind that no matter what the changes are, the endings of all these verbs are those of regular **-er** verbs, like **parler** (*to speak*). (Check out Chapter 2 for information about conjugating regular verbs.)

Taking a Stab at Spelling-Change Verbs

When speaking French, sometimes you encounter regular **-er** verbs that have a slight spelling change. Don't worry about difficult spelling. I don't ask you to spell "hors-d'oeuvre" or "Versailles" in this section. Instead, this section focuses on the **-er** verbs that have spelling changes within their conjugations. I show you these changes, but note that the endings of these verbs are the same as those of regular **-er** verbs.

Managing -ger verbs

The verbs that end in **-ger**, like **manger** (*to eat*) have a spelling change in the **nous** form only. Unlike the regular **-er** verbs, **-ger** verbs need to keep the **e** before the **-ons** in the **nous** form. To form the present tense, drop the **-er** of the infinitive and add the following endings, just like you do for the regular **-er** verbs:

Common Spelling Change for -ger Verb Endings	
je **-e**	nous **-eons**
tu **-es**	vous **-ez**
il/elle/on **-e**	ils/elles **-ent**

As you may have noticed, the only difference between **-er** and **-ger** verbs is in the **nous** form where you add the **e** before the **ons.** This difference occurs because the **e** after the **g** in front of an **a, o,** or **u** softens the pronunciation of the **g,** which is pronounced like the **s** in the word *pleasure.* If the **e** isn't in front of **ons,** then the **g** is pronounced like the **g** in the word *guess.*

Check out the following example of the conjugation of **manger** (*to eat*).

manger (*to eat*)	
je mang**e**	nous mang**eons**
tu mang**es**	vous mang**ez**
il/elle/on mang**e**	ils/elles mang**ent**
Je **mange** une salade. (*I eat a salad,* or *I am eating a salad.*)	

Table 3-1 provides you with a list of some common **-ger** verbs that have the same conjugation as **manger.**

Table 3-1	Common Spelling-Change Verbs
Verb	*Translation*
changer	*to change*
mélanger	*to mix*
nager	*to swim*
obliger	*to oblige, to force*
partager	*to share*
plonger	*to dive*
voyager	*to travel*

I provide a few practice problems for you. Try conjugating these verbs.

Q. Nous _____ (partager) le bureau.

A. Nous **partageons** le bureau. (*We share the office.*)

1. Tu _____ (mélanger) les ingrédients.

2. Nous _____ (plonger).

3. Ils _____ (voyager).

4. Elle _____ (changer).

5. Nous _____ (nager).

Working with -cer verbs

Verbs whose infinitive ends in **-cer** are similar to those whose infinitive ends in **-ger** (see the previous section). Both are conjugated exactly like regular **-er** verbs, except for the **nous** form. The **nous** form of the **-cer** verbs requires a cedilla on the **c (ç)**. These **-cer** verbs are also common, everyday verbs. When you want to begin something (**commencer**), announce something (**annoncer**), influence someone (**influencer**), or make progress in something (**avancer**), you use **-cer** verbs.

Notice that with the exception of the **nous** form, the conjugation exactly matches the regular **-er** verbs. (Check out Chapter 2 for details on how to conjugate a regular **-er** verb.)

Common Spelling Change for -cer Verb Endings	
je **-e**	nous **-çons**
tu **-es**	vous **-ez**
il/elle/on **-e**	ils/elles **-ent**

Check out the following example of **commencer** (*to begin*):

commencer (*to begin*)	
je commenc**e**	nous commen**çons**
tu commenc**es**	vous commenc**ez**
il/elle/on commenc**e**	ils/elles commen**cent**
Je **commence** mon travail. (*I begin my work,* or *I am beginning my work.*)	

Now that you have an understanding of how to conjugate **-cer** verbs, check out Table 3-2 for a list of some other useful **-cer** verbs.

Table 3-2	Common -cer Verbs
Verb	**Translation**
annoncer	*to announce*
avancer	*to advance, to make progress*
influencer	*to influence*
lancer	*to throw*
menacer	*to threaten*
placer	*to place*
remplacer	*to replace*

Practice conjugating the verbs in parentheses.

Q. Il _____ (influencer) ses amis.

A. Il **influence** ses amis. (*He influences his friends.*)

    6. Nous _____ (avancer).

    7. Je _____ (annoncer) les prix.

    8. Ils _____ (menacer) les enfants.

    9. Elle _____ (remplacer) Paul.

    10. Vous _____ (lancer) la balle.

In these practice problems, I put the **-ger** and **-cer** verbs together. Conjugate the verbs in parentheses.

    11. Jean et Marie-Claire _____ (annoncer) leurs fiançailles.

    12. Mon patron _____ (voyager) en France.

    13. Nous _____ (placer) nos affaires dans l'armoire.

    14. Mes parents _____ (commencer) à apprendre le japonais.

    15. Je _____ (nager) très bien.

    16. Nous _____ (partager) une bouteille de vin.

    17. Tu _____ (changer) d'avis.

    18. Les étudiants _____ (avancer) en mathématiques.

    19. Le chat _____ (menacer) la souris.

    20. Nous _____ (manger) un grand repas le dimanche.

Keeping an eye on the silent types

Two other types of **-er** verbs have a mute or silent **e** in the infinitive. In order to conjugate these types of verbs, you must pronounce the **e** in all but the **nous** and **vous** forms, and therefore spelling changes occur in the rest of the conjugation for phonetic reasons. What do you do to the verb in order to pronounce the **e?** You either add an accent grave (`) to the **e** (**è**) or double the consonant after it. Note that the endings of these verbs are like all regular **-er** verbs. Just drop the **-er** from the infinitive and stick to the endings in the following chart.

Common Spelling-Change Verb Endings	
je -**e**	nous -**ons**
tu -**es**	vous -**ez**
il/elle/on -**e**	ils/elles -**ent**

First, I begin with verbs to which you add the accent grave, like **acheter** (*to buy*).

acheter (*to buy*)	
j'achète	nous achetons
tu achètes	vous achetez
il/elle/on achète	ils/elles achètent
J'**achète** des légumes. (*I buy vegetables,* or *I am buying vegetables.*)	

You add the accent grave only to the entire singular and third person plural (**je, tu, il/elle/on,** and **ils/elles**). The **nous** and **vous** forms don't have an accent grave. *Note:* When you have an irregularity in the conjugation of a verb, usually the **nous** and **vous** forms resemble the infinitive. In other words, the infinitive has no accent grave, so the **nous** and **vous** forms have no accent grave. Notice also that the endings are the same as regular **-er** verbs. Check out Table 3-3 for other verbs like **acheter.**

Table 3-3	Adding an Accent Grave (è) to the Mute e
Verb	*Translation*
amener	*to bring*
geler	*to freeze*
lever	*to raise*
mener	*to lead, to take along*
peser	*to weigh*
promener	*to take a person or a pet for a walk*
***se lever**	*to get up, to stand*
***se promener**	*to take a stroll, to take a walk*

* *se lever* and ***se promener*** are reflexive verbs; see Chapter 5 for more information.

See whether you can work through the following practice problems that help you with this verb type.

Q. Elle _____ (acheter) des fruits.

A. Elle **achète** des fruits. (*She buys fruit.*)

21. Ils _____ (promener) le chien.

22. Nous _____ (geler).

23. Tu _____ (peser) 60 kilos.

24. Je _____ (amener) mes enfants.

25. Vous _____ (lever) la main.

Handling é verbs

Verbs that have an **é** or **e accent aigu** in the second to the last syllable in their infinitive also undergo changes. The accent aigu (**é**) changes to an accent grave (**è**) in the entire singular and the third person plural (**je, tu, il/elle/on,** and **ils/elles**). Note that the **nous** and **vous** forms don't change and have the same accents as the infinitives. Remember that the endings are like the regular **-er** verbs (check out Chapter 2 to see how to conjugate regular **-er** verbs).

espérer (to hope)	
j'espère	nous espérons
tu espères	vous espérez
il/elle/on espère	ils/elles espèrent
J'espère que tu vas bien. (*I hope you're doing well.*)	

Check out the list of verbs that are similar to **espérer** in Table 3-4.

Table 3-4	Changing the é to è
Verb	*Translation*
céder	*to give up, to yield*
exagérer	*to exaggerate*
***préférer**	*to prefer*
protéger	*to protect*
***répéter**	*to repeat*
suggérer	*to suggest*

Note:* The first **é in the verbs **préférer** and **répéter** never changes; the second **é** changes to **è** in all the subject pronouns except for **nous** and **vous**.

Try conjugating verbs that have an **é** in the following exercise.

Q. Il _____ (céder) sa place.

A. Il **cède** sa place. (*He gives up his seat.*)

26. Je _____ (préférer) la soupe.

27. Les étudiants _____ (répéter).

28. Tu _____ (exagérer).

29. Nous _____ (protéger) les petits chats. (*the kittens*)

30. Elles _____ (espérer).

Figuring out -eter and -eler verbs

Some verbs that end in **-eter** and **-eler** double the **t** or **l** after the mute **e** (except with **nous** and **vous**) in order to pronounce the **e.** The endings are the same as those of regular **-er** verbs.

See the following example of **jeter** (*to throw*).

jeter (*to throw*)	
je je**tte**	nous je**tons**
tu je**ttes**	vous je**tez**
il/elle/on je**tte**	ils/elles je**ttent**
Je **jette** la balle. (*I throw the ball,* or *I am throwing the ball.*)	

For a list of some of the more common types of these verbs, check out Table 3-5.

Table 3-5	Common -eter and -eler Verbs
Verb	*Translation*
appeler	*to call*
épeler	*to spell*
rappeler	*to call back*
rejeter	*to reject*
***s'appeler**	*to be called* (*to be named*)
***se rappeler**	*to remember*

*Refer to Chapter 5 for more on these pronominal verbs.

Take the time to work on these practice problems and perfect your use of **-eter** and **-eler** verbs.

Q. Je _____ (rejeter) l'idée.

A. Je **rejette** l'idée. (*I reject the idea.*)

31. Nous _____ (épeler) notre nom.

32. Ils _____ (rejeter) la proposition.

33. Tu _____ (appeler) le docteur.

34. Vous _____ (jeter) des cailloux.

35. Je _____ (rappeler) mes enfants.

Dotting the i in -yer verbs

The last group of spelling-change verbs with regular endings is the group of infinitives that ends in **-yer**. In this group, the **y** changes to an **i** in front of a mute **e**. Use the following example as a guide for conjugating the **-yer** verbs.

I conjugate the verb **essayer** (*to try*) as an example of this type of verb.

essayer (to try)	
j'essaie	nous essayons
tu essaies	vous essayez
il/elle/on essaie	ils/elles essaient
J'essaie le vin. (*I try the wine*, or *I am trying the wine.*)	

The spelling changes of this type of verb occur only in the entire singular and the third person plural. Spell the **nous** and **vous** forms just like the infinitive form of the verb and add the endings **-ons** and **-ez** after you drop the **-er.**

Do you want a few more verbs to practice? Table 3-6 covers some important **-yer** verbs that are conjugated similarly.

Table 3-6	Common -yer Verbs
Verb	*Translation*
employer	*to use*
ennuyer	*to bother*
envoyer	*to send*
essuyer	*to wipe*
nettoyer	*to clean*
payer	*to pay*
s'ennuyer	*to be bored*
tutoyer	*to address someone using the **tu** form, informally*
vouvoyer	*to address someone using the **vous** form, formally*

Try conjugating some of these **-yer** verbs.

0. Tu _____ (envoyer) une lettre.

A. Tu **envoies** une lettre. (*You send a letter.*)

36. Elle _____ (payer).

37. Nous _____ (nettoyer).

38. Tu _____ (essuyer) la table.

39. Ils _____ (employer) le dictionnaire.

40. Il _____ (ennuyer) Luc.

Now that you're familiar with many of these spelling-change verbs, take the time to conjugate some of these different types of verbs in the following problems, and then translate the sentences.

Q. Suzanne _____ (essayer) les escargots.

A. Suzanne **essaie** les escargots. *Suzanne tries the snails.*

41. Tu _____ (appeler) ton ami.

_____

42. L'épicier _____ (peser) les tomates.

_____

43. Les enfants _____ (s'ennuyer) à la maison.

_____

44. Je _____ (acheter) les billets pour le théâtre.

_____

45. Ils _____ (répéter) après le professeur.

_____

46. Nous _____ (nettoyer) la maison.

_____

47. Le sommelier _____ (lever) le verre de vin.

_____

48. L'équipe _____ (jeter) la balle.

_____

49. Tu _____ (amener) ton frère à l'école.

_____

50. Les Martin nous _____ (envoyer) des cadeaux.

_____

51. Elle _____ (espérer) continuer ses études.

_____

52. La neige _____ (geler) l'étang.

_____

53. Je _____ (essuyer) les meubles.

_____

54. Tu _____ (essayer) le foie gras.

_____

55. Nous _____ (préférer) la soupe à l'oignon.

_____

56. Marc _____ (épeler) son nom avec un **c.**

_____

57. Les parents _____ (protéger) leurs enfants.

_____

58. Ils _____ (rejeter) le candidat.

_____

59. Tu _____ (exagérer) vraiment!

_____

60. Elle _____ (mener) son chien.

_____

Building Sentences: Word by Word

Do you have a grasp of the verbs in this chapter? Do you feel comfortable putting them into complete sentences? If you don't, I suggest you revisit any verb type that's causing you concern.

To actually build a sentence with these verbs, take the verb and conjugate it in the present tense. You can also add adverbs to give further meaning or emphasis to the verbs. (See Chapter 2 for more information on adverbs.) You can say how frequently, how well, how seriously, or even how attentively you do something. Then add appropriate nouns to form a complete sentence. Remember that along with the conjugation of these verbs, you also acquire new vocabulary by knowing what they mean.

Tu voyages fréquemment. (*You travel frequently.*)

Il appelle souvent son ami. (*He often calls his friend.*)

Try translating the following sentences. If you get stuck, refer to the tables earlier in this chapter. Note that the present tense in French has three meanings in English. For example, **Jean et Marie-Claire annoncent leurs fiançailles** means *Jean and Marie-Claire announce, do announce,* or *are announcing their engagement.*

I complete the first one for you. Check out the following example.

0. I am constantly traveling.

A. **Je voyage constamment.**

61. They wipe the table.

_____

62. We mix the ingredients well.

_____

63. The students repeat frequently after the professor.

_____

64. I send e-mails often.

_____

65. Michelle rarely calls.

_____

66. We are changing our phone number.

_____

67. The people are influencing the politicians.

_____

68. Tim is really annoying his sister.

_____

69. I am walking my dog.

_____

70. The clients are paying the bill.

_____

Answer Key

In this section, I give you the answers to all the practice problems in this chapter. I also provide the most common translations to help you improve your French vocabulary. (Remember that the present tense in French has three potential translations.)

1 Tu **melanges** les ingrédients. (*You mix the ingredients.*)

2 Nous **plongeons.** (*We dive.*)

3 Ils **voyagent.** (*They travel.*)

4 Elle **change.** (*She changes.*)

5 Nous **nageons.** (*We swim.*)

6 Nous **avançons.** (*We advance.*)

7 J'**annonce** les prix. (*I am announcing the prizes.*)

8 Ils **menacent** les enfants. (*They threaten the children.*)

9 Elle **remplace** Paul. (*She replaces Paul.*)

10 Vous **lancez** la balle. (*You throw the ball.*)

11 Jean et Marie-Claire **annoncent** leurs fiançailles. (*Jean and Marie-Claire announce their engagement.*)

12 Mon patron **voyage** en France. (*My boss is traveling to France.*)

13 Nous **plaçons** nos affaires dans l'armoire. (*We are placing our things in the armoire.*)

14 Mes parents **commencent** à apprendre le japonais. (*My parents are beginning to learn Japanese.*)

15 Je **nage** très bien. (*I swim very well.*)

16 Nous **partageons** une bouteille de vin. (*We are sharing a bottle of wine.*)

17 Tu **changes** d'avis. (*You are changing your mind.*)

18 Les étudiants **avancent** en mathématiques. (*The students are advancing in mathematics.*)

19 Le chat **menace** la souris. (*The cat is threatening the mouse.*)

20 Nous **mangeons** un grand repas le dimanche. (*We eat a big meal on Sundays.*)

21 Ils **promènent le chien.** (*They take the dog for a walk.*)

22 Nous **gelons.** (*We are freezing.*)

23 Tu **pèses** 60 kilos. (*You weigh 60 kilograms.*)

24 J'**amène** mes enfants. (*I am bringing my children.*)

25 Vous **levez** la main. (*You raise your hand.*)

26 Je **préfère la soupe.** (*I prefer the soup.*)

27 Les étudiants **répètent.** (*The students repeat.*)

28 Tu **exagères.** (*You exaggerate.*)

29 Nous **protégeons** les petits chats. (*We protect the kittens.*)

30 Elles **espèrent.** (*They hope.*)

31 Nous **épelons** notre nom. (*We spell our name.*)

32 Ils **rejettent** la proposition. (*They reject the proposal.*)

33 Tu **appelles** le docteur. (*You call the doctor.*)

34 Vous **jetez** des cailloux. (*You throw pebbles.*)

35 Je **rappelle** mes enfants. (*I call my children back.*)

36 Elle **paie.** (*She is paying.*)

37 Nous **nettoyons.** (*We clean.*)

38 Tu **essuies** la table. (*You wipe the table.*)

39 Ils **emploient** le dictionnaire. (*They use the dictionary.*)

40 Il **ennuie** Luc. (*He bothers Luc.*)

41 Tu **appelles** ton ami. *You call your friend.*

42 L'épicier **pèse** les tomates. *The grocer weighs the tomatoes.*

43 Les enfants **s'ennuient** à la maison. *The children are bored in the house.*

44 J'**achète** les billets pour le théâtre. *I am buying the tickets for the theater.*

45 Ils **répètent** après le professeur. *They repeat after the professor.*

46 Nous **nettoyons** la maison. *We are cleaning the house.*

47 Le sommelier **lève** le verre de vin. *The wine steward is raising the glass of wine.*

48 L'equipe **jette** la balle. *The team throws the ball.*

49 Tu **amènes** ton frère à l'école. *You bring your brother to school.*

50 Les Martin nous **envoient** des cadeaux. *The Martins send us gifts.*

Elle **espère** continuer ses études. *She hopes to continue her studies.*

La neige **gèle** l'étang. *The snow freezes the pond.*

J'**essuie** les meubles. *I am wiping the furniture.*

Tu **essaies** le foie gras. *You are trying the foie gras.*

Nous **préférons** la soupe à l'oignon. *We prefer the onion soup.*

Marc **épelle** son nom avec un **c.** *Marc spells his name with a **c.***

Les parents **protègent** leurs enfants. *The parents protect their children.*

Ils **rejettent** le candidat. *They reject the candidate.*

Tu **exagères** vraiment! *You really exaggerate!*

Elle **mène** son chien. *She is bringing her dog.*

Ils essuient la table.

Nous mélangeons bien les ingrédients.

Les étudiants répètent fréquemment après le professeur.

J'envoie souvent des e-mails tous.

Michelle appelle rarement.

Nous changeons notre numéro de téléphone.

Les gens influencent les politiciens.

Tim ennuie vraiment sa soeur.

Je promène mon chien.

Les clients paient l'addition.

Chapter 4

Wrestling with Some Irregular Conjugations

· ·

In This Chapter

▶ Breaking down irregular verbs

▶ Putting different irregular verbs together

· ·

*I*n Chapter 2, I introduce the regular verbs whose infinitives end in **-er, -ir,** and **-re.** Some verbs with these endings, however, have an irregular conjugation. They're harder to conjugate because they don't have a consistent stem throughout their conjugation, but most have similar endings, making them a little easier to figure out.

In this chapter, I start with the most common and most frequently used irregular verbs. I then focus on different groupings of irregular verbs and show you how to conjugate them all. (If you want to work on other not-quite-so-common irregular verbs, you can find more in Appendix C.)

Conjugating Irregular Verbs

From your experiences, you probably realize that nothing is run-of-the-mill. Just like in life where you may know a few eccentric people, French is similar with its own unique verbs. They're not at all like the regular verbs you find in Chapter 2 (or even Chapter 3). These verbs are irregular and in a world of their own.

This section first covers the four most commonly used irregular verbs in the French language and then delves into other frequently used irregular verbs.

Focusing on the four most common irregular verbs

The following are the most common irregular verbs in the French language. I wish I had a clear-cut, easy way for you to master these irregular beasts. The only suggestion I can make is that you study each one and practice using it; I'm sure each will be become second nature to you in no time. A good way to make these verbs your own is to practice saying them out loud to try to build up a certain rhythm. You may even try making a song out of the conjugations, using your favorite melody.

Even with the following irregular conjugations, you may notice some consistencies; for example, the **nous** form in French always ends in **-ons,** and the **vous** form almost always ends in **-ez** (exceptions include **être, dire,** and **faire,** whose **vous** forms end in **-es** instead). Because the verbs in this section are irregular, I bold the entire conjugation and not just the ending in the following tables. From these four verbs, **avoir** and **être** are the two auxiliary verbs. That means that you always use them when forming the compound past tenses, which I discuss in Part III.

avoir (*to have*)	
j'**ai**	nous **avons**
tu **as**	vous **avez**
il/elle/on **a**	ils/elles **ont**
J'**ai** trois enfants. (*I have three children.*)	

être (*to be*)	
je **suis**	nous **sommes**
tu **es**	vous **êtes**
il/elle/on **est**	ils/elles **sont**
Ils **sont** gentils. (*They are nice.*)	

aller (*to go*)	
je **vais**	nous **allons**
tu **vas**	vous **allez**
il/elle/on **va**	ils/elles **vont**
Nous **allons** au cinéma. (*We are going to the movies.*)	

faire (*to do, to make*)	
je **fais**	nous **faisons**
tu **fais**	vous **faites**
il/elle/on **fait**	ils/elles **font**
Tu **fais** du bruit. (*You are making noise.*)	

Other verbs conjugated like **faire** are **refaire** (*to redo*), **défaire** (*to dismantle*), and **satisfaire** (*to satisfy*).

The four verbs in this section are the most common irregular verbs in French. Try the following practice problems to double-check how well you know them. I've conjugated the verbs in the following sentences, but I may not have conjugated them correctly. Check to see whether they're right, and correct the ones that are wrong by writing the correct conjugation in the provided blank. If you come across any that are already correct, simply write "yes" in the blank.

Q. Tu va à l'université.

A. No. Tu **vas** à l'université. (*You are going to the university.*)

1. Tu fait ton lit.

2. Ils vont à la plage.

_____

3. Claudine es canadienne.

_____

4. J'ai de la chance.

_____

5. Vous faitez du ski.

_____

6. Les touristes disont au revoir.

_____

7. Tu vas bien.

_____

8. Vous sommes formidable.

_____

9. Philippe as un sac de couchage.

_____

10. Nous faisons une quiche.

_____

Working through other "helpful" irregular verbs

This next section of verbs focuses on important helping verbs. **Vouloir** (*to want to*), **pouvoir** (*to be able to*), and **devoir** (*to have to*) help the main verb, which is in the infinitive form. For example, **Je veux voyager** means *I want to travel;* **Je peux voyager** means *I am able to travel;* and **Je dois voyager** means *I have to travel.* The verbs **vouloir** and **devoir** can also be followed by nouns. For example, **Je veux du café** means *I want some coffee.* Usually the verb **vouloir** is in the conditional form when followed by a noun. (See Chapter 17 for the lowdown on the conditional tense.) When the verb **devoir** is followed by a noun, it means *to owe,* as in the example **Il me doit de l'argent,** which means *He owes me money.*

Look at the following conjugations to see how you handle these three common helping verbs. You may notice a lot of similarities between **pouvoir** and **vouloir,** such as their endings and their vowel sequence (**eu** in all the singular — **je, tu, il/elle/on** — and the third person plural — **ils/elles;** and **ou** in the **nous** and **vous** forms within the conjugation).

pouvoir (*to be able to*)	
je **peux**	nous **pouvons**
tu **peux**	vous **pouvez**
il/elle/on **peut**	ils/elles **peuvent**
Je **peux** parler français. (*I can [am able to] speak French.*)	

vouloir (*to want to*)	
je **veux**	nous **voulons**
tu **veux**	vous **voulez**
il/elle/on **veut**	ils/elles **veulent**
Nous **voulons** apprendre le français. (*We want to learn French.*)	

devoir (*to have to*)	
je **dois**	nous **devons**
tu **dois**	vous **devez**
il/elle/on **doit**	ils/elles **doivent**
Ils **doivent** lire. (*They have to read.*)	

Now it's your turn to conjugate these verbs and add the infinitives to make complete sentences. Work through the following practice questions and compare your answers to those in the key at the end of the chapter. Translate the sentences after you conjugate the verbs.

Q. Tu _____ (pouvoir) conduire.

A. Tu **peux** conduire. *You can drive.*

11. Nous _____ (vouloir) dormir.

_____

12. Ils _____ (pouvoir) lire.

_____

13. Je _____ (pouvoir) venir.

_____

14. Isabelle _____ (vouloir) sortir.

_____

15. Tu _____ (devoir) travailler.

_____

16. Vous _____ (pouvoir) parler français.

_____

17. Tout le monde _____ (vouloir) avoir de l'argent.

_____

18. Les filles _____ (vouloir) voyager.

_____

19. Je _____ (devoir) manger.

_____

20. Tu _____ (pouvoir) chanter.

_____

Grouping Irregular Verbs

Although many verbs have an irregular conjugation, you may be able to group them according to the ending of their infinitive or the similarity of their conjugation. For instance, many **-ir** verbs are irregular, but you can put them into three groups. If you remember the conjugation of one verb in a group, then you know the conjugation of all the verbs in that group. The following sections show each of the three groups and give you tips on how to remember each.

Looking at the "pseudo" -ir verbs

The following are irregular verbs that end in **-ir.** To conjugate these verbs, you need to keep the singular conjugation (the **je, tu,** and **il/elle/on**) separate from the plural conjugation (the **nous, vous,** and **ils/elles**). For the singular conjugation, get rid of not only the **-ir** of the infinitive, but also the consonant before the **-ir.** For example, for the verb **partir,** get rid of the **-tir** for the singular and add **-s, -s, -t.** Now for the plural, bring back the **t** from the infinitive and add **-ons, -ez, -ent.** For the verb **servir,** drop the **-vir** from the infinitive, add the ending **-s, -s, -t;** bring the **v** back for the plural and add **-ons, -ez, -ent.** Do this with all the verbs in this group.

"Pseudo" -ir Verb Endings	
je **-s**	nous **-ons**
tu **-s**	vous **-ez**
il/elle/on **-t**	ils/elles **-ent**

I use the verb **partir** (*to leave*) as an example. Check out the following conjugation.

partir (*to leave*)	
je par**s**	nous par**tons**
tu par**s**	vous par**tez**
il/elle/on par**t**	ils/elles par**tent**
Ils **partent** de l'école. (*They are leaving [from] school.*)	

Check out Table 4-1 for more examples of these types of verbs.

Table 4-1	Common "Pseudo" -ir Verbs	
Verb	*Translation*	*Where to Break the Infinitive*
dormir	*to sleep*	dor/mir
mentir	*to lie*	men/tir
ressentir	*to feel*	ressen/tir
se sentir	*to feel* (*well/unwell*)	se sen/tir
sentir	*to smell, to feel*	sen/tir
servir	*to serve*	ser/vir
sortir	*to go out*	sor/tir

Use the following practice exercises to double-check that you have a good grasp of these types of verbs. In each blank, write the correctly conjugated form of the verb in parentheses. I provide the translations in the Answer Key.

Q. Nous _____ (partir) demain matin.

A. Nous **partons** demain matin. (*We are leaving tomorrow morning.*)

21. Tu _____ (servir) les hors-d'oeuvre.

22. Nous _____ (dormir) tard le weekend.

23. Je _____ (sortir) le vendredi soir.

24. Elle _____ (mentir) quelquefois.

25. Ils _____ (servir) de la glace.

26. Vous _____ (sentir) bon.

27. Il _____ (partir) demain.

28. Tu _____ (dormir) trop.

29. Marie _____ (sortir) souvent.

30. Elles _____ (partir) pour l'Australie.

The "wannabes": -ir verbs acting like -er verbs

You conjugate this set of irregular **-ir** verbs like **-er** verbs, such as the verb **parler** (*to speak*). Drop the **-ir** of the infinitive and add the endings in the following table. (Don't the endings look familiar?)

The "Wannabe" Endings: -ir Verbs Acting Like -er Verbs	
je **-e**	nous **-ons**
tu **-es**	vous **-ez**
il/elle/on **-e**	ils/elles **-ent**

Check out the following example of the verb **ouvrir** (*to open*), conjugated.

ouvrir (*to open*)	
j'ouvr**e**	nous ouvr**ons**
tu ouvr**es**	vous ouvr**ez**
il/elle/on ouvr**e**	ils/elles ouvr**ent**
Nous **ouvrons** la porte. (*We open the door.*)	

Table 4-2 has some examples of this type of verb.

Table 4-2	Common "Wannabe" -ir Verbs
Verb	*Translation*
accueillir	*to welcome*
couvrir	*to cover*
cueillir	*to pick, to gather (flowers, vegetables, and so on)*
découvrir	*to discover*
offrir	*to offer*
souffrir	*to suffer*

Work through these practice problems for a quick review of the "wannabe" verbs. Conjugate the verb in parentheses and write your answer in the blank. (I provide the translation in the answers.)

Q. Tu _____ (souffrir) de la chaleur.

A. Tu **souffres** de la chaleur. (*You suffer/are suffering from the heat.*)

31. Nous _____ (cueillir) des fleurs.

32. Ils _____ (accueillir) leurs invités.

33. Je _____ (couvrir) mon livre.

34. Elle _____ (découvrir) la vérité.

35. Vous _____ (offrir) des bonbons.

"Deceptive" -ir verbs: Same endings, different stem

One more set of irregular verbs that end in **-ir** are verbs that are all alike, yet irregular compared to regular **-ir** verbs. These verbs have a conjugating pattern all their own. If you know how to conjugate one of them, then you can conjugate them all.

These **-ir** verbs have the same endings as regular **-ir** verbs but without the double **s** in the plural (check out Chapter 2). The irregularity here is in the stem. In fact, these verbs have two stems, one for the entire singular and third person plural and another for the **nous** and **vous** forms. To begin the conjugation, get rid of **-enir** from the infinitive and add **-iens, -iens, -ient,** or **-iennent** for the singular forms or third person plural (**ils/elles**). For the **nous** and **vous** forms, add **-enons** and **-enez**. Look at the example.

The "Deceptive" -ir Verb Endings	
je **-iens**	nous **-enons**
tu **-iens**	vous **-enez**
il/elle/on **-ient**	ils/elles **-iennent**

venir (*to come*)	
je v**iens**	nous v**enons**
tu v**iens**	vous v**enez**
il/elle/on v**ient**	ils/elles v**iennent**
Elle **vient** ici souvent. (*She comes here often.*)	

Table 4-3 provides a list of verbs that follow the same type of conjugation.

Table 4-3	Alike But Unique Irregular -ir Verbs
Verb	*Translation*
appartenir à	*to belong to*
contenir	*to contain*
devenir	*to become*
maintenir	*to maintain*
obtenir	*to obtain*
retenir	*to retain*
revenir	*to come back*
se souvenir	*to remember*

Verb	Translation
soutenir	to support
tenir	to hold

Conjugate the verb in each set of parentheses and write your answers in the blanks provided. I provide the translations in the Answer Key.

Q. Le lait _____ (contenir) des vitamines.

A. Le lait **contient** des vitamines. (*Milk contains vitamins.*)

36. Conjugate the verb **tenir** (*to hold*) from start to finish. Use the verb **venir** from earlier in this section as an example.

je _____   nous _____

tu _____   vous _____

il/elle/on _____   ils/elles _____

37. Nous _____ (revenir) du cinéma.

38. Les boîtes _____ (contenir) des cadeaux.

39. Paul _____ (tenir) le chien par la laisse.

40. Tu _____ (obtenir) ton diplôme.

41. Le dictionnaire _____ (appartenir) à mon grand-père.

42. Les invités _____ (venir) à huit heures.

43. Le douanier _____ (retenir) les journalistes.

44. Nous _____ (devenir) influents.

45. Je _____ (obtenir) la permission de mon patron.

Comprehending irregular -re verbs

Many irregular verbs in French have infinitives that end in **-re**. Just like the irregular **-ir** verbs, these verbs can be put into various groups. I start off with verbs that build off the verb **prendre** (*to take*). If you know how to conjugate **prendre,** you can also conjugate verbs that end in **-prendre.** To conjugate these verbs, drop the **-re** off the infinitive for the singular forms (**je, tu,** and **il/elle/on**) and add the following endings: **-s, -s,** nothing. For the plural forms, drop the **-dre** and add the following ending: **-ons, -ez, -nent.**

The -prendre Verb Endings	
je **-s**	nous **-ons**
tu **-s**	vous **-ez**
il/elle/on (nothing)	ils/elles **-nent**

With **il, elle,** and **on,** remember that you don't add any endings. Just drop the **-re.**

For an example, check out the conjugation of **prendre.**

prendre (*to take*)	
je prend**s**	nous pren**ons**
tu prend**s**	vous pren**ez**
il/elle/on prend	ils/elles pren**nent**
Tu **prends** le métro. (*You take/are taking the subway.*)	

Table 4-4 lists other common **-prendre** verbs. Look through this list and practice conjugating them.

Table 4-4	Common -prendre Verbs
Verb	*Translation*
apprendre	*to learn*
comprendre	*to understand*
entreprendre	*to undertake*
reprendre	*to take back, to recapture*
surprendre	*to surprise*

Are the following verbs conjugated correctly? If not, correct them. If you find one that's right, simply write "yes" in the blank after the question.

Q. Nous **prennons** un taxi.

A. No. Nous **prenons** un taxi. (*We take/are taking a taxi.*)

46. J'apprends le français.

_____

47. Ils comprenent le russe.

_____

48. Elle prends le train.

_____

49. Je surprends mes amis.

_____

50. Nous comprendons la leçon.

_____

Remembering the "mets"

Like the verb **prendre,** other irregular **-re** verbs have one stem in the singular and another stem in the plural. This is the case for the verb **mettre** (*to put, to place*) and verbs that end in **-mettre.** To form the singular conjugation, just drop the **-tre** from the infinitive and add **-s, -s,** nothing. For the plural, bring back the **t** and add **-ons, -ez, -ent.**

The -mettre Verb Endings	
je **-s**	nous **-tons**
tu **-s**	vous **-tez**
il/elle/on (nothing)	ils/elles **-tent**

In this example, I conjugate **mettre.** If you know how to conjugate this verb, then you can conjugate others like it.

mettre (*to put, to place*)	
je mets	nous met**tons**
tu mets	vous met**tez**
il/elle/on met	ils/elles met**tent**
Je **mets** mon manteau. (*I put my coat on.*)	

Table 4-5 lists the other common **-mettre** verbs. Look through this list and practice conjugating the verbs.

Table 4-5	Common -mettre Verbs
Verb	*Translation*
admettre	*to admit*
permettre	*to allow*
promettre	*to promise*
soumettre	*to submit, to subject*
transmettre	*to transmit, to convey*

Conjugate the verb in the following practice problems.

Q. Tu _____ (admettre) ton erreur.

A. Tu **admets** ton erreur. (*You admit your error.*)

51. Conjugate the verb **permettre** (*to allow*) from start to finish. Use **mettre** from earlier in this section as an example.

je _____   nous _____

tu _____   vous _____

il/elle/on _____   ils/elles _____

52. Les enfants _____ (promettre) d'être sages.

53. Les chaînes de télévision _____ (transmettre) les nouvelles.

54. Le professeur _____ (permettre) aux étudiants de partir.

55. Nous _____ (mettre) nos gants.

Continuing with irregular -re verbs

The following irregular **-re** verbs all have the same endings but different stems. For the verb **écrire** (*to write*), as well as other verbs conjugated like it, drop the **-re** off the infinitive and add **-s, -s, -t** for the singular. For the plural, add a **v** before the **-ons, -ez,** and **-ent.**

The following is an example of this type of conjugation.

écrire (*to write*)	
j'écris	nous écri**vons**
tu écris	vous écri**vez**
il/elle/on écrit	ils/elles écri**vent**
Il **écrit** une lettre. (*He writes a letter.*)	

Other verbs conjugated like **écrire** include the following: **décrire** (*to describe*), **inscrire** (*to inscribe*), **récrire** (*to rewrite*), and **transcrire** (*to transcribe*).

Lire (*to read*) is very similar in its conjugation. First, drop the **-re** from the infinitive, and add the endings you see in this table. Remember to add an **s** in the plural.

lire (*to read*)	
je lis	nous li**sons**
tu lis	vous li**sez**
il/elle/on lit	ils/elles li**sent**
Ils **lisent** le journal. (*They read the newspaper.*)	

Élire (*to elect*), **relire** (*to reread*), **traduire** (*to translate*), and **conduire** are conjugated like **lire.**

You conjugate **dire** (*to say*) exactly like **lire** and **conduire** (*to drive*) with the exception of the **vous** form. The **vous** form of **dire** ends in **-tes** just like the verbs **être** (*to be*) and **faire** (*to do, to make*).

Note the following conjugation:

dire (*to say*)	
je dis	nous di**sons**
tu dis	vous di**tes**
il/elle/on dit	ils/elles di**sent**
Elle **dit** bonjour. (*She says hello.*)	

Other verbs conjugated like **dire** include the following: **contredire** (*to contradict*), **interdire** (*to forbid*), **prédire** (*to predict*), and **redire** (*to repeat*). You may want to note that the **vous** forms of **contredire, interdire,** and **prédire** end in **-disez.**

The verb **boire** (*to drink*) is in a place all its own. It starts out like the other irregular **-re** verbs. Drop the **-re** from the infinitive, and add **-s, -s, -t** for the singular forms. However, the plural forms have a different stem. Note this transformation in the following conjugation.

boire (*to drink*)	
Je bo**is**	nous b**uvons**
Tu bo**is**	vous b**uvez**
il/elle/on boi**t**	ils/elles boi**vent**
Je **bois** du café. (*I drink coffee.*)	

Try conjugating these irregular **-re** verbs. I provide the translations in the Answer Key.

Q. La loi _____ (interdire) le vol.

A. La loi **interdit** le vol. (*The law forbids theft.*)

56. Ils _____ (lire) des magazines.

57. Vous _____ (dire) au revoir.

58. Tu _____ (conduire) une Mercedes.

59. Elle _____ (écrire) des poèmes.

60. Nous _____ (traduire) en français.

61. Je _____ (décrire) Paris.

62. Vous _____ (boire) du thé.

63. Ils _____ (élire) le Président.

64. Nous _____ (écrire) une pièce.

65. Tu _____ (dire) bon appétit.

Looking at other odd irregular verbs

Some verbs don't necessarily follow a set pattern. Unfortunately, the only way to remember them is to practice saying them and writing them over and over until they sink in.

Verbs such as **voir** (*to see*) and **croire** (*to believe*) are verbs with regular endings: **-s, -s, -t, -ons, -ez,** and **-ent.** However, in the **nous** and **vous** forms, you need to change the **i** to a **y,** as in the following examples.

voir (*to see*)	
je vois	nous vo**yons**
tu vois	vous vo**yez**
il/elle/on voi**t**	ils/elles voi**ent**
Nous **voyons** le drapeau. (*We see the flag.*)	

croire (*to believe*)	
je crois	nous cro**yons**
tu crois	vous cro**yez**
il/elle/on croit	ils/elles croi**ent**
Je **crois** l'article. (*I believe the article.*)	

Don't be fooled by the verb **recevoir** (*to receive*). It contains the verb **voir,** but it's conjugated very differently. The endings are regular, but take a look at the stem. Oh, la, la. In Chapter 1, I explain when you add the accent cédille on the **c.** You add it when the **c** is followed by an **a, o,** or **u.** That way the **c** is always pronounced **c** and not **k.** Take a look at the conjugation of **recevoir.**

recevoir (*to receive*)	
je re**ç**ois	nous recev**ons**
tu re**ç**ois	vous recev**ez**
il/elle/on re**ç**oit	ils/elles re**ç**oivent
Elle **reçoit** un cadeau. (*She receives a present.*)	

Verbs conjugated like **recevoir** include the following: **apercevoir** (*to notice, to perceive*), **concevoir** (*to conceive*), **décevoir** (*to deceive*), and **percevoir** (*to perceive*).

Craindre (*to fear*) is another verb that has a unique conjugation. Drop the **-dre** and add **-s, -s, -t** for the singular. For the plural, drop the **-ndre** and add **-gn** before the regular endings, **-ons, -ez, -ent.**

craindre (*to fear*)	
je crain**s**	nous crai**gn**on**s**
tu crain**s**	vous crai**gn**ez
il/elle/on crain**t**	ils/elles crai**gn**ent
Ils **craignent** l'ouragan. (*They fear the hurricane.*)	

Other verbs similar to **craindre** include the following: **plaindre** (*to pity, to feel sorry for*), **se plaindre** (*to complain*), and **contraindre** (*to compel, to force someone to do something*).

Now you can practice your skills by conjugating these verbs. You can also take it a step further and translate the sentences.

Q. Ils _____ (prévoir) le mauvais temps. _____

A. Ils **prévoient** le mauvais temps. *They foresee bad weather.*

66. Nous _____ (recevoir) des e-mails.

_____

67. Les Français _____ (boire) du vin au dîner.

_____

68. Je _____ (conduire) prudemment.

_____

69. Vous _____ (voir) le pont.

_____

70. Michelle _____ (traduire) du français en anglais.

_____

71. Nous _____ (craindre) les araignées.

_____

72. Tu _____ (lire) le journal tous les jours.

_____

73. Vous _____ (croire) l'histoire.

_____

74. Je _____ (recevoir) de bonnes notes.

_____

75. Il _____ (écrire) des poèmes.

_____

Answer Key

The following section includes the answers for all the practice problems in this chapter. How did you do? If one type of irregular verb gives you trouble, take a few minutes to review it.

1 No. Tu **fais** ton lit. (*You make/are making your bed.*)

2 Yes. Ils **vont** à la plage. (*They are going to the beach.*)

3 No. Claudine **est** canadienne. (*Claudine is Canadian.*)

4 Yes. J'**ai** de la chance. (*I am lucky.*)

5 No. Vous **faites** du ski. (*You are skiing.*)

6 No. Les touristes **disent** au revoir. (*The tourists say goodbye.*)

7 Yes. Tu **vas** bien. (*You are well.*)

8 No. Vous **êtes** formidable. (*You are wonderful.*)

9 No. Philippe **a** un sac de couchage. (*Philippe has a sleeping bag.*)

10 Yes. Nous **faisons** une quiche. (*We are making a quiche.*)

11 Nous **voulons** dormir. *We want to sleep.*

12 Ils **peuvent** lire. *They can read.*

13 Je **peux** venir. *I can come.*

14 Isabelle **veut** sortir. *Isabelle wants to go out.*

15 Tu **dois** travailler. *You have to/must/ought to work.*

16 Vous **pouvez** parler français. *You can speak French.*

17 Tout le monde **veut** avoir de l'argent. *Everyone wants to have money.*

18 Les filles **veulent** voyager. *The girls want to travel.*

19 Je **dois** manger. *I have to eat.*

20 Tu **peux** chanter. *You can/are able to sing.*

21 Tu **sers** les hors-d'oeuvre. (*You serve the hors-d'oeuvres.*)

22 Nous **dormons** tard le weekend. (*We sleep late on the weekends.*)

23 Je **sors** le vendredi soir. (*I go out Friday evenings.*)

24 Elle **ment** quelquefois. (*She lies sometimes.*)

25 Ils **servent** de la glace. (*They serve ice cream.*)

26 Vous **sentez** bon. (*You smell good.*)

27 Il **part** demain. (*He's leaving tomorrow.*)

28 Tu **dors** trop. (*You sleep too much.*)

29 Marie **sort** souvent. (*Mary goes out often.*)

30 Elles **partent** pour l'Australie. (*They are leaving for Australia.*)

31 Nous **cueillons** des fleurs. (*We pick flowers.*)

32 Ils **accueillent** leurs invités. (*They welcome their guests.*)

33 Je **couvre** mon livre. (*I cover my book.*)

34 Elle **découvre** la vérité. (*She discovers the truth.*)

35 Vous **offrez** des bonbons. (*You offer candy.*)

36
je **tiens**	nous **tenons**
tu **tiens**	vous **tenez**
il/elle/on **tient**	ils/elles **tiennent**

37 Nous **revenons** du cinéma. (*We are coming back from the movies.*)

38 Les boîtes **contiennent** des cadeaux. (*The boxes contain gifts.*)

39 Paul **tient** le chien par la laisse. (*Paul is holding the dog by the leash.*)

40 Tu **obtiens** ton diplôme. (*You are obtaining your diploma.*)

41 Le dictionnaire **appartient** à mon grand-père. (*The dictionary belongs to my grandfather.*)

42 Les invités **viennent** à huit heures. (*The guests are coming at 8 o'clock.*)

43 Le douanier **retient** les journalistes. (*The customs officer is retaining the journalists.*)

44 Nous **devenons** influents. (*We are becoming influential.*)

45 J'**obtiens** la permission de mon patron. (*I'm obtaining my boss's permission.*)

46 Yes. J'**apprends** le français. (*I am learning French.*)

47 No. Ils **comprennent** le russe. (*They understand Russian.*)

48 No. Elle **prend** le train. (*She takes the train.*)

49 Yes. Je **surprends** mes amis. (*I surprise my friends.*)

50 No. Nous **comprenons** la leçon. (*We understand the lesson.*)

je **permets**	nous **permettons**
tu **permets**	vous **permettez**
il/elle/on **permet**	ils/elles **permettent**

Les enfants **promettent** d'être sages. (*The children promise to be good.*)

Les chaînes de télévision **transmettent** les nouvelles. (*The TV channels transmit the news.*)

Le professeur **permet** aux étudiants de partir. (*The professor allows the students to leave.*)

Nous **mettons** nos gants. (*We put on our gloves.*)

Ils **lisent** des magazines. (*They read magazines.*)

Vous **dites** au revoir. (*You say goodbye.*)

Tu **conduis** une Mercedes. (*You drive a Mercedes.*)

Elle **écrit** des poèmes. (*She writes poems.*)

Nous **traduisons** en français. (*We translate in French.*)

Je **décris** Paris. (*I describe Paris.*)

Vous **buvez** du thé. (*You drink tea.*)

Ils **élisent** le Président. (*They elect the President.*)

Nous **écrivons** une pièce. (*We are writing a play.*)

Tu **dis** bon appétit. (*You say bon appétit.*)

Nous **recevons** des e-mails. *We receive e-mails.*

Les Français **boivent** du vin au dîner. *The French drink wine at dinner.*

Je **conduis** prudemment. *I drive carefully.*

Vous **voyez** le pont. *You see the bridge.*

Michelle **traduit** du français en anglais. *Michelle translates from French to English.*

Nous **craignons** les araignées. *We fear spiders.*

Tu **lis** le journal tous les jours. *You read the newspaper every day.*

Vous **croyez** l'histoire. *You believe the story.*

Je **reçois** de bonnes notes. *I get (receive) good grades.*

Il **écrit** des poèmes. *He writes poems.*

Chapter 5

Reflecting on Pronominal Verbs (Reflexive, Reciprocal, and Idiomatic)

. . . .

In This Chapter

▶ Explaining reflexive verbs

▶ Clarifying reciprocal verbs

▶ Discussing idiomatic verbs

. . . .

The pronominal verb is one of the trickiest concepts for native English-speakers to understand. You may be scratching your head, wondering how you can tell whether a verb is pronominal or not. Don't worry. You can easily tell because the infinitive is preceded by the pronoun **se** (or **s'** if the verb begins with a vowel or a mute **h**). For example, **se laver** (*to wash oneself*), **s'amuser** (*to have fun*), and **s'habiller** (*to get dressed*) are all pronominal verbs.

This chapter focuses on the three types of pronominal verbs: reflexive, reciprocal, and idiomatic. They may seem tricky, but you do catch a few breaks: You conjugate pronominal verbs the same way you conjugate regular French verbs, and the pronominal pronouns (which each verb has) are the same whether the verb is reflexive, reciprocal, or idiomatic. If you want more information about reflexive verbs and giving commands, check out Chapter 8, and see Chapter 7 for information on using reflexive verbs when answering negatively.

Understanding Reflexive Verbs

Every pronominal verb has a pronominal pronoun in front of it. With reflexive verbs, this pronoun is often referred to as the reflexive pronoun. The addition of the reflexive pronoun doesn't necessarily change the meaning of the verb, but it alerts you that the subject is doing the action on itself. **Laver** (*to wash*) and **se laver** (*to wash oneself*) are a great example. **Je lave la voiture** means *I'm washing the car.* The subject, **je**, is performing an action on something or someone else — in this case, **la voiture**. Add a reflexive pronoun and you get **Je me lave,** which means *I wash/am washing myself.* Now the subject is performing the action on itself.

Before you can conjugate reflexive verbs, you need to know about their unique pronouns. Table 5-1 shows a list of subject pronouns and their corresponding reflexive pronouns. You use these pronouns when you want to imply that the subject is doing the action on itself.

Table 5-1	Subject Pronouns and the Corresponding Reflexive Pronouns
Subject Pronouns	*Reflexive Pronouns*
je	me
tu	te
il/elle/on	se
nous	nous
vous	vous
ils/elles	se

I conjugate the verb **laver** first as nonreflexive and then as reflexive so that you can compare the two. Remember that **laver** is a regular **-er** verb. (You can check out Chapter 2 for more about present-tense regular verb conjugations.)

laver (*to wash something or someone*)	
je lave	nous lavons
tu laves	vous lavez
il/elle/on lave	ils/elles lavent
Je **lave** le bébé. (*I am washing the baby.*)	

se laver (*to wash oneself*)	
je **me** lave	nous **nous** lavons
tu **te** laves	vous **vous** lavez
il/elle/on **se** lave	ils/elles **se** lavent
Elle **se** lave. (*She washes/is washing herself.*)	

With **Je lave la voiture** and **Je lave le bébé,** the subject is performing the action on something (the car) or someone (the baby) else. However, with **Je me lave,** the subject is doing the action on itself. Thus, you use a reflexive verb.

Drop the **e** from the pronouns **me, te,** and **se** and add an apostrophe before a verb that begins with a vowel or a mute **h.** The verb **s'habiller** (*to dress*) serves as an example.

s'habiller (*to dress oneself/to get dressed*)	
je **m'**habille	nous **nous** habillons
tu **t'**habilles	vous **vous** habillez
il/elle/on **s'**habille	ils/elles **s'**habillent
Nous **nous** habillons. (*We get/are getting dressed.*)	

The following verbs in Table 5-2 can be reflexive or nonreflexive. When the subject is doing the action not on itself but on someone or something else, don't use a reflexive pronoun. When the subject is doing the action on itself, use the reflexive pronoun.

Table 5-2	Common French Reflexive Verbs
Verb	*Translation*
s'appeler	to call oneself, to be named
s'arrêter	to stop oneself
s'habiller	to dress oneself, to get dressed
se baigner	to bathe oneself
se brosser	to brush oneself
se coiffer	to do/style one's hair
se coucher	to go to bed, to put oneself to bed
se couper	to cut oneself
se laver	to wash oneself
se lever	to get up, to get oneself up
se maquiller	to put makeup on oneself
se peigner	to comb one's hair (literally, *to comb oneself*)
se promener	to take oneself for a walk, to stroll
se raser	to shave oneself
se réveiller	to wake oneself up

When you use a part of the body with a reflexive verb, you need definite articles before the part of the body rather than the possessive adjectives that you use in English. A definite article means **the** in English and in French is **le** (masculine singular), **la** (feminine singular), **l'** (masculine or feminine singular beginning with a vowel or mute **h**), or **les** (masculine or feminine plural). For example, *I wash **my** face* in French is "Je **me** lave **la** figure." It literally means *I wash the face to myself.*

Now it's your turn to take a stab. The following practice exercises can help you get a better grasp of reflexive verbs. In these exercises, determine whether the subject is doing the action on itself or on someone/something else. Choose the reflexive or non-reflexive verb and conjugate it in the sentence. I provide the translations in the Answer Key.

Q. Elle _____ (peigner/se peigner) les cheveux.

A. Elle **se peigne** les cheveux. (*She is combing her hair.*)

Q. Nous _____ (brosser/se brosser) les dents.

A. Nous **nous brossons** les dents. (*We are brushing our teeth.*)

1. Elle _____ (maquiller/se maquiller) la poupée.

2. Je _____ (réveiller/se réveiller) à six heures.

3. Tu _____ (couper/se couper) ton bifteck.

4. Ils _____ (laver /se laver).

5. Nous _____ (brosser/se brosser) les cheveux.

Looking At Reciprocal Verbs

Reciprocal verbs are another type of pronominal verb and they reciprocate the action of the subject pronouns. The meaning is *each other* or *to each other*. **Nous nous aimons** (*we love each other*) and **ils se parlent** (*they are speaking to each other*) are two examples. Because the subject pronoun **on** can often refer to a plural subject pronoun like *we* or even *they*, it can also be used in reciprocal constructions. Check out the following examples:

On **s'écrit** tous les jours. (*We write to each other every day.*)

On **se voit** souvent. (*We see each other often.*)

Remember that even when **on** has a plural meaning, you always conjugate the verb in the third person singular.

Table 5-3 lists the common reciprocal verbs.

Table 5-3	Common French Reciprocal Verbs
Verb	*Translation*
s'aimer	*to love each other*
s'écrire	*to write to each other*
s'embrasser	*to kiss each other*
se comprendre	*to understand each other*
se connaître	*to know each other*
se dire	*to say to each other*
se disputer	*to argue with each other*
se parler	*to speak to each other*
se promettre	*to promise each other*
se quitter	*to leave each other*
se regarder	*to look at each other*
se rencontrer	*to meet each other*
se retrouver	*to find each other*
se téléphoner	*to call each other*
se voir	*to see each other*

After you've had a chance to familiarize yourself with reciprocal verbs, take a moment to try the following practice exercises. In these exercises, conjugate the following verbs and then translate the sentences.

Q. Nous _____ (se rencontrer) souvent.

A. Nous **nous rencontrons** souvent. (We meet each other often.)

6. Ils _____ (se promettre).

_____

7. Vous _____ (se dire) au revoir.

_____

8. Nous _____ (se voir).

_____

9. On _____ (s'écrire).

_____

10. Elles _____ (se comprendre).

_____

Attempting Idiomatic Verbs

The last type of pronominal verbs is idiomatic — those verbs whose meaning can't be understood from the usual meaning of the verb. In other words, the same verb has one meaning when it is nonpronominal and a different meaning when it is pronominal.

To help you understand the difference between the idiomatic and the usual meaning of a verb, check out the following example:

> **Il ennuie sa soeur.** (*He is bothering his sister.*)
>
> **Il s'ennuie.** (*He is bored.*)

As you notice from the preceding example, when you use the verb **ennuyer** in its non-pronominal form, it means something completely different than in its pronominal form. This is the case for all idiomatic pronominal verbs. These verbs become idiomatic when you use them in their pronominal form because their meaning changes, some-times even drastically. You can't translate idiomatic expressions word for word because separately they have a different meaning than when they're idiomatic.

If you already know that **ennuyer** means *to bother,* you may have difficulty translating **il s'ennuie** correctly. Why does it refer to boredom instead? That's just the nature of idiomatic verbs or expressions in any language. Imagine trying to tell a nonnative English-speaker that she's the "apple of your eye" or that you "got up on the wrong side of the bed," and you'll see what I mean. To a native speaker, it's a common enough phrase; translated literally into another language, it doesn't make much sense. The bottom line: If you're aware of what an idiom is and you try to remember the idioms in this chapter, you'll end up understanding more French and sounding more like a native when you speak.

These idiomatic verbs include the pronominal pronouns, just like the reflexive and reciprocal verbs do, and are conjugated the same way.

Table 5-4 compares the "plain" usual verb with its idiomatic counterpart.

Table 5-4		Comparing the Usual Verb with the Idiomatic Verb	
Usual Verb	*Translation*	*Idiomatic Verb*	*Translation*
aller	*to go*	s'en aller	*to go away, to leave*
amuser	*to amuse, to entertain*	s'amuser	*to have fun*
débrouiller	*to disentangle*	se débrouiller	*to manage*
demander	*to ask*	se demander	*to wonder*
dépêcher	*to dispatch*	se dépêcher	*to hurry, to be in a hurry*
douter	*to doubt*	se douter de	*to suspect*
ennuyer	*to bother*	s'ennuyer	*to be bored*
entendre	*to hear*	s'entendre	*to get along*
inquiéter	*to disturb someone*	s'inquiéter	*to become worried*
mettre	*to put, to place*	se mettre à + infinitive	*to begin (to do something)*
occuper	*to occupy, to hold*	s'occuper de	*to be in charge of, to take care of, to deal with*
passer	*to go, to pass*	se passer de	*to do without*
rappeler	*to call back*	se rappeler	*to remember, to recall*
rendre	*to give back, to return*	se rendre compte de	*to realize*
servir	*to serve*	se servir de	*to use*
tromper	*to deceive, to disappoint*	se tromper de	*to be mistaken, to be wrong*

Try translating these sentences and conjugating the pronominal verbs.

Q. Mom takes care of the children.

A. **Maman s'occupe des enfants.**

11. We get along.

_____

12. I am going away.

_____

13. They are seeing each other.

_____

14. David is in a hurry.

_____

15. We are bored.

_____

In the following group of practice exercises, conjugate the verb and then translate the sentence. In each question, I add some adverbs after the verbs to make the sentences more interesting. (Check out Chapter 2 for common adverbs.)

0. Nous _____ (s'écrire) souvent.

_____

A. Nous **nous écrivons** souvent. *We write to each other often.*

16. Tu _____ (s'énerver) rarement.

_____

17. Vous _____ (se disputer) souvent.

_____

18. Je _____ (s'habiller) vite.

_____

19. Ils _____ (se coucher) tard.

_____

20. Nous _____ (s'entendre) bien.

_____

Answer Key

In this section you can find all the answers to the problems in this chapter. I also provide the translations for these questions to help you understand what you're conjugating.

1. Elle **maquille** la poupée. (*She puts makeup on the doll.*)

2. Je **me réveille** à six heures. (*I get up at 6 o'clock.*)

3. Tu **coupes** ton bifteck. (*You are cutting your steak.*)

4. Ils **se lavent.** (*They get/are getting washed.*)

5. Nous **nous brossons** les cheveux. (*We are brushing our hair.*)

6. Ils **se promettent.** (*They promise each other.*)

7. Vous **vous dites** au revoir. (*You are saying goodbye to each other.*)

8. Nous **nous voyons.** (*We see each other.*)

9. On **s'écrit.** (*We write to each other,* or *they write to each other.*)

10. Elles **se comprennent.** (*They understand each other.*)

11. **Nous nous entendons.**

12. **Je m'en vais.**

13. **Ils se voient.**

14. **David se dépêche.**

15. **Nous nous ennuyons.**

16. Tu **t'énerves** rarement. *You rarely become irritated.*

17. Vous **vous disputez** souvent. *You argue with each other often.*

18. Je **m'habille** vite. *I get dressed quickly.*

19. Ils **se couchent** tard. *They go to bed late.*

20. Nous **nous entendons** bien. *We get along well.*

Chapter 6

Forming the Present Participle and the Gerund

In This Chapter

▶ Explaining the present participle

▶ Practicing gerunds

▶ Figuring out the past present participle

ow do you do your daily chores? Do you work or drive to work while singing, talking, listening to the radio, or keeping quiet? Well, you can describe how you do things as well as why and under which circumstances with the present participle and the gerund.

In this chapter I cover the present participle, show you how to form a gerund, and then show you how to use them.

Introducing the Present Participle

The present participle is used to express the way things are done, as well as why and how they're done. It expresses manner, cause, and circumstances. The present participle answers the questions "why" and "how." In English, it always ends in -*ing* — examples include *singing, walking,* and so on. In French, the present participle ends in **-ant** — examples include **chantant** and **marchant.** Forming the present participle is easy for regular verbs and for most irregular verbs. Simply take the first person plural (the **nous** form) of any present tense verb, drop the **-ons** ending, and add **-ant.**

(**Nous**) **allons** (*We go/are going*) becomes **allant** (*going*) when you drop the **-ons** and add **-ant** to the verb.

The subject pronoun **nous** isn't part of the present participle. Table 6-1 forms the present participle for some regular and irregular verbs.

Table 6-1	Forming the Present Participle	
Infinitive	*Nous Form*	*Present Participle*
aller	all**ons**	all**ant** (*going*)
appeler	appel**ons**	appel**ant** (*calling*)
commencer	commenç**ons**	commenç**ant** (*beginning*)

(continued)

Table 6-1 (continued)

Infinitive	Nous Form	Present Participle
faire	faisons	faisant (*doing*)
finir	finissons	finissant (*finishing*)
manger	mangeons	mangeant (*eating*)
parler	parlons	parlant (*speaking*)
partir	partons	partant (*leaving*)
préférer	préférons	préférant (*preferring*)
prendre	prenons	prenant (*taking*)
vendre	vendons	vendant (*selling*)
venir	venons	venant (*coming*)
voir	voyons	voyant (*seeing*)

Only three verbs have an irregular present participle. They are

✔ **avoir** (*to have*), which becomes **ayant** (*having*)

✔ **être** (*to be*), which becomes **étant** (*being*)

✔ **savoir** (*to know*), which becomes **sachant** (*knowing*)

Using the Present Participle

The present participle has many functions. In fact, you can use the present participle in the following three ways:

✔ **To indicate cause or circumstances.** When you use the present participle to indicate cause or circumstances, it's always in the same form and doesn't have to agree with anything (such as a pronoun). For example, **Comprenant le français, j'ai regardé le film en version originale** means *Understanding French, I watched the film in its original version.* **Ayant de l'argent, elle a pu voyager** means *Having some money, she was able to travel.*

✔ **As an adjective.** When you use the present participle as an adjective, it agrees in gender and number with the noun it modifies. For example, **C'est une histoire intéressante** means *It is an interesting story.*

✔ **As a noun.** Some nouns in French are derived from the present participle. For example, **L'assistante du cadre est très efficace** means *The manager's assistant is very efficient.* **Du café Dôme, on regarde les passants** means *From the café Dôme, we watch the passersby.*

Now it's your turn. Put the following verbs in the present participle. I provide the translations in the Answer Key.

Q. Rire _____

A. **Riant** (*laughing*)

1. Boire _____

2. Mettre _____

3. Savoir _____

4. Tenir _____

5. Ecrire _____

6. Vouloir _____

7. Craindre _____

8. Faire _____

9. Avoir _____

10. Nager _____

Forming the Gerund

A *gerund* is a verb-noun. It looks like a verb, but actually works as a noun. For example, in the sentence *walking to the store is fun, walking* looks like a verb, but it's in fact a noun. In this phrase, *walking* is a gerund.

In French, to form the gerund, just add the preposition **en** in front of the present participle. The gerund in English translates to *while, by, upon,* or *in doing something.* Remember that the gerund often indicates a simultaneous action.

La fille chante en marchant. (*The girl is singing while walking.*)

Les étudiants écoutent de la musique en faisant leurs devoirs. (*The students listen to music while doing their homework.*)

In this section I show you how to form the gerund as well as how you use it in French. I then provide you with some practice problems to ensure that you understand gerunds.

Using the gerund

In addition to indicating a simultaneous action, you can use the gerund to express manner or circumstances.

En entrant dans le bâtiment, j'ai vu Paul. (*Upon/In entering the building, I saw Paul.*)

J'ai compris la situation politique en lisant les journaux. (*I understood the political situation upon/in/by reading the newspapers.*)

You can add **tout** in front of the gerund in order to make the simultaneous actions stronger, generally to stress a contradiction. For example, Elle lit le journal **tout en regardant** la télévision means *She is reading the newspaper while watching television.*

The gerund is also used in many famous proverbs in French. For example, **C'est en forgeant que l'on devient forgeron** means *It is by blacksmithing that one becomes a blacksmith.* Or as you say in English, practice makes perfect.

Now take the time to make your own proverbs by putting the verbs in parentheses in the gerund form. I provide the translations in the Answer Key.

Q. C'est _____ (faire) la cuisine que l'on devient cuisinier.

A. C'est **en faisant** la cuisine que l'on devient cuisinier. (*It's by cooking that one becomes a cook.*)

11. C'est _____ (nager) que l'on devient nageur.

12. C'est _____ (jardiner) que l'on devient jardinier.

13. C'est _____ (peindre) que l'on devient peintre.

14. C'est _____ (écrire) que l'on devient écrivain.

15. C'est _____ (chanter) que l'on devient chanteur.

16. C'est _____ (danser) que l'on devient danseur.

17. C'est _____ (sculpter) que l'on devient sculpteur.

18. C'est _____ (composer) que l'on devient compositeur.

19. C'est _____ (juger) que l'on devient juge.

20. C'est _____ (parler) beaucoup de langues que l'on devient interprète.

Pronominal verbs: Corresponding to the subject

With pronominal verbs, the pronominal pronoun corresponds to the subject. See Chapter 5 for more information on reflexive verbs.

En nous promenant, nous avons trouvé dix euros. (*While strolling/taking a walk, we found ten euros.*)

Jean s'est coupé en se rasant. (*Jean cut himself while shaving.*)

J'étais toujours fatiqué en me réveillant. (*I was still tired in waking up.*)

One general difference between the present participle and the gerund is that the present participle is linked to the noun, whereas the gerund is linked to the verb. For example, **J'ai vu Olivier sortant du café** means *I saw Olivier leaving the café*. The present participle is associated with Olivier, who is the noun. (Olivier was leaving the café.) Whereas in the sentence **J'ai vu Olivier en sortant du café** (*I saw Olivier while [I was] leaving the café*), the use of the gerund, which is linked to the verb, says that I saw Olivier while I was leaving the café.

In the following exercises, choose between the present participle and the gerund and fill in the blanks. I provide the translations in the Answer Key.

Q. La petite fille chante _____ (jouer) du piano.

A. La petite fille chante **en jouant** du piano. (*The little girl is singing while playing the piano.*)

21. C'est une idée _____ (encourager).

22. Il parle à sa femme _____ (conduire).

23. Vous demandez pardon _____ (savoir) que vous avez tort.

24. On maigrit _____ (manger) moins.

25. Elle fait des gestes _____ (raconter) des histoires.

26. Je me sens mieux _____ (faire) de l'exercice.

27. Les enfants _____ (sourire) ouvrent leurs cadeaux.

28. Le bébé se calme _____ (entendre) la voix de sa mère.

29. _____ (vouloir) apprendre l'italien, nous allons en Italie.

30. Ce sont des chiens _____ (obéir).

Forming and Using the Past Present Participle

The present participle also has a past form. To create this form, you need an *auxiliary verb* (**avoir** or **être**), which is a verb that's used to help form all the compound past tenses of verbs. In English, this form is called the perfect participle and is indicated by adding a past participle to the present participle of the auxiliary, as in the phrases *having eaten, having left,* and so on. In French, simply put the auxiliaries **avoir** and **être** in the present participle (**ayant** and **étant**) and add the past participle of the verb you want — for example, **ayant mangé** (*having eaten*) and **étant parti** (*having left*). (Check out Chapter 12 for more on the passé composé if you need help with the translations.)

How do you use this past form of the present participle? Use it when its action comes before the action of the main verb.

> **Ayant lu l'article, il a découvert la vérité.** (*Having read the article, he discovered the truth.*)
>
> **Étant arrivé en retard, il a manqué le début du film.** (*Having arrived late, he missed the beginning of the movie.*)

Now try something challenging. Transform these sentences by changing the auxiliaries **avoir** and **être** into the present participle form and getting rid of the subject pronoun and the conjunction, like in the example. Then translate the sentences. I give you the past participles to help you get started.

Q. J'ai écouté la musique classique et je me suis calmé. (*I listened to classical music and I calmed down.*)

A. **Ayant écouté** la musique classique, je me suis calmé.

Having listened to classical music, I calmed down.

31. Il avait trop mangé et il s'est endormi dans le sofa. (*He had eaten too much and he fell asleep on the sofa.*)

_____

_____

32. Nous étions en retard et nous avons couru. (*We were late and we ran.*)

_____

_____

33. Ils avaient raté le train et ils sont rentrés en retard. (*They had missed the train and they came home late.*)

_____

_____

34. Elle avait réussi à l'examen et elle était très heureuse. (*She had passed the exam and she was very happy.*)

_____

_____

35. Tu étais rentré tard et tu es monté tout de suite dans ta chambre. (*You had come home late and you went to your room right away.*)

_____

_____

36. J'étais resté dans la maison tout le weekend et je me suis ennuyé. (*I had stayed home all weekend and I was bored.*)

_____

_____

37. Vous aviez pris une douche et vous vous êtes habillé. (*You had taken a shower and you got dressed.*)

_____

_____

38. Il avait suivi un régime et il a maigri. (*He had gone on a diet and he lost weight.*)

_____

_____

39. J'étais tombé de l'escalier et je me suis cassé la jambe. (*I had fallen from the staircase and I broke my leg.*)

_____

_____

40. Ils avaient fait leurs devoirs et ils sont sortis. (*They had done their homework and they went out.*)

_____

_____

Answer Key

In this section I give you the answers to all the problems in this chapter. I also provide translations to help you know what you've just conjugated. How did you do?

1. **buvant** (*drinking*)

2. **mettant** (*putting*)

3. **sachant** (*knowing*)

4. **tenant** (*holding*)

5. **écrivant** (*writing*)

6. **voulant** (*wanting*)

7. **craignant** (*fearing*)

8. **faisant** (*doing*)

9. **ayant** (*having*)

10. **nageant** (*swimming*)

11. C'est **en nageant** que l'on devient nageur. (*It's by swimming that one becomes a swimmer.*)

12. C'est **en jardinant** que l'on devient jardinier. (*It's by gardening that one becomes a gardener.*)

13. C'est **en peignant** que l'on devient peintre. (*It's by painting that one becomes a painter.*)

14. C'est **en écrivant** que l'on devient écrivain. (*It's by writing that one becomes a writer.*)

15. C'est **en chantant** que l'on devient chanteur. (*It's by singing that one becomes a singer.*)

16. C'est **en dansant** que l'on devient danseur. (*It's by dancing that one becomes a dancer.*)

17. C'est **en sculptant** que l'on devient sculpteur. (*It's by sculpting that one becomes a sculptor.*)

18. C'est **en composant** que l'on devient compositeur. (*It's by composing that one becomes a composer.*)

19. C'est **en jugeant** que l'on devient juge. (*It's by judging that one becomes a judge.*)

20. C'est **en parlant** beaucoup de langues que l'on devient interprète. (*It's by speaking many languages that one becomes an interpreter.*)

21. C'est une idée **encourageante.** (*It's an encouraging idea.*)

22. Il parle à sa femme **en conduisant.** (*He speaks to his wife while driving.*)

23. Vous demandez pardon **sachant** que vous avez tort. (*You ask for forgiveness knowing that you are wrong.*)

24. On maigrit **en mangeant** moins. (*One loses weight by eating less.*)

25 Elle fait des gestes **en racontant** des histoires. (*She makes gestures while telling stories.*)

26 Je me sens mieux **en faisant** de l'exercice. (*I feel better by exercising.*)

27 Les enfants **souriants** ouvrent leurs cadeaux. (*The smiling children open their presents.*)

28 Le bébé se calme **en entendant** la voix de sa mère. (*The baby calms himself by hearing his mother's voice.*)

29 **Voulant** apprendre l'italien, nous allons en Italie. (*Wanting to learn Italian, we are going to Italy.*)

30 Ce sont des chiens **obéissants.** (*They are obedient dogs.*)

31 **Ayant** trop **mangé**, il s'est endormi dans le sofa.

   Having eaten too much, he fell asleep on the sofa.

32 **Ayant été** en retard, nous avons couru.

   Having been late, we ran.

33 **Ayant raté** le train, ils sont rentrés en retard.

   Having missed the train, they came home late.

34 **Ayant réussi** à l'examen, elle était très heureuse.

   Having passed the exam, she was very happy.

35 **Etant rentré** tard, tu es monté tout de suite dans ta chambre.

   Having come home late, you went to your room right away.

36 **Etant resté** dans la maison tout le weekend, je me suis ennuyé.

   Having stayed home all weekend, I was bored.

37 **Ayant pris** une douche, vous vous êtes habillé.

   Having taken a shower, you got dressed.

38 **Ayant suivi** un régime, il a maigri.

   Having gone on a diet, he lost weight.

39 **Etant tombé** de l'escalier, je me suis cassé la jambe.

   Having fallen from the staircase, I broke my leg.

40 **Ayant fait** leurs devoirs, ils sont sortis.

   Having done their homework, they went out.

Part II
Using Verbs Correctly with Questions, Commands, and Such

The 5th Wave   By Rich Tennant

"Here's something. It's a language school that will teach you to speak French for $500, or for $200 they'll just give you an accent."

In this part . . .

You use verbs to ask questions, give answers, order someone around, or order something to eat. You use verbs for description, for action, to recount past events, to express the future, or even to express your wishes and desires. This part shows you how to use the verbs to ask and answer questions (Chapter 7); to give commands (Chapter 8); to incorporate **aller** (*to go*) and **venir** (*to come*), and to form the immediate future and the immediate past (Chapter 9); and to use certain verbs correctly to form some popular expressions (Chapter 10). Furthermore, this part is a guide to help you use certain tricky verbs correctly. Some verbs (such as **connaître** and **savoir**) have the same meaning in English (*to know*) but are used differently in French. This part tells you which French verb to choose even though you see no distinction between them in English.

Chapter 7

Inquisitive Minds Want to Know: Asking and Answering Questions

● ●

In This Chapter

▶ Asking questions with inversion

▶ Responding in the negative

▶ Making pronominal verbs and infinitives negative

● ●

In any language, being able to ask questions is important. Questions can range from the most simple (those requiring a yes or no answer) to more complex (those requiring detailed information, such as the date, time, and location for your party). Furthermore, you can use many styles to ask questions, ranging from informal, conversational styles (How ya doin'?) to the most formal styles, which you probably use mostly in writing and in polite situations (May I inquire as to your health?). Therefore, the way you ask a question depends on the circumstances and the environment you're in.

French has four main ways to ask a question. They are as follows:

✔ **Intonation:** The most common and conversational way of asking a question, you simply raise your voice at the end of the sentence.

For example, **Tu regardes la télé?** (*Are you watching television?*)

✔ **N'est-ce pas:** Another conversational way you can ask a question is to add this phrase at the end of the sentence.

For example, **Nous déjeunons ensemble, n'est-ce pas?** (*We're having lunch together, right?*)

✔ **Est-ce que:** The third conversational way of asking a question is by using this expression at the beginning of a sentence.

For example, **Est-ce que tu cherches tes clés?** (*Are you looking for your keys?*)

✔ **Inversion:** The fourth way to ask a question is by inverting or switching the place of the subject and verb and adding a hyphen.

For example, **Vas-tu au cinéma ce soir?** (*Are you going to the movies this evening?*)

In this chapter I focus on using the inversion method to ask questions. Because this book is a verb book, I look closely at how inversion can affect the verb. This chapter also addresses how answering a question can affect the verb.

Using Inversion to Ask Questions

Inversion means that you invert or switch the places of the subject and verb and add a hyphen. In fact, with inversion you have to add a **t** in the third person singular between the verb and the subject pronoun if the verb ends in a vowel. Although you use inversion in conversational French, you also need to know it for formal situations, such as in speeches, polite conversation, and writing.

Check out the following two examples. In order to turn the statement into a question, simply switch the place of the subject and verb and add a hyphen, like so:

Tu prends le train tous les jours. (*You take the train every day.*)

Prends-tu le train tous les jours? (*Do you take the train every day?*)

Vous parlez français. (*You speak French.*)

Parlez-vous français? (*Do you speak French?*)

You usually don't use inversion with the first person singular **je.** This rule has a few exceptions, such as **Puis-je?** (*May I?*), **Suis-je?** (*Am I?*), and **Sais-je?** (*Do I know?*). In most cases, you use **est-ce que** with **je** instead of using inversion.

Inversion with vowels

You probably already know that pronunciation is very important in French. It's all about sound. If two vowels meet head-to-head in an inversion, add the letter **t** between the two vowels and surround it with hyphens. This only happens in the third person singular with **il, elle,** and **on.**

Il cherche le livre. (*He is looking for the book.*)

Cherche-t-il le livre? (*Is he looking for the book?*)

If the verb doesn't end in a vowel but the subject pronoun begins with a vowel, you don't add a **t.** You only add the **t** when you have two vowels head-to-head.

Il attend l'autobus. (*He is waiting for the bus.*)

Attend-il l'autobus? (*Is he waiting for the bus?*)

Note that the pronunciation of the **d** is a **t.**

You don't need to add a **t** with the plural subjects **ils/elles** because the third person plural verb always ends in a consonant, specifically a **t.**

Ils nagent bien. (*They swim well.*)

Nagent-ils bien? (*Do they swim well?*)

You try it. Use inversion to transform these statements into questions. Check out the sample if you have any questions.

Q. Elle écoute la radio. (*She is listening to the radio.*)

A. Écoute-t-elle la radio? (*Is she listening to the radio?*)

1. Vous comprenez le film. (*You understand the film.*)

_____

2. Il voyage souvent. (*He travels often.*)

_____

3. Tu cherches tes clés. (*You are looking for your keys.*)

_____

4. Elle nettoie la maison. (*She is cleaning the house.*)

_____

5. Ils mangent bien. (*They eat well.*)

_____

Inversion with a noun

What happens when the sentence has a proper noun (or any noun for that matter) for its subject? Keep the noun before the verb and add a subject pronoun that corresponds to the noun with a hyphen.

Marc écrit des poèmes. (*Marc writes poems.*)

Marc, écrit-il des poèmes? (*Does Marc write poems?*)

Les enfants aiment le théâtre. (*The children like the theater.*)

Les enfants, aiment-ils le théâtre? (*Do the children like the theater?*)

Inversion with pronominal verbs

Inversion is a little trickier with pronominal verbs, because you have to consider the pronominal pronoun. (Check out Chapter 5 for the lowdown on pronominal verbs.) Keep the pronominal pronoun exactly where it is — in front of the verb — and place the subject pronoun after the verb, as you can see in the following examples:

Il se rase. (*He is shaving.*)

Se rase-t-il? (*Is he shaving?*)

Tu te lèves de bonne heure. (*You wake up early.*)

Te lèves-tu de bonne heure? (*Do you wake up early?*)

Because in the **nous** and **vous** forms the subject pronouns and the pronominal pronouns look exactly the same, it can be difficult to know which is which. Just remember that the pronoun after the verb and the hyphen is the subject pronoun.

Nous nous aimons. (*We love each other.*)

Nous aimons-nous? (*Do we love each other?*)

Now it's your turn to practice: Transform these statements into questions by using inversion.

Q. Il s'amuse. (*He is having fun.*)

A. **S'amuse-t-il?** (*Is he having fun?*)

6. Tu mets ton chapeau. (*You are putting on your hat.*)

_____

7. Nous nous dépêchons. (*We are hurrying.*)

_____

8. Elle boit du vin. (*She is drinking wine.*)

_____

9. Nous payons l'addition. (*We are paying the check.*)

_____

10. Ils achètent un lecteur de CD. (*They are buying a CD palyer.*)

_____

Inversion with two verbs in a sentence

If a sentence has two verbs, how do you know which verb to invert? You invert the conjugated verb with the subject pronoun.

> **Tu veux sortir.** (*You want to go out.*)
>
> **Veux-tu sortir?** (*Do you want to go out?*)

The same holds true for other compound verbs. For example, this rule applies to the passé composé (see Chapter 12), where you place the subject pronoun after the auxiliary, which is the conjugated verb.

Use inversion to transform these statements into questions. Remember, that you invert the conjugated verb with the subject pronoun.

Q. Tu vas dîner avec nous. (*You are going to have dinner with us.*)

A. **Vas-tu dîner avec nous?** (*Are you going to have dinner with us?*)

11. Il faut faire de l'exercice. (*It is necessary to exercise.*)

_____

12. Nous pouvons chanter. (*We can sing.*)

_____

13. Ils veulent aller au cinéma. (*They want to go to the movies.*)

_____

14. Géraldine va voir ses amis cet après-midi. (*Géraldine is going to see her friends this afternoon.*)

_____

15. Tu peux conduire. (*You can drive.*)

_____

Responding in the Negative

If you decide to answer *yes* to a question, you typically only have to add **oui** (*yes*) to your answer. However, you can't say yes all the time. Sometimes you have to refuse to do something or express your dislike for something or someone. To do this, you use the negative. The negative consists of two parts: **ne**, which is placed before the conjugated verb, and **pas**, which is placed after the verb. Just think of **ne . . . pas** as surrounding the conjugated verb. **Pas** means *step*, like in the ballet terms **pas de deux** or **pas de trois** (*a dance for two* or *a dance for three dancers*). Check out the following example.

> **Je parle italien.** (*I speak Italian.*)
>
> **Je ne parle pas italien.** (*I do not speak Italian.*)

With pronominal verbs, the **ne** precedes the pronominal pronoun, which precedes the verb, and you place the **pas** after the conjugated verb. See the following example.

> **Nous nous amusons.** (*We are having fun.*)
>
> **Nous ne nous amusons pas.** (*We are not having fun.*)

When the verb begins with a vowel or a mute **h**, drop the **e** of **ne** and add an apostrophe.

> **Elle habite à Paris.** (*She lives in Paris.*)
>
> **Elle n'habite pas à Paris.** (*She doesn't live in Paris.*)

Try making the following sentences negative. Add **ne** before the conjugated verb and **pas** after it. If the verb begins with a vowel, remember to drop the **e** and add an apostrophe. Also remember that when a pronoun precedes the verb, the **ne** precedes the pronoun.

Q. Elle sort tous les soirs. (*She goes out every evening.*)

A. **Elle ne sort pas tous les soirs.** (*She doesn't go out every evening.*)

16. Je nage bien. (*I swim well.*)

_____

17. Ils comprennent la leçon. (*They understand the lesson.*)

_____

18. Nous nous ennuyons. (*We are bored.*)

_____

19. Elle aime danser. (*She likes to dance.*)

_____

20. Tu crains les souris. (*You are afraid of mice.*)

_____

When walking the streets in France, you may hear the French stress the **pas** and omit the **ne**. This custom is a very informal way of expressing the negative, such as **Je sais pas** (*I don't know*) or **Je comprends pas** (*I don't understand*).

However, in formal writing, you may come across a sentence where the **pas** is eliminated, as with the verbs **oser** (*to dare*), **cesser** (*to stop, to cease*), **pouvoir** (*to be able to*), and **savoir** (*to know*). Examples include **Je n'ose vous interrompre** (*I don't dare interrupt you*) and **Il ne cesse de parler!** (*He doesn't stop talking!*)

After the negative in French, certain changes can occur with the articles. In fact, I could write an entire chapter on just these pronouns, but I want to stay focused on verbs, so I suggest you check out *French For Dummies* by Dodi-Katrin Schmidt, Michelle M. Williams, and Dominique Wenzel (Wiley), or ask your French teacher for extra help.

Here are some more problems for you to work on. Try making the following sentences negative. Add **ne** before the conjugated verb and **pas** after it. If the verb begins with a vowel, remember to drop the **e** and add an apostrophe. Also remember that when a pronoun precedes the verb, the **ne** precedes the pronoun.

Q. Antoine attend ses amis. (*Antoine is waiting for his friends.*)

A. **Antoine n'attend pas ses amis.** (*Antoine is not waiting for his friends.*)

21. Tu peux venir avec nous. (*You can come with us.*)

_____

22. J'essaie les choux de Bruxelles. (*I'm trying Brussels sprouts.*)

_____

23. Nous avons la motocyclette de Paul. (*We have Paul's motorcycle.*)

_____

24. C'est du fromage. (*It is cheese.*)

_____

25. Elle va faire les courses. (*She is going to run errands.*)

_____

Forming the Negative with Inversion

In the previous section, you can see how to form the negative. (You just add **ne** before the conjugated verb and **pas** after it.) With inversion, the **ne** still precedes the conjugated verb, but the negative expression follows the subject pronoun, like it does in the following examples:

> **Ne parle-t-il pas français?** (*Doesn't he speak French?*)
>
> **Ne vendent-ils pas leur maison?** (*Are they not selling their house?*)
>
> **Corinne, ne veut-elle pas venir avec nous?** (*Doesn't Corinne want to come with us?*)

Make the following sentences negative. Just follow the sample Q and A.

Q. Répondez-vous aux questions? (*Do you answer the questions?*)

A. Ne répondez-vous pas aux questions? (*Don't you answer the questions?*)

26. Philippe prend-il des médicaments? (*Does Philippe take medication?*)

_____

27. Réussissent-ils aux éxamens? (*Do they pass the exams?*)

_____

28. Vas-tu voyager cet été? (*Are you going to travel this summer?*)

_____

29. Nous rencontrons-nous souvent? (*Do we meet each other often?*)

_____

30. Avez-vous de l'argent? (*Do you have any money?*)

_____

Making the Infinitive Negative

Earlier in this chapter, in the "Forming the Negative with Inversion" section, I show you the basic negative structure (**ne** + conjugated verb + negative word). That basic structure doesn't work if you want to make an infinitive negative. If you want to say, for example, *to be or not to be,* you have to put the **ne** and the **pas** together before the infinitive. Use this structure and you come up with **Être ou ne pas être** (*To be or not to be*). Note the negative in front of the following infinitives.

> **J'espère ne pas oublier mes clés.** (*I hope not to forget my keys.*)
>
> **Il promet de ne pas fumer.** (*He promises not to smoke.*)

Using Verbs Correctly with Questions, Commands, and Such

Translate the following sentences into French. Remember to make the infinitive negative. (I provide some helpful hints so that you can translate the sentence.)

Q. **Nous/préférons/sortir.** (*We prefer not to go out.*)

A. Nous préférons **ne pas sortir.**

31. Ils/promettre/boire. (*They promise not to drink.*)

_____

32. Il/espérer/être en retard. (*He hopes not to be late.*)

_____

33. Nous/détester/pouvoir/aider. (*We hate not to be able to help.*)

_____

34. Tu/regretter/être en France. (*You regret not to be in France.*)

_____

35. Je/essayer/rire. (*I am trying not to laugh.*)

_____

Answer Key

The following section provides all the answers to the problems in this chapter. Compare your answers to the correct answers to see how you did.

1 **Comprenez-vous le film?** (*Do you understand the film?*)

2 **Voyage-t-il souvent?** (*Does he travel often?*)

3 **Cherches-tu tes clés?** (*Are you looking for your keys?*)

4 **Nettoie-t-elle la maison?** (*Is she cleaning the house?*)

5 **Mangent-ils bien?** (*Do they eat well?*)

6 **Mets-tu ton chapeau?** (*Are you putting on your hat?*)

7 **Nous dépêchons-nous?** (*Are we hurrying?*)

8 **Boit-elle du vin?** (*Is she drinking wine?*)

9 **Payons-nous l'addition?** (*Are we paying the check?*)

10 **Achètent-ils un lecteur de CD?** (*Are they buying a CD player?*)

11 **Faut-il faire de l'exercice?** (*Is it necessary to exercise?*)

12 **Pouvons-nous chanter?** (*Can we sing?*)

13 **Veulent-ils aller au cinéma?** (*Do they want to go to the movies?*)

14 **Géraldine va-t-elle voir ses amis cet après-midi?** (*Is Géraldine going to see her friends this afternoon?*)

15 **Peux-tu conduire?** (*Can you drive?*)

16 **Je ne nage pas bien.** (*I don't swim well.*)

17 **Ils ne comprennent pas la leçon.** (*They don't understand the lesson.*)

18 **Nous ne nous ennuyons pas.** (*We aren't bored.*)

19 **Elle n'aime pas danser.** (*She doesn't like to dance.*)

20 **Tu ne crains pas les souris.** (*You aren't afraid of mice.*)

21 **Tu ne peux pas venir avec nous.** (*You can't come with us.*)

22 **Je n'essaie pas les choux de Bruxelles.** (*I'm not trying the Brussels sprouts.*)

23 **Nous n'avons pas la motocyclette de Paul.** (*We don't have Paul's motorcycle.*)

24 **Ce n'est pas du fromage.** (*It isn't cheese.*)

25 **Elle ne va pas faire les courses.** (*She isn't going to run errands.*)

26 **Philippe ne prend-il pas de médicaments?** (*Doesn't Philippe take medication?*)

27 **Ne réussissent-ils pas aux éxamens?** (*Don't they pass the exams?*)

28 **Ne vas-tu pas voyager cet été?** (*Aren't you going to travel this summer?*)

29 **Nous ne rencontrons-nous pas souvent?** (*Don't we meet each other often?*)

30 **N'avez-vous pas d'argent?** (*Don't you have any money?*)

31 **Ils promettent de ne pas boire.**

32 **Il espère ne pas être en retard.**

33 **Nous détestons ne pas pouvoir aider.**

34 **Tu regrettes de ne pas être en France.**

35 **J'essaie de ne pas rire.**

Chapter 8

Telling People What to Do: The Regular, Irregular, and Pronominal Commands

In This Chapter

▶ Forming the imperative with regular and irregular verbs

▶ Making the imperative negative

▶ Including pronominal verbs in a command

▶ Putting pronouns in the mix to make commands

How do you tell people what to do, like bring you coffee, clean your house, go to the market, or even leave? You can tell people to do all these things and more by using the imperative mood, more commonly known as the command.

This chapter shows you how to transform regular, irregular, and pronominal verbs into commands as well as how to create negative commands. Then I show you how to add pronouns to your commands.

Forming Commands with Regular Verbs

The technical term for giving commands or orders is *the imperative*. In this chapter, I use the terms interchangeably. You give orders in English as well as in French by using the verb directly and eliminating the subject pronoun. For example, you may say *Set the table, Wash the dishes,* and so on. In the following sections, I show you how to form commands with regular verbs.

Making -er verbs into commands

The commands come from the **tu, nous**, and **vous** forms of the present tense. Note that the subject pronouns are never used in the command, just their verb forms. In English, you don't command someone by saying *You speak*. Instead, you simply say *Speak!* It's the same in French.

For all **-er** verbs (as well as the irregular verb **aller** [*to go*]), you drop the **s** from the **tu** form in the imperative.

This rule also applies to irregular **-ir** verbs, which are conjugated like regular **-er** verbs — like **ouvrir** (*to open*), **souffrir** (*to suffer*), and **offrir** (*to offer*). The **s** reappears when the verb is followed by the pronouns **y** or **en** for pronunciation reasons. Examples include **Parles-en!** (*Speak about it!*), **Vas-y!** (*Go there!*), and **Offres-en!** (*Offer some!*). However, the **s** is dropped in the imperative negative: **N'en parle pas** (*Don't speak about it!*), **N'y va pas!** (*Don't go there!*), and **N'en offre pas!** (*Don't offer any!*). The **nous** and **vous** forms don't have any changes.

Use the **tu** command when speaking to one person with whom you're familiar. You use the **vous** command when speaking to one person with whom you aren't familiar, a superior (like your boss or your professor), or someone older than you; and when you're speaking to more than one person. When you use the **nous** command, you're including yourself in the group. For example, **Allons au centre commercial** (*Let's go to the mall*).

Take a look at the verb **parler** (*to speak*) in Table 8-1 as an example of **-er** verbs.

Table 8-1	Parler (*to speak*) in the Imperative Form
Present Tense	*Imperative Form*
Tu parles	**Parle!** (*Speak!*)
Nous parlons	**Parlons!** (*Let's speak!*)
Vous parlez	**Parlez!** (*Speak!*)

Try putting some regular **-er** verbs in their three imperative forms: **tu, nous,** and **vous.** Check out the example problem first.

Q. Chanter (*to sing*) _____ _____ _____

A. **Chante!** (*Sing!*), **Chantons!** (*Let's sing!*), **Chantez!** (*Sing!*)

1. Arrêter (*to stop*) _____ _____ _____

2. Regarder (*to watch*) _____ _____ _____

3. Écouter (*to listen*) _____ _____ _____

4. Décider (*to decide*) _____ _____ _____

5. Répéter (*to repeat*) _____ _____ _____

Making -ir verbs into commands

Regular **-ir** verbs follow the same pattern in commands as the verbs that end in **-er.** You use the **tu, nous,** and **vous** forms of the verbs without the subject pronouns. Unlike the **-er** verbs, however, you don't drop the **s** from the verb in the **tu** form. Check out Table 8-2 for an example of **-ir** verbs in the imperative.

Table 8-2	Finir (*to finish*) in the Imperative Form
Present Tense	*Imperative Form*
Tu finis	**Finis!** (*Finish!*)
Nous finissons	**Finissons!** (*Let's finish!*)
Vous finissez	**Finissez!** (*Finish!*)

Put the following **-ir** verbs in the imperative form. For each question, write out the **tu, nous,** and **vous** forms.

Q. Réunir (*to reunite*) _____ _____ _____

A. **Réunis!** (*Reunite!*), **Réunissons!** (*Let's reunite!*), **Réunissez!** (*Reunite!*)

6. Choisir (*to choose*) _____ _____ _____

7. Réfléchir (*to think*) _____ _____ _____

8. Obéir (*to obey*) _____ _____ _____

9. Applaudir (*to applaud*) _____ _____ _____

10. Réussir (*to succeed*) _____ _____ _____

Making -re verbs into commands

The **-re** verbs are no different than the **-ir** and **-re** verbs in the command form. Just take the **tu, nous,** and **vous** forms of the present tense and drop the subject pronouns. Take a look at Table 8-3 for an example **-re** verb.

Table 8-3	Attendre (*to wait*) in the Imperative Form
Present Tense	*Imperative Form*
Tu attends	**Attends!** (*Wait!*)
Nous attendons	**Attendons!** (*Let's wait!*)
Vous attendez	**Attendez!** (*Wait!*)

Try putting regular **-re** verbs in their imperative **tu, nous,** and **vous** forms.

Q. Défendre (*to defend*) _____ _____ _____

A. Défends! (*Defend!*), Défendons! (*Let's defend!*), Défendez! (*Defend!*)

11. Descendre (*to go downstairs*) _____ _____ _____

12. Répondre (*to answer*) _____ _____ _____

13. Vendre (*to sell*) _____ _____ _____

14. Rendre (*to give back*) _____ _____ _____

15. Entendre (*to hear*) _____ _____ _____

Forming Commands with Irregular Verbs

Irregular verbs work exactly the same way as regular verbs (see the previous section). All you have to worry about is remembering the conjugation of the irregular verbs and you can put them in the **tu, nous,** and **vous** forms. (You can find the conjugation of the irregular verbs in Chapter 4.) Check out the examples in Table 8-4 and Table 8-5.

Table 8-4	Prendre (*to take*) in the Imperative Form
Present Tense	*Imperative Form*
Tu prends	**Prends!** (*Take!*)
Nous prenons	**Prenons!** (*Let's take!*)
Vous prenez	**Prenez!** (*Take!*)

Table 8-5	Lire (*to read*) in the Imperative Form
Present Tense	*Imperative Form*
Tu lis	**Lis!** (*Read!*)
Nous lisons	**Lisons!** (*Let's read!*)
Vous lisez	**Lisez!** (*Read!*)

As you can see, even most irregular verbs have the same pattern as the regular verbs. That is, you use their **tu, nous,** and **vous** present tense verb forms, minus the subject pronouns. Try putting the following verbs in the imperative form.

Q. Écrire (*to write*) _____ _____ _____

A. Écris! (*Write!*), Écrivons! (*Let's write!*), Écrivez! (*Write!*)

16. Faire (*to do, to make*) _____ _____ _____

17. Aller (*to go*) _____ _____ _____

18. Sortir (*to go out*) _____ _____ _____

19. Venir (*to come*) _____ _____ _____

20. Dormir (*to sleep*) _____ _____ _____

Four irregular verbs, however, also have irregular imperative forms, which are not the same as their present tenses. Check out Tables 8-6, 8-7, 8-8, and 8-9 to see these verbs.

Table 8-6	Avoir (*to have*) in the Imperative Form
Present Tense	*Imperative Form*
Tu as	Aie! (*Have . . .!*)
Nous avons	Ayons! (*Let's have . . .!*)
Vous avez	Ayez! (*Have . . .!*)

Table 8-7	Être (*to be*) in the Imperative Form
Present Tense	*Imperative Form*
Tu es	Sois! (*Be . . .!*)
Nous sommes	Soyons! (*Let's be . . .!*)
Vous êtes	Soyez! (*Be . . .!*)

Table 8-8	Savoir (*to know*) in the Imperative Form
Present Tense	*Imperative Form*
Tu sais	Sache! (*Know . . .!*)
Nous savons	Sachons! (*Let's know . . .!*)
Vous savez	Sachez! (*Know . . .!*)

Table 8-9	Vouloir (*to want*) in the Imperative Form
Present Tense	*Imperative Form*
Tu veux	Veuille! (*Please . . .!*)
Nous voulons	Veuillons! (*Please . . .!*)
Vous voulez	Veuillez! (*Please . . .!*)

For the verb **vouloir,** you mostly use the **veuillez** form when giving commands, and you usually follow it with the infinitive. This word is a polite way to give commands and is often translated as *please,* as it is with **Veuillez entrer** (*Please come in*) and **Veuillez me suivre** (*Please follow me*).

Put the following verbs in their imperative forms for the subject pronoun indicated in parentheses.

Q. Fermer la porte. (nous)

A. **Fermons la porte!** (*Let's close the door!*)

21. Être gentil. (tu)

_____

22. Obéir à tes parents. (tu)

_____

23. Manger. (nous)

_____

24. Faire vos devoirs. (vous)

_____

25. Avoir de la patience. (tu)

_____

Creating the Negative Imperative

What if you want to tell people not to do something? Imagine telling your little sister, your child, or even your dog not to do something. For example, you tell them don't yell, don't run, and don't touch. This section shows you how to use the negative command. In order to use the negative command, just add **ne** before the imperative form and **pas** or any other negative expression after the imperative form. (For more on the negative, look at Chapter 7.) Check out the following examples.

Ne parle pas! (_Don't speak!_)

Ne parlons pas! (_Let's not speak!_)

If the verb begins with a vowel or a mute **h,** drop the **e** from **ne** and add an apostrophe.

N'attends pas! (_Don't wait!_)

N'attendons pas! (_Let's not wait!_)

Note that when the infinitive is negative, the **ne** and **pas** are placed together and they precede the infinitive.

Veuillez ne pas fumer! (_Please don't smoke!_)

Veuillez ne pas toucher! (_Please don't touch!_)

Put the following verbs in the negative imperative for the **tu, nous,** or **vous** form, as indicated in parentheses.

Q. Ne pas venir. (vous) _____

A. **Ne venez pas!** (_Don't come!_)

26. Ne pas commencer les devoirs. (nous)

_____

27. Ne pas dormir. (tu)

_____

28. Ne pas mettre les pieds sur la table. (tu)

_____

29. Ne pas aller au magasin. (nous)

_____

30. Ne pas téléphoner à Marc. (tu)

_____

Using Pronominal Verbs to Make Commands

You eliminate the subject pronouns in the imperative form, but you still have to keep the pronominal pronouns when you're working with pronominal verbs (see Chapter 5 for the lowdown on pronominal verbs). In the affirmative imperative, the pronominal pronouns follow a verb-hyphen combination. In the negative imperative, the pronominal pronouns precede the verb. *Note:* **Ne** precedes the pronouns and **pas** follows the verb. Check out the following example in Table 8-10.

Table 8-10	Se Lever (*to get up*) in the Imperative Form	
Present Tense	*Affirmative Imperative*	*Negative Imperative*
Tu te lèves	**Lève-toi!** (*Get up!*)	**Ne te lève pas!** (*Don't get up!*)
Nous nous levons	**Levons-nous!** (*Let's get up!*)	**Ne nous levons pas!** (*Let's not get up!*)
Vous vous levez	**Levez-vous!** (*Get up!*)	**Ne vous levez pas!** (*Don't get up!*)

Note that the pronominal pronoun **te** becomes **toi** in the imperative affirmative but then returns to being **te** in the negative. If the verb begins with a vowel or a mute **h,** drop the **e** from **te** and add an apostrophe. An example is the verb **s'habiller** (*to get dressed*), which you can see in Table 8-11. (Both **se lever** and **s'habiller** are **-er** verbs, so remember to drop the **s** from the **tu** form of their present conjugation.)

Table 8-11	S'habiller (*to get dressed*) in the Imperative Form	
Present Tense	*Affirmative Imperative*	*Negative Imperative*
Tu t'habilles	**Habille-toi!** (*Get dressed!*)	**Ne t'habille pas!** (*Don't get dressed!*)
Nous nous habillons	**Habillons-nous!** (*Let's get dressed!*)	**Ne nous habillons pas!** (*Let's not get dressed!*)
Vous vous habillez	**Habillez-vous!** (*Get dressed!*)	**Ne vous habillez pas!** (*Don't get dressed!*)

Now it's your turn. Put the following pronominal verbs in the three imperative forms, first in the affirmative and then in the negative.

0. Se maquiller (*to put on makeup*)

A. (tu) **Maquille-toi!** (*Put on makeup!*), **Ne te maquille pas!** (*Don't put on makeup!*)

(nous) **Maquillons-nous!** (*Let's put on makeup!*), **Ne nous maquillons pas!** (*Let's not put on makeup!*)

(vous) **Maquillez-vous!** (*Put on makeup!*), **Ne vous maquillez pas!** (*Don't put on makeup!*)

31. Se coucher (*to go to bed*)

(tu) _____ _____

(nous) _____ _____

(vous) _____ _____

32. Se réveiller (*to wake up*)

(tu) _____ _____

(nous) _____ _____

(vous) _____ _____

33. Se laver (*to get washed*)

(tu) _____ _____

(nous) _____ _____

(vous) _____ _____

34. Se brosser les dents (*to brush one's teeth*)

(tu) _____ _____

(nous) _____ _____

(vous) _____ _____

35. Se raser (*to shave*)

(tu) _____ _____

(nous) _____ _____

(vous) _____ _____

Adding Pronouns to Commands

If you want to add pronouns to commands, with comments such as *take it, give it to us,* or *offer her some,* use the verb in the imperative affirmative and then the pronoun, and you join the two with a hyphen. Use the following order separated by hyphens:

Verb in the imperative- + direct object- + indirect object- + y- + en

You never use all these pronouns at once, but you often use two of them, and this chart shows the order you use them in. For example, to say *give it to her,* put the verb in the imperative, add a hyphen, the direct object, another hyphen, and the indirect object, like so: **Donne-le-lui!**

Before you practice adding pronouns to commands, you need to know the direct and indirect object pronouns. Table 8-12 lists them with their English counterparts.

Table 8-12	Direct and Indirect Object Pronouns		
Direct Object Pronoun (English)	*Direct Object Pronoun (French)*	*Indirect Object Pronoun (English)*	*Indirect Object Pronoun (French)*
me	**me**	to me	**me**
you	**te**	to you	**te**
him/it (masculine singular)	**le**	to him	**lui**
her/it (feminine singular)	**la**	to her	**lui**
us	**nous**	to us	**nous**
you	**vous**	to you	**vous**
them	**les**	to them	**leur**

In the negative command, the **ne** precedes the pronoun or pronouns and the **pas** or another negative word follows the verb in the command form. Check out the following examples of affirmative and negative imperatives with direct and indirect object pronouns.

Parle-lui! (*Speak to him/her!*), **Ne lui parle pas!** (*Don't speak to him/her!*)

Finis-le! (*Finish it!*), **Ne le finis pas!** (*Don't finish it!*)

Commençons-la! (*Let's begin it!*), **Ne la commençons pas!** (*Let's not begin it!*)

Écrivez-nous! (*Write to us!*), **Ne nous écrivez pas!** (*Don't write to us!*)

The following are examples of both direct and indirect objects together. Note that the direct object precedes the indirect object and that **me** and **te** change to **moi** and **toi** when they're at the end of the imperative construction. In the negative, however, they go back to **me** and **te.** *Note:* You usually never have more than two pronouns in a sentence, but Figure 8-1 shows the order the pronouns come in.

Donnez-les-moi! (*Give them to me!*), **Ne me les donnez pas!** (*Don't give them to me!*)

Envoyons-le-leur! (*Let's send it to them!*), **Ne le leur envoyons pas!** (*Let's not send it to them!*)

Vends-les-nous! (*Sell them to us!*), **Ne nous les vends pas!** (*Don't sell them to us!*)

Figure 8-1:
The order of pronouns for the negative commands.

	me							
	te	le						
ne +	se +	la +	lui +	y +	en +	verb +	pas
	nous	les	leur				
	vous						

The pronoun **y** means *there* or *in it* and is a pronoun of place. It replaces phrases starting with prepositions of place such as **à, en, dans, sur, sous,** and **à + noun** (things, not people). For example, **à + la musique** means *in music* in the sentence **Je m'intéresse à la musique** (*I am interested in music*). You replace **à la musique** with **y.**

The pronoun **en** replaces the prepositions **de, du, de l',** and **des + noun,** and it means *some, any, from there,* or *of them,* depending on what it's replacing.

Offres-en! (*Offer some!*), **N'en offre pas!** (*Don't offer any!*)

Prends-en! (*Take some!*), **N'en prends pas!** (*Don't take any!*)

Allons-y! (*Let's go [there]!*), **N'y allons pas!** (*Let's not go [there]!*)

Don't forget to add the **s** to the **tu** form of **-er** verbs if the pronoun begins with a vowel and the verb ends in a vowel. However, in the negative, the **s** is dropped.

Entres-y! (*Enter [there]!*), **N'y entre pas!** (*Don't enter [there]!*)

Check out these examples with more added pronouns.

Mets-les-y! (*Put them there!*), **Ne les y mets pas!** (*Don't put them there!*)

Parlez-lui-en! (*Speak to him/her about it!*), **Ne lui en parlez pas!** (*Don't speak to him/her about it!*)

Place-l'y! (*Place it there!*), **Ne l'y place pas!** (*Don't place it there!*)

Translate the following sentences by putting the verb in the imperative form and adding the appropriate pronouns by looking at Table 8-12. (Remember that some verbs are transitive in French but intransitive in English and vice versa, so check out Chapter 1 if you need additional help.)

Q. Let's ask him!

A. **Demandons-lui!**

36. Finish them!

_____

37. Let's speak to them!

_____

38. Go there!

_____

39. Open it!

_____

40. Close it!

_____

Answer Key

This section provides the answers for all the problems in this chapter. Compare your answers to the correct ones. How did you do? Remember that some of these verbs usually appear with a noun, so the literal translation may appear a bit odd.

1 **Arrête!** (*Stop!*), **Arrêtons!** (*Let's stop!*), **Arrêtez!** (*Stop!*)

2 **Regarde!** (*Watch!*), **Regardons!** (*Let's watch!*), **Regardez!** (*Watch!*)

3 **Écoute!** (*Listen!*), **Écoutons!** (*Let's listen!*), **Écoutez!** (*Listen!*)

4 **Décide!** (*Decide!*), **Décidons!** (*Let's decide!*), **Décidez!** (*Decide!*)

5 **Répète!** (*Repeat!*), **Répétons!** (*Let's repeat!*), **Répétez!** (*Repeat!*)

6 **Choisis!** (*Choose!*), **Choisissons!** (*Let's choose!*), **Choisissez!** (*Choose!*)

7 **Réfléchis!** (*Think!*), **Réfléchissons!** (*Let's think!*), **Réfléchissez!** (*Think!*)

8 **Obéis!** (*Obey!*), **Obéissons!** (*Let's obey!*), **Obéissez!** (*Obey!*)

9 **Applaudis!** (*Applaud!*), **Applaudissons!** (*Let's applaud!*), **Applaudissez!** (*Applaud!*)

10 **Réussis!** (*Succeed!*), **Réussissons!** (*Let's succeed!*), **Réussissez!** (*Succeed!*)

11 **Descends!** (*Go down [the stairs]!*), **Descendons!** (*Let's go down [the stairs]!*), **Descendez!** (*Go down [the stairs]!*)

12 **Réponds!** (*Answer!*), **Répondons!** (*Let's answer!*), **Répondez!** (*Answer!*)

13 **Vends!** (*Sell!*), **Vendons!** (*Let's sell!*), **Vendez!** (*Sell!*)

14 **Rends!** (*Give back!*), **Rendons!** (*Let's give back!*), **Rendez!** (*Give back!*)

15 **Entends!** (*Hear!*), **Entendons!** (*Let's hear!*), **Entendez!** (*Hear!*)

16 **Fais!** (*Do!*), **Faisons!** (*Let's do!*), **Faites!** (*Do!*)

17 **Va!** (*Go!*), **Allons!** (*Let's go!*), **Allez!** (*Go!*)

18 **Sors!** (*Go out!*), **Sortons!** (*Let's go out!*), **Sortez!** (*Go out!*)

19 **Viens!** (*Come!*), **Venons!** (*Let's come!*), **Venez!** (*Come!*)

20 **Dors!** (*Sleep!*), **Dormons!** (*Let's sleep!*), **Dormez!** (*Sleep!*)

21 **Sois gentil!** (*Be nice!*)

22 **Obéis à tes parents!** (*Obey your parents!*)

23 **Mangeons!** (*Let's eat!*)

24 **Faites vos devoirs!** (*Do your homework!*)

25 **Aie de la patience!** (*Have patience!*)

26 **Ne commençons pas les devoirs!** (*Let's not begin the homework!*)

27 **Ne dors pas!** (*Don't sleep!*)

28 **Ne mets pas les pieds sur la table!** (*Don't put your feet on the table!*)

29 **N'allons pas au magasin!** (*Let's not go to the store!*)

30 **Ne téléphone pas à Marc!** (*Don't call Marc!*)

31 (tu) **Couche-toi!** (*Go to bed!*), **Ne te couche pas!** (*Don't go to bed!*)

(nous) **Couchons-nous!** (*Let's go to bed!*), **Ne nous couchons pas!** (*Let's not go to bed!*)

(vous) **Couchez-vous!** (*Go to bed!*), **Ne vous couchez pas!** (*Don't go to bed!*)

32 (tu) **Réveille-toi!** (*Wake up!*), **Ne te réveille pas!** (*Don't wake up!*)

(nous) **Réveillons-nous!** (*Let's wake up!*), **Ne nous réveillons pas!** (*Let's not wake up!*)

(vous) **Réveillez-vous!** (*Wake up!*), **Ne vous réveillez pas!** (*Don't wake up!*)

33 (tu) **Lave-toi!** (*Wash yourself!*), **Ne te lave pas!** (*Don't wash yourself!*)

(nous) **Lavons-nous!** (*Let's wash ourselves!*), **Ne nous lavons pas!** (*Let's not wash ourselves!*)

(vous) **Lavez-vous!** (*Wash yourself/yourselves!*), **Ne vous lavez pas!** (*Don't wash yourself/ yourselves!*)

34 (tu) **Brosse-toi les dents!** (*Brush your teeth!*), **Ne te brosse pas les dents!** (*Don't brush your teeth!*)

(nous) **Brossons-nous les dents!** (*Let's brush our teeth!*), **Ne nous brossons pas les dents!** (*Let's not brush our teeth!*)

(vous) **Brossez-vous les dents!** (*Brush your teeth!*), **Ne vous brossez pas les dents!** (*Don't brush your teeth!*)

35 (tu) **Rase-toi!** (*Shave!*), **Ne te rase pas!** (*Don't shave!*)

(nous) **Rasons-nous!** (*Let's shave!*), **Ne nous rasons pas!** (*Let's not shave!*)

(vous) **Rasez-vous!** (*Shave!*), **Ne vous rasez pas!** (*Don't shave!*)

36 **Finis-les!** Or, **Finissez-les!**

37 **Parlons-leur!**

38 **Vas-y!** Or, **Allez-y!**

39 **Ouvre-le/la!** Or, **Ouvrez-le/la!**

40 **Ferme-le/la!** Or, **Fermez-le/la!**

Chapter 9

Looking Forward and Back: The Immediate Future and Past

In This Chapter
▶ Forming the immediate future
▶ Forming the immediate past
▶ Using prepositions with verbs of coming and going

*T*he two types of future tense are the simple future, which I discuss in Chapter 15, and the immediate future, which I talk about in this chapter. Although the two types of future tenses can be and are used interchangeably, you use the immediate future to express something that you're going to do pretty soon in the future, as the name indicates. Similarly to the immediate future, the immediate past expresses actions that you've just done. For example, *I have just taken a test* or *She has just eaten.* In this chapter, I show you how to form the immediate future and the immediate past.

Creating the Immediate Future Tense

In order to form the immediate future, conjugate the verb **aller** (*to go*) in the present tense and add the infinitive of a verb of your choice. Because **aller** is an irregular verb, check out the following conjugations in the present tense to refresh your memory.

aller (*to go*)	
je **vais**	nous **allons**
tu **vas**	vous **allez**
il/elle/on **va**	ils/elles **vont**

Now add an infinitive to form the immediate future. The following examples show you how to do it.

> **Je vais lire.** (*I'm going to read.*)
>
> **Nous allons sortir.** (*We are going to go out.*)

To construct the immediate future with pronominal verbs, place the pronominal pronoun, which agrees with the subject, before the infinitive.

> **Je vais me promener dans le parc.** (*I'm going to walk in the park.*)
>
> **Elle va se reposer.** (*She is going to rest.*)

In order to make the immediate future negative, simply place **ne** before the conjugated **aller** and **pas,** or any other negative word you want to use, after the conjugated verb.

> **Nous n'allons pas voyager cet été.** (*We are not going to travel this summer.*)

Now take the time to try it. Work through the following practice problems and conjugate the verb so that the sentence is in the immediate future tense.

Q. Je dors. (*I am sleeping.*)

A. Je **vais dormir.** (*I am going to sleep.*)

1. Il mange.

_____

2. Nous nageons.

_____

3. Tu ne travailles pas.

_____

4. Les clients paient.

_____

5. Elle se maquille.

_____

Creating the Immediate Past Tense

Just like the immediate future (see the previous section), you also have an immediate past tense, which you use when you've just done something. Form the immediate past tense with the verb **venir** conjugated in the present tense, the preposition **de,** and the infinitive (**venir de + infinitive**). (Note that the immediate future has no preposition in front of the infinitive, but the immediate past does). **Venir** by itself means *to come,* but when it's followed by **de + infinitive,** it means *to have just done something.* I conjugate **venir** in the present tense for you in the following table.

venir (*to come*)	
je **viens**	nous **venons**
tu **viens**	vous **venez**
il/elle/on **vient**	ils/elles **viennent**

> **Nous venons d'acheter les billets.** (*We have just bought the tickets.*)

How do you construct the immediate past with pronominal verbs? (Check out Chapter 5 for a complete discussion on pronominal verbs in the present tense.) Just place the pronominal pronoun before the infinitive, like so:

Je viens de me réveiller. (*I just woke up.*)

Elle vient de se coucher. (*She has just gone to bed.*)

In order to make the immediate past negative, simply place **ne** before the conjugated verb **(venir)** and **pas,** or any other negative word you want to use, after the conjugated verb.

Ils ne viennent pas de manger. (*They have not just eaten.*)

Transform the following sentences from the present to the immediate past, as in the example. If the sentence is negative, keep it negative in your answer.

Q. Nous jouons au tennis. (*We are playing tennis.*)

A. Nous **venons de jouer** au tennis. (*We have just played tennis.*)

6. Il se coupe les cheveux.

_____

7. Vous attendez.

_____

8. Je pleure.

_____

9. Je me mets à travailler.

_____

10. Elle se coiffe.

_____

Going and Coming with Aller and Venir

How do you go to the movies or the market and most importantly, how do you come back from these and other places? Well, you use the same verbs you did to form the immediate future and the immediate past (see the two previous sections), but they're followed by nouns instead of by infinitives. In this section, I show you what prepositions to use to get to where you are going **aller** (*to go*) and what prepositions you use to come back **venir** (*to come*).

Going to and coming back

Go anywhere you want to go by adding the preposition **à** to **aller,** thus forming **aller à** (*to go to*).

Je vais au cinéma. (*I am going to the movies.*)

The preposition **à** contracts with the definite article **le** (masculine singular) to form **au** and with the plural **les** to form **aux**. It doesn't contract with the feminine singular **la** or with the **l'**.

Tu vas à la banque. (*You are going to the bank.*)

Now that you can go anywhere in town, how do you get back? You get back with the verb **venir** and the preposition **de**, which means *to come (back) from.*

Je viens du marché. (*I'm coming back from the market.*)

Elle vient de l'école. (*She's coming back from school.*)

The same types of transformations occur with the preposition **de** as with the preposition **à**. The two contractions are **de + le**, which form **du**, and **de + les**, which form **des**. Table 9-1 shows you a list of the two prepositions with the definite articles so that you can keep track of them when you use them.

Table 9-1	Combining Definite Articles and Prepositions	
Preposition	*Definite Article*	*Combined Form*
à	le	au
à	la	à la
à	l'	à l'
à	les	aux
de	le	du
de	la	de la
de	l'	de l'
de	les	des

Before you work on the practice problems, review this list of places around town that you can go to and come back from.

- l'aéroport (*the airport*)
- la banque (*the bank*)
- la bibliothèque (*the library*)
- la boîte de nuit (*the nightclub*)
- la boulangerie (*the bakery*)
- le café (*the café*)
- le centre commercial (*the mall*)
- le cinéma (*the movies*)
- le club (*the club*)
- le collège (*middle school*)
- l'école (*the school*)

- l'église (*the church*)
- l'épicerie (*the grocery store*)
- la gare (*the train station*)
- le grand magasin (*the department store*)
- l'hôtel (*the hotel*)
- la librairie (*the bookstore*)
- le lycée (*high school*)
- le magasin (*the store*)
- la maison (*the house*)
- le marché (*the market*)
- le musée (*the museum*)

✔ l'opéra (*the opera*)

✔ la pharmacie (*the pharmacy*)

✔ la piscine (*the swimming pool*)

✔ la plage (*the beach*)

✔ la poste (*the post office*)

✔ le restaurant (*the restaurant*)

✔ le stade (*the stadium*)

✔ le supermarché (*the supermarket*)

✔ le théâtre (*the theater*)

Go to the following places and come back by conjugating the verbs **aller** in the first sentence and **venir** in the second sentence. Make sure you add the correct prepositions. Check out the example. I provide the translations in the Answer Key.

Q. Il _____ le lycée.

_____

A. Il **va au** lycée. (*He is going to high school.*)

Il **vient du** lycée. (*He is coming back from high school.*)

11. Nous _____ le magasin.

_____

12. Ils _____ la pharmacie.

_____

13. Ma sœur _____ le centre commercial.

_____

14. Papa _____ la gare.

_____

15. Tu _____ la librairie.

_____

Going to and coming from

If you want to get out of town and go to Morocco or Australia, for example, you need the verbs **aller** and **venir** again. All you have to do is change the prepositions. To go to any city, use the preposition **à** + the name of the city. To come back, use the preposition **de** + the name of the city. Most islands follow this rule as well.

Je vais à Bruxelles. (*I am going to Brussels.*)

Je viens de Bruxelles. (*I come/am coming from Brussels.*)

Je vais à Hawaii. (*I am going to Hawaii.*)

Je viens d'Hawaii. (*I come/am coming from Hawaii.*)

Countries, provinces, and states are divided into masculine, feminine, and plural nouns. What determines gender for these geographic areas is a matter of spelling. Aside from some exceptions, countries, provinces, and states that end in an **e** or begin with a vowel are considered feminine, and they use the prepositions **en** (*to, in, at*) and **de** (*from*). Those that don't end in an **e** or that begin with a consonant are considered masculine, and they use the prepositions **au** (*to, in, at*) and **du** (*from*). For plural countries like the United States, use **aux** (*to, in, at*) and **des** (*from*).

Nous allons en France. (*We are going to France.*)

Nous venons de France. (*We are coming from France.*)

Tu vas au Canada. (*You are going to Canada.*)

Tu viens du Canada. (*You are coming from Canada.*)

Il va aux Pays-Bas. (*He is going to the Netherlands.*)

Il vient des Pays-Bas. (*He's coming from the Netherlands.*)

Table 9-2 puts everything together.

Table 9-2	Prepositions to Use for Going and Coming			
Location	*Prepositions for Going to or Being in*	*Examples of Going Verbs*	*Prepositions for Coming from*	*Examples of Coming Verbs*
Cities and islands	à	Je **vais à** Paris. Je **vais à** Tahiti.	de	Je **viens de** Paris. Je **viens de** Tahiti.
Countries, states, provinces, and continents that end in **e** or begin with a vowel	en	Je **vais en** Grèce. Je **vais en** Californie. Je **vais en** Normandie.	de	Je **viens de** Grèce. Je **viens de** Californie. Je **viens de** Normandie.
Countries, states, and provinces that begin with a consonant	au	Je **vais au** Canada. Je **vais au** Texas. Je **vais au** Québec.	du	Je **viens du** Canada. Je **viens du** Texas. Je **viens du** Québec.
Plural countries	aux	Je **vais aux** États-Unis. Je **vais aux** Pays-Bas.	des	Je **viens des** États-Unis. Je **viens des** Pays-Bas.

Table 9-2 shows the general rules for verbs of coming and going, but some exceptions do exist. Some cities have an article in conjunction with the preposition. For example, if you want to say I am going to or am in New Orleans, Mans, Havre, and Cairo, you say **à la Nouvelle Orléans, au Mans, au Havre, au Caire.** And if you're coming from these places, **de la Nouvelle Orléans, du Mans, du Havre, du Caire.** Also, some countries do end in an **e** but are considered masculine. For example, if you go to or are in Mexico, you say **au Mexique,** and coming back from Mexico is **du Mexique.**

Form sentences by conjugating the verbs and putting in the correct preposition. I provide the translations in the Answer Key.

Q. Nous _____ (aller/Irlande).

A. Nous **allons en Irlande.** (*We are going to Ireland.*)

16. Mes parents _____ (aller/Tunisie).

17. Tu _____ (aller/Suisse).

18. Nous _____ (venir/Sénégal).

19. Mon assistante _____ (venir/San Francisco).

20. Vous _____ (venir/Chine).

Answer Key

This section contains the answers for all the practice problems in this chapter. Compare your answers to see how well you did.

1 Il **va manger.** (*He is going to eat.*)

2 Nous **allons nager.** (*We are going to swim.*)

3 Tu **ne vas pas travailler.** (*You are not going to work.*)

4 Les clients **vont payer.** (*The clients are going to pay.*)

5 Elle **va se maquiller.** (*She is going to put on makeup.*)

6 Il **vient de se couper** les cheveux. (*He has just cut his hair.*)

7 Vous **venez d'attendre.** (*You have just waited.*)

8 Je **viens de pleurer.** (*I have just cried.*)

9 Je **viens de me mettre** à travailler. (*I have just begun to work.*)

10 Elle **vient de se coiffer.** (*She has just done her hair.*)

11 Nous **allons au** magasin. (*We are going to the store.*)

Nous **venons du** magasin. (*We are coming back from the store.*)

12 Ils **vont à** la pharmacie. (*They are going to the drugstore.*)

Ils **viennent de** la pharmacie. (*They are coming back from the drugstore.*)

13 Ma sœur **va au** centre commercial. (*My sister is going to the mall.*)

Ma sœur **vient du** centre commercial. (*My sister is coming back from the mall.*)

14 Papa **va à** la gare. (*Dad is going to the train station.*)

Papa **vient de** la gare. (*Dad is coming from the train station.*)

15 Tu **vas à** la librairie. (*You are going to the bookstore.*)

Tu **viens de** la librarie. (*You are coming back from the bookstore.*)

16 Mes parents **vont en** Tunisie. (*My parents are going to Tunisia.*)

17 Tu **vas en** Suisse. (*You are going to Switzerland.*)

18 Nous **venons du** Sénégal. (*We are coming back from Senegal.*)

19 Mon assistante **vient de** San Francisco. (*My assistant comes from San Francisco.*)

20 Vous **venez de** Chine. (*You come from China.*)

Chapter 10

Correctly Using Often Misused Verbs in Daily Conversation

In This Chapter

▶ Knowing the verbs **connaître** and **savoir**

▶ Identifying the differences between **jouer à** and **jouer de**

▶ Forming expressions with **avoir**

▶ Understanding how to use **faire**

*E*very language has different ways of saying things and of expressing yourself that can't be translated into another language word for word. French is no exception. For instance the phrases *How are you doing?* or *How are you?* are expressed in French not by the verbs **faire** (*to do, to make*) or **être** (*to be*), but by the verb **aller** (*to go*). To ask these questions in French, you say **Comment allez-vous?** or **Comment vas-tu?**

In this chapter, I focus on some verbs that have the same meaning in English, but different usage in French. You want to make sure you use the right verb so that people know what you're talking about. I also cover two common verbs: **avoir** (*to have*) and **faire** (*to do, to make*) and how you can correctly utilize these verbs in your conversations. (You can also check out Chapter 23, which focuses on ten often-misused verbs.)

Knowing the Difference between Connaître and Savoir

French has two verbs that mean *to know.* One is **connaître,** and the other is **savoir.** Even though the English language translates them the same, the French language uses them in different circumstances. In this section, I show you how to use each verb. Both verbs are irregular.

connaître (*to know*)	
je **connais**	nous **connaissons**
tu **connais**	vous **connaissez**
il/elle/on **connaît**	ils/elles **connaissent**
Je **connais** Aix-en-Provence. (*I know Aix-en-Provence.*)	

savoir (*to know*)	
je **sais**	nous **savons**
tu **sais**	vous **savez**
il/elle/on **sait**	ils/elles **savent**
Nous **savons** la date de ton anniversaire. (*We know your birthday.*)	

So are you wondering what the differences are between the two verbs? Well, you use the two verbs with different types of information. For example, use **connaître** when you mean *to know* or *to be acquainted with a person, a place, or a thing.* Meanwhile, use **savoir** when you mean *to know a fact, to know something by heart,* or *to know specific information,* such as a telephone number, an address, or someone's name.

You can also use **savoir** with the clauses in Table 10-1.

Table 10-1		Clauses That Use Savoir (*to know*)	
Common Clause	***Translation***	***Example***	***Translation***
savoir à quelle heure	*to know (at) what time*	**Je sais à quelle heure il va venir.**	*I know (at) what time he is going to come.*
savoir combien	*to know how much*	**Je sais combien ça coûte.**	*I know how much that costs.*
savoir comment	*to know how*	**Je sais comment conjuguer connaître.**	*I know how to conjugate connaître.*
savoir où	*to know where*	**Je sais où est la classe.**	*I know where the class is.*
savoir pourquoi	*to know why*	**Je sais pourquoi Henri est en retard.**	*I know why Henri is late.*
savoir quand	*to know when*	**Je sais quand le train part.**	*I know when the train is leaving.*
savoir que	*to know that*	**Je sais que tu aimes le chocolat.**	*I know that you like chocolate.*
savoir quel, quelle, quels, quelles	*to know which*	**Je sais quelle heure il est.**	*I know what time it is.*
savoir qui	*to know who*	**Je sais qui est là.**	*I know who is there.*
savoir si	*to know if*	**Je sais si tu regardes la télé.**	*I know if you're watching TV.*

To say *I know!* or *I don't know,* you simply say **Je sais** or **Je ne sais pas.**

You can also follow **savoir** with an infinitive, but you can't do that with **connaître**. In this way, **savoir** means *to know how to do something.* For example, **Tu sais parler français** means *You know how to speak French,* and **Nous savons faire du ski** means *We know how to ski.*

Which verb, **connaître** or **savoir,** do you use in the following sentences? Conjugate the verbs and translate the sentences.

Q. Les enfants _____ compter en français.

A. Les enfants **savent** compter en français. (*The children know how to count in French.*)

1. Est-ce que tu _____ New York?

_____

2. Marie ne _____ pas parler japonais.

_____

3. Nous _____ où il habite.

_____

4. Ils ne _____ pas la famille du professeur.

_____

5. Vous _____ conduire.

_____

Identifying What to Play

Jouer is a regular **-er** verb that is used with different prepositions in order to convey either playing a sport or playing a musical instrument. More specifically, **jouer à** is used with sports and **jouer de** with instruments. If the sport or instrument is masculine, make the necessary contractions: **à + le = au; de + le = du.** See the following examples.

> **Je joue au tennis**. (*I play tennis.*)
>
> **Je joue du piano.** (*I play the piano.*)

Check out Table 10-2 for playing other sports and games or playing other instruments.

Table 10-2	The Different Ways to Play
Jouer à (+ *sports or games*)	*Jouer de* (+ *instruments*)
Je joue au basket(ball). (*I play basketball.*)	Je joue du saxophone. (*I play the saxophone.*)
Je joue au foot. (*I play soccer.*)	Je joue du violon. (*I play the violin.*)
Je joue au volley. (*I play volleyball.*)	Je joue de la batterie. (*I play the drums.*)
Je joue au golf. (*I play golf.*)	Je joue de la flûte. (*I play the flute.*)
Je joue au hockey. (*I play hockey.*)	Je joue de la guitare. (*I play the guitar.*)
Je joue au bridge. (*I play bridge.*)	Je joue de la trompette. (*I play the trumpet.*)

(continued)

Table 10-2 *(continued)*	
Jouer à (+ sports or games)	*Jouer de (+ instruments)*
Je joue aux cartes. (*I play cards.*)	Je joue du violoncelle. (*I play the cello.*)
Je joue aux dames. (*I play checkers.*)	Je joue de la basse. (*I play bass.*)
Je joue aux échecs. (*I play chess.*)	Je joue de la clarinette. (*I play the clarinet.*)

In the negative, the prepositions **à, au, à la, à l',** and **aux** don't change. However, **du, de la, de l',** and **des** do change to **de** or **d'** after the negative, such as **Je ne joue pas de piano,** which means *I don't play the piano.*

Now, it's your turn. Conjugate the verb **jouer** (*to play*) and provide the correct prepositions. Translate the following sentences.

O. Mon père _____ (jouer) golf.

A. Mon père **joue au** golf. *My father plays golf.*

6. Georges _____ (jouer) violon.

_____

7. Ils _____ (ne pas jouer) batterie.

_____

8. Je _____ (jouer) échecs.

_____

9. Mon frère _____ (jouer) guitare.

_____

10. Les enfants _____ (jouer) basketball.

_____

Keeping Avoir and Faire in Line

French has two very important verbs, **avoir** (*to have*) and **faire** (*to do, to make*), that are responsible for many sentence formations. From these two simple verbs you can form dozens of everyday expressions.

This section looks at each verb, **avoir** and **faire,** and helps you with any questions you may have. I show you the correct conjugations (you can also find them in Chapter 4) as well as several common expressions formed with these two verbs.

Using avoir

The verb **avoir** is very versatile in French and has several meanings in English. This verb is living proof that translating literally from one language to another doesn't always work. Check out the conjugation in the present tense.

avoir (*to have*)	
j'**ai**	nous **avons**
tu **as**	vous **avez**
il/elle/on **a**	ils/elles **ont**
Ils **ont** trois enfants. (*They have three children.*)	

In French, one isn't a certain age, but has a certain age. Therefore, the question *How old are you?* is *What age do you have?* In French if someone asks you **Quel âge as-tu/ avez-vous?** (*How old are you?*), you respond as follows: **J'ai** (your age) **ans.** For example, **J'ai vingt ans** (*I am 20 years old*).

Check out Table 10-3 for other important **avoir** expressions.

Table 10-3	Important Avoir Expressions
Avoir Expression	*Translation*
avoir faim	*to be hungry*
avoir soif	*to be thirsty*
avoir sommeil	*to be sleepy*
avoir tort (de)	*to be wrong*
avoir raison (de)	*to be right*
avoir chaud	*to be hot*
avoir froid	*to be cold*
avoir peur (de)	*to be afraid (of)*
avoir besoin de	*to need*
avoir envie de	*to want, to feel like*
avoir l'intention de	*to have the intention of*
avoir l'habitude de	*to be accustomed to, to be used to*
avoir l'occasion de	*to have the chance to, to have the opportunity to*
avoir de la chance	*to be lucky*
avoir honte (de)	*to be ashamed of*
avoir mal (à + a part of the body)	*to ache, to have pain in a part of the body*

You can use the expressions in Table 10-3 with the preposition **de** in parentheses alone or followed by an infinitive or a noun. For example, **J'ai tort** means _I am wrong_ and **J'ai tort de mentir** means _I am wrong to lie_. When these expressions are followed by an infinitive, you must use the preposition **de** in front of the infinitive, as in the following examples:

> **J'ai l'occasion de voyager cet été.** (_I have the chance/the opportunity to travel this summer._)
>
> **Nous avons l'habitude de sortir le samedi soir.** (_We are used [accustomed] to going out Saturday evenings._)

Avoir besoin de and **avoir envie de** can be followed by an infinitive or a noun. In either case, the preposition **de** is necessary before the infinitive or the noun.

> **Tu as besoin d'étudier.** (_You need to study._)
>
> **J'ai envie de chanter.** (_I feel like singing._)
>
> **J'ai envie de chocolat.** (_I feel like chocolate._)

To make these expressions negative, add **ne** before the verb and **pas** or another negative word after it.

> **Je n'ai pas envie de chanter.** (_I don't feel like singing._)

You can also add adverbs to these sentences. Check out _French For Dummies_ by Dodi-Katrin Schmidt, Michelle M. Williams, and Dominique Wenzel (Wiley) for more specific information about French grammar.

The expression **avoir mal** is the only one from the list in Table 10-3 that's followed by the preposition **à.** Conjugate the verb **avoir** in the present and add **mal,** the preposition **à,** and the part of the body that's hurting now. For example, if you have a backache, you say **J'ai mal au dos.** The preposition **à** is followed by the part of the body that is hurting along with the definite article.

> **J'ai mal aux pieds.** (_My feet hurt._)
>
> **J'ai mal à l'épaule.** (_My shoulder hurts._)

Now translate some of these expressions into French.

_Q._ He doesn't feel like going out.

_A._ **Il n'a pas envie de sortir.**

11. We are thirsty.

_____

12. They are right.

_____

13. You need to read.

_____

14. Michael is lucky.

_____

15. Her head hurts.

_____

Trying faire

Another important verb used in many common expressions is **faire** (*to do, to make*). You need to know how to correctly use it because it's very versatile and can be used to express playing both an instrument and a sport without switching prepositions. This section shows you how to conjugate it and then provides numerous expressions using this verb.

faire (*to do, to make*)	
je **fais**	nous **faisons**
tu **fais**	vous **faites**
il/elle/on **fait**	ils/elles **font**
Il **fait** du tennis. (*He plays tennis.*)	

Table 10-4 shows many of the ways that you can use **faire** when talking about sports as well as instruments. When you use **faire** with sports and instruments, remember that it has the same meaning as the verb **jouer à** or **de** (*to play*). These two verbs are used interchangeably. However, remember to use the correct prepositions. Unlike **jouer, faire** is followed by the preposition **de** whether you're talking about a sport or an instrument.

Table 10-4	Using Faire with Sports and Instruments
Faire Expression	*Translation*
faire de l'alpinisme	to mountain climb
faire de la planche à voile	to windsurf
faire de la voile	to sail, sailing
faire des randonnées	to hike
faire du baseball	to play baseball
faire du foot, football	to play soccer
faire du football américain	to play football
faire du karaté	to do karate
faire du ski	to ski
faire du tennis	to play tennis

(continued)

Table 10-4 *(continued)*

Faire Expression	Translation
faire du vélo	to ride a bike
faire du volley	to play volleyball
faire de la batterie	to play the drums
faire de la flûte	to play the flute
faire de la guitare	to play the guitar
faire de la trompette	to play the trumpet
faire du piano	to play the piano
faire du saxophone	to play the saxophone
faire du violon	to play the violin

In addition to sports and instruments, you can also use **faire** in other ways. Table 10-5 shows many common expressions that utilize **faire**.

Table 10-5   Faire in Everyday Conversation

Faire Expression	Translation
faire attention	to pay attention
faire la connaissance de	to make someone's acquaintance
faire la cuisine	to cook, to do the cooking
faire la grasse matinée	to sleep in late
faire la lessive	to do laundry
faire la liste	to make a list
faire la queue	to form a line, to wait in line
faire la sieste	to take a nap
faire la vaisselle	to do the dishes
faire le marché	to do the shopping
faire le ménage	to do the housework
faire les courses	to run errands, to do the shopping
faire les devoirs	to do the homework
faire les provisions	to do the grocery shopping
faire les valises/bagages	to pack
faire un voyage	to take a trip
faire une promenade	to take a walk/stroll

Translate the following sentences and correctly conjugate **faire** in the appropriate form. Remember that some may have more than one answer. (I provide the most common answer in the answer key.)

Q. The baby is taking a nap.

A. **Le bébé fait la sieste.**

16. My mother does the cooking.

_____

17. The children do the dishes.

_____

18. I play tennis.

_____

19. We pay attention.

_____

20. You sleep in late.

_____

Answer Key

This section contains all the answers for the practice problems in this chapter. Compare your answers to the correct answers to see how you fared.

1 Est-ce que tu **connais** New York? *Do you know New York?*

2 Marie ne **sait** pas parler japonais. *Marie doesn't know how to speak Japanese.*

3 Nous **savons** où il habite. *We know where he lives.*

4 Ils ne **connaissent** pas la famille du professeur. *They don't know the professor's family.*

5 Vous **savez** conduire. *You know how to drive.*

6 Georges **joue du** violon. *Georges plays the violin.*

7 Ils **ne jouent pas de** batterie. *They don't play the drums.*

8 Je **joue aux** échecs. *I play chess.*

9 Mon frère **joue de la** guitare. *My brother plays the guitar.*

10 Les enfants **jouent au** basketball. *The children play basketball.*

11 **Nous avons soif.**

12 **Ils ont raison.**

13 **Tu as besoin de lire.**

14 **Michael a de la chance.**

15 **Elle a mal à la tête.**

16 **Ma mère fait la cuisine.**

17 **Les enfants font la vaisselle.**

18 **Je fais du tennis.**

19 **Nous faisons attention.**

20 **Tu fais la grasse matinée.**

Part III
Taking a Look Back: The Past Tenses

The 5th Wave   By Rich Tennant

"I'm pretty sure you're supposed to just 'smell' the cork."

In this part . . .

Humankind can't live on bread alone, and a language isn't nearly as interesting or as complete if it has only one tense. Think of the confusion just one tense could cause — how would you tell your friends whether you're waiting for them at the restaurant now, will be waiting for them later, or were waiting for them earlier? In this part, you look at how to form the many past tenses in French: the imperfect, the passé composé (compound past), the pluperfect, and the passé simple (the simple past). You can use these past tenses to recount, or describe, events in the past, such as your childhood, your high school prom, your family's last vacation, or even the movie you saw last weekend. Sometimes, you may even want to explain the sequence of past events, those that happened prior to other past events. That's why you need all those different past tenses, all of which are introduced in this part one by one. So go ahead, reminisce! You can do it with the past tenses.

Chapter 11

No Tense Is Perfect: The Imperfect Tense

In This Chapter

▶ Forming the imperfect with regular, irregular, and pronominal verbs

▶ Using the imperfect tense

D o you ever get nostalgic about the past? Do you want to be able to say what you used to do when you were a child, to describe a wonderful family tradition, or to recall how blue the sky was on your favorite vacation? Well, you can with the imperfect tense. You use the imperfect tense to describe a continuous or habitual action in the past, or an action that you did a nonspecific number of times. The English translation of the imperfect is *was doing something, used to do something,* or *would do something* in the past. *Note:* One of the translations of the imperfect tense in English is *would*. However this translation isn't the same as the *would* of the conditional tense, which expresses the present and the future. An example of the *would* in the imperfect is **Quand j'habitais à Paris, je prenais souvent le métro** (*When I lived in Paris, I would often take the train*). (See Chapter 17 for more on the conditional tense.)

This chapter shows you how to form the imperfect tense for regular, irregular, and pronominal verbs, as well as the many ways you can correctly use the tense.

Making Regular Verbs Imperfect

The imperfect is a simple tense to form; the verb is conjugated by itself without an auxiliary. The stem for the imperfect comes from the **nous** form of the present tense of the verb, minus the **-ons**. This rule applies to all regular, irregular, and pronominal **-er, -ir,** and **-re** verbs. (Check out Chapters 2, 3, 4, and 5 for more about the present tense.) Only one verb, **être** (*to be*), is irregular in the imperfect tense; the stem is **ét** (check out "The one true irregular imperfect verb — **être**" later in this chapter). However, the endings are all the same, even for this irregular verb. The imperfect endings are as follows:

Imperfect Tense Verb Endings	
je **-ais**	nous **-ions**
tu **-ais**	vous **-iez**
il/elle/on **-ait**	ils/elles **-aient**

So the imperfect tense conjugations for a regular verb are as follows:

parler (*to speak*)	
Present-tense nous form: parl**ons**	
je parl**ais**	nous parl**ions**
tu parl**ais**	vous parl**iez**
il/elle/on parl**ait**	ils/elles parl**aient**
Il **parlait** à ses parents. (*He was speaking to his parents.*)	

finir (*to finish*)	
Present-tense nous form: finiss**ons**	
je finiss**ais**	nous finiss**ions**
tu finiss**ais**	vous finiss**iez**
il/elle/on finiss**ait**	ils/elles finiss**aient**
Je **finissais** mon déjeuner. (*I was finishing my lunch.*)	

vendre (*to sell*)	
Present-tense nous form: vend**ons**	
je vend**ais**	nous vend**ions**
tu vend**ais**	vous vend**iez**
il/elle/on vend**ait**	ils/elles vend**aient**
Nous **vendions** notre maison. (*We were selling our house.*)	

Pronominal verbs don't pose a problem either. Just remember to add the pronominal pronouns (see Chapter 5 for a refresher on pronominal verbs). The stem and the endings are the same as those of the nonpronominal verbs.

se promener (*to take a walk/a stroll*)	
Present-tense nous form: nous nous promen**ons**	
je me promen**ais**	nous nous promen**ions**
tu te promen**ais**	vous vous promen**iez**
il/elle/on se promen**ait**	ils/elles se promen**aient**
Je **me promenais** chaque jour. (*I would/used to take a walk every day.*)	

Now it's your turn to try. Conjugate the following verbs into the imperfect tense.

Q. Tu _____ (chercher) les enfants.

A. Tu **cherchais** les enfants. (*You were looking for/were picking up the children.*)

1. Nous _____ (répondre) aux questions.

2. Mes parents nous _____ (punir).

3. Corinne _____ (chanter) bien.

4. Je _____ (perdre) toujours mes clés.

5. Vous _____ (travailler) beaucoup.

6. Les enfants _____ (se coucher) à 8 heures.

7. Philippe _____ (marcher) six kilomètres.

8. Nous _____ (se réunir) régulièrement.

9. Tu _____ (arriver) à l'heure.

10. Je _____ (choisir) le train.

Forming the Imperfect with Irregular Verbs

Unlike many of the other tenses, irregular verbs (see Chapter 4) aren't irregular in the imperfect tense. In fact, even the irregular verbs are regular in the imperfect tense, albeit with one major exception. This section focuses on the regular irregular verbs as well as the true irregular verb in the imperfect tense.

To create the imperfect tense of irregular verbs, simply take their **nous** form, drop the **-ons,** and add the appropriate endings: **-ais, -ais, -ait, -ions, -iez,** and **-aient.** Check out Table 11-1, which lists several verbs in their **nous** form.

Table 11-1	Nous Forms of Irregular Verbs	
Infinitive	*Nous form*	*Stem*
aller (*to go*)	Nous **allons**	all
avoir (*to have*)	Nous **avons**	av
boire (*to drink*)	Nous **buvons**	buv
craindre (*to fear*)	Nous **craignons**	craign
croire (*to believe*)	Nous **croyons**	croy

(continued)

Table 11-1 *(continued)*		
devoir (*to owe, to have to, must*)	Nous **devons**	dev
dire (*to say*)	Nous **disons**	dis
écrire (*to write*)	Nous **écrivons**	écriv
faire (*to do, to make*)	Nous **faisons**	fais
lire (*to read*)	Nous **lisons**	lis
mettre (*to put, to place*)	Nous **mettons**	mett
ouvrir (*to open*)	Nous **ouvrons**	ouvr
partir (*to leave*)	Nous **partons**	part
pouvoir (*to be able to*)	Nous **pouvons**	pouv
prendre (*to take*)	Nous **prenons**	pren
recevoir (*to receive*)	Nous **recevons**	recev
venir (*to come*)	Nous **venons**	ven
voir (*to see*)	Nous **voyons**	voy
vouloir (*to want to*)	Nous **voulons**	voul

Il pouvait travailler. (*He was able to work.*)

Conjugate the following verbs into the imperfect tense.

0. Les étudiants _____ (dire) la vérité.

A. Les étudiants **disaient** la vérité. (*The students were telling the truth.*)

11. Nous _____ (prendre) des notes.

12. Je _____ (sortir) tous les soirs.

13. Vous _____ (lire) des romans.

14. Les enfants _____ (craindre) des moustiques.

15. Tu _____ (boire) du vin.

16. Nous _____ (s'écrire) quelquefois.

17. Mathilde _____ (faire) des études.

18. Vous _____ (croire) aux contes de fées.

19. Je _____ (recevoir) des cadeaux.

20. Nous _____ (vouloir) partir.

"Eyeing" verb stems

What if the stem of the verb in the **nous** form ends in an **i**, like **étudier** (*to study*), **rire** (*to smile*), or **crier** (*to scream*)? Just keep the **i** and add the endings. Doing so may look funny to native English speakers, especially in the **nous** and **vous** forms in the imperfect, but the rules of the imperfect never change. Look at the following example.

étudier (*to study*)	
Present-tense nous form: étud**ons**	
j'étudi**ais**	nous étudi**ions**
tu étudi**ais**	vous étudi**iez**
il/elle/on étudi**ait**	ils/elles étudi**aient**
Il **étudiait.** (*He was studying.*)	

Working with -cer and -ger verbs

Verbs that end in **-cer** and **-ger** also have imperfect forms. These imperfect forms use the same endings (from the present-tense **nous** form) as other imperfect verbs, but you have to remember the rules that you use for the present tense. To make their **nous** form, for the **-cer** verbs, you need to add the cedilla on the **c,** and for the **-ger** verbs, you add the **e** before the **ons.** In Chapter 3, I explain why and when the cedilla and the **e** are added to the present tense. In the imperfect, the pronunciations of the **c** and the **g** aren't affected when followed by an **i** but are affected when followed by an **a.** How does this affect the imperfect form of these types of verbs? Check out the following examples.

commencer (*to begin*)	
Present-tense nous form: commen**çons**	
je commen**çais**	nous commenc**ions**
tu commen**çais**	vous commenc**iez**
il/elle/on commen**çait**	ils/elles commen**çaient**
Nous **commencions** à jouer. (*We were beginning to play.*)	

manger (*to eat*)	
Present-tense nous form: mange**ons**	
je mange**ais**	nous mang**ions**
tu mange**ais**	vous mang**iez**
il/elle/on mange**ait**	ils/elles mange**aient**
Ils **mangeaient** des croissants chaque jour. (*They would eat croissants every day.*)	

The one true irregular imperfect verb — être

Only one French verb has an irregular stem: **être** (*to be*). The stem of **être** isn't derived from its **nous** form but from the stem **ét**. Its endings, however, are regular.

être (*to be*)	
j'**ét**ais	nous **ét**ions
tu **ét**ais	vous **ét**iez
il/elle/on **ét**ait	ils/elles **ét**aient
Elle **était** occupée. (*She was busy.*)	

Put the verbs in parentheses in the imperfect tense.

Q. Ils _____ (annoncer) leurs fiançailles.

A. Ils **annonçaient** leurs fiançailles. (*They were announcing/would announce their engagement.*)

21. Tu _____ (aller) au marché.

22. Ils _____ (acheter) du pain.

23. Elle _____ (lire).

24. Nous _____ (travailler).

25. Je _____ (nager).

26. Vous _____ (s'ennuyer).

27. Tu _____ (faire) de la voile.

28. Nous _____ (rire).

29. Il _____ (neiger).

30. Je _____ (conduire).

Using the Imperfect

You can use the imperfect tense in many different situations. For example, you can use it to express a habitual and continuous action in the past as well as in all kinds of descriptions. You can recall what the weather was like, what someone was wearing, or what the surroundings you're describing were like. Because of its versatility, the imperfect tense has many meanings in English. You can translate it as *used to, would, was, were, was doing,* or *were doing something.* You can choose whichever translation best suits what you want to say.

This section looks at the main ways that you can use the imperfect tense. Check out Table 11-2 to see some specific expressions that imply a general and nonspecific time in the past. These expressions usually indicate a habitual and continuous action.

Expressing habitual and continuous actions

Habitual action means something that you would do or used to do over and over again for an unspecified number of times. The following example illustrates how you use imperfect verbs to express habitual and continuous actions. (The French verbs are bolded; the English translation verbs are italicized.) Remember that you can also say *used to* instead of *would* in the translation.

Chez ses grands-parents, Michelle **jouait** tous les jours avec ses petits cousins, et **nageait** dans la mer. Sa grand-mère **préparait** toujours des repas délicieux qui **sentaient** si bons. Le soir, ses grands-parents **amenaient** Michelle au centre ville et lui **achetaient** de la glace. Puis, ils **s'asseyaient** à la terrasse d'un café et ils **regardaient** les gens qui **passaient.**

At her grandparents' house, Michelle *would play* every day with her little cousins and *would swim* in the sea. Her grandmother *would* always *prepare* delicious meals, which *smelled* so good. In the evenings, her grandparents *would bring* Michelle to town and *would buy* her ice cream. Then, they *would sit* at the terrace of the café and *watch* the people who *would pass by.*

Table 11-2	Common Expressions in the Imperfect Tense
Expression	*Translation*
autrefois	*in the past*
chaque année	*each year*
chaque fois	*each time*
chaque jour	*each day*
chaque mois	*each month*
chaque semaine	*each week*
d'habitude/habituellement	*usually*
en général/généralement	*in general/generally*
le lundi	*on Mondays, or every Monday*
le mardi	*on Tuesdays, or every Tuesday*
le mercredi	*on Wednesdays, or every Wednesday*
le jeudi	*on Thursdays, or every Thursday*
le vendredi	*on Fridays, or every Friday*
le samedi	*on Saturdays, or every Saturday*
le dimanche	*on Sundays, or every Sunday*
le weekend	*on the weekends, or every weekend*
quelquefois	*sometimes, at times*
souvent	*often*
toujours/tout le temps	*always*
tous les ans	*every year*
tous les jours	*every day*
tous les mois	*every month*
toutes les semaines	*every week*

Form sentences in the past from the given elements. Remember to put the verb in the imperfect tense.

Q. Elle/choisir/toujours/le coq au vin.

A. Elle **choisissait** toujours le coq au vin. (*She would always choose the coq au vin.*)

31. Autrefois/je/prendre/le train. (*In the past, I used to/would take the train.*)

_____

32. Nous/aller/à l'école/tous les jours. (*We used to/would go to school every day.*)

_____

33. Ils/jouer/au golf/le weekend. (*They would play golf on the weekends.*)

_____

34. Je/faire/souvent/des promenades. (*I would often take walks.*)

_____

35. D'habitude/il/rencontrer/ses amis/au café. (*Usually, he would meet his friends at the café.*)

_____

36. Vous/se dépêcher/tout le temps. (*You were always in a hurry.*)

_____

37. Le vendredi/elle/sortir/avec ses amis. (*On Fridays she would go out with her friends.*)

_____

38. Nous/partir/en vacances/chaque été. (*We would leave for vacation each summer.*)

_____

39. Tu/manger/toujours vite. (*You would always eat quickly.*)

_____

40. En général/les étudiants/parler/français en classe. (*Generally, the students would speak French in class.*)

_____

Describing the past

If you want to set the background of the past by describing physical, mental, and emotional conditions, then you use the imperfect tense. These conditions include the description of weather, scenery, appearances, and feelings. Some examples include what the beach looked like from your hotel window, what your best friend was wearing at yesterday's party, or what you were thinking when you first met the love of your life.

The following paragraph provides an example. All the imperfect verbs are bolded in the French version and italicized in the English translation.

Quand Michelle **était** jeune, elle **passait** tous les étés avec ses grands-parents qui **habitaient** en Provence. Parce qu'il **faisait toujours** très chaud, elle **portait** toujours un chapeau pour la protéger du soleil. Elle **pensait** qu'elle **voulait** y rester toute sa vie.

When Michelle *was* young, she *would spend* all the summers with her grandparents who *lived/used to live* in Provence. Because it *was* always very hot, she *would wear* a hat to protect her from the sun. She *thought* that she *wanted* to stay there all her life.

Interrupting actions in progress

What if you were doing something and all of a sudden something happened and interrupted what you were doing? For example, you were watching a great movie when your children came in asking for a snack. Here, you would use two tenses, the imperfect of the verb *to watch* (were watching) and the completed past (see Chapter 12) of the verb *to come* (came).

Je **regardais** un très bon film quand mes enfants **sont venus** me demander un casse-croûte. (*I was watching a very good film when my children came in asking me for a snack.*)

Les enfants **jouaient** au foot quand il **a commencé** à pleuvoir. (*The children were playing soccer when it began to rain.*)

In the second example, *were playing* is in the imperfect tense and *began* is in the passé composé, which is a completed action in the past. (Check out Chapter 12 for more on the passé composé.)

Using the imperfect with certain constructions

You use the imperfect tense with the following constructions in order to express ongoing actions in the past: **être en train de** (*to be in the middle of something*) and **venir de + infinitive** (*to have just done something*).

Elle **était en train de** faire la cuisine quand elle a brûlé la sauce. (*She was in the middle of cooking when she burned the sauce.*)

Nous **venions de travailler** toute la journée alors nous étions fatigués (*We had just worked the whole day so we were tired.*)

Describing simultaneous actions

When two actions occur at the same time in the past, the imperfect tense is used for both verbs in order to express continuous simultaneous action. Usually, the expression **pendant que** (*while*) is used to link these two actions.

Il **conduisait** pendant que je **lisais** la carte routière. (*He was driving while I was reading the directions.*)

Tu **jouais** au tennis pendant qu'il **nageait**. (*You were playing tennis while he was swimming.*)

Making suggestions and expressing wishes

You can use the imperfect tense to make suggestions to your friends, your parents, your spouse, or your children, or to express a wish. You can do this by using **si** (*if*) followed by the imperfect. Check out the following examples.

Si nous **allions** au cinéma? (*What if we went to the movies?* or *How about going to the movies?*)

Si tu **étais** un peu plus patient! (*If only you were a little more patient!*)

Hypothesizing with the imperfect

The imperfect is part of a construction of a hypothetical sentence. A hypothetical sentence is composed of two clauses, the **si** (*if*) *clause* and the result clause. You use the imperfect in the **si** clause and the conditional tense in the result clause (see Chapter 17 for more on hypothetical sentences). Check out the following example:

Si **j'avais** de l'argent, je **voyagerais.** (*If I had money/were to have money, I would travel.*)

Avais is in the imperfect tense and **voyagerais** is in the conditional tense.

Match the following sentences with one of the categories that best describes it. Write the appropriate letter in each blank. I show you how in the example.

Q. Il jouait du piano pendant qu'elle chantait.

A. **e.** Simultaneous action

41. _____ Quand j'étais à Paris, je prenais toujours le métro.

42. _____ Si on faisait un pique-nique?

43. _____ Il pleuvait en avril.

44. _____ Nous étudiions pendant que tu regardais la télévision.

45. _____ Je lisais quand le téléphone a sonné.

46. _____ Elle portait une robe blanche et un chapeau rose.

47. _____ Tu écrivais toujours à tes amis.

48. _____ Ils mangeaient quand je suis entré.

49. _____ Il faisait beau en été mais il neigeait beaucoup en hiver.

50. _____ Je pensais qu'il était formidable.

a. Description of weather and time

b. Physical and mental description

c. Habitual action

d. Interrupted action

e. Simultaneous action

f. Wishing or suggesting with **si**

Answer Key

This section contains all the answers to the practice problems in this chapter. Compare your answers with the correct answers. Remember that the imperfect tense has several meanings in English: *were doing something, used to do something,* or *would do something.* The choice often depends on the context or connotation of the sentence.

1 Nous **répondions** aux questions. (*We were answering/would answer the questions.*)

2 Mes parents **nous punissaient.** (*My parents used to punish/would punish us.*)

3 Corinne **chantait** bien. (*Corinne used to sing well.*)

4 Je **perdais** toujours mes clés. (*I would always lose my keys.*)

5 Vous **travailliez** beaucoup. (*You were working a lot.*)

6 Les enfants **se couchaient** à 8 heures. (*The children would go to bed at 8 o'clock.*)

7 Philippe **marchait** six kilomètres. (*Philippe would walk six kilometers.*)

8 Nous **nous réunissions** régulièrement. (*We would reunite regularly.*)

9 Tu **arrivais** à l'heure. (*You used to arrive on time.*)

10 Je **choisissais** le train. (*I would choose the train.*)

11 Nous **prenions** des notes. (*We would take notes.*)

12 Je **sortais** tous les soirs. (*I used to go out every evening.*)

13 Vous **lisiez** des romans. (*You used to read novels.*)

14 Les enfants **craignaient** des moustiques. (*The children used to fear mosquitoes.*)

15 Tu **buvais** du vin. (*You used to drink wine.*)

16 Nous **nous écrivions** quelquefois. (*We would write to each other sometimes.*)

17 Mathilde **faisait** des études. (*Mathilde was taking classes.*)

18 Vous **croyiez** aux contes de fées. (*You used to believe in fairy tales.*)

19 Je **recevais** des cadeaux. (*I used to receive gifts.*)

20 Nous **voulions** partir. (*We wanted to leave.*)

21 Tu **allais** au marché. (*You used to go to the market.*)

22 Ils **achetaient** du pain. (*They were buying bread.*)

23 Elle **lisait.** (*She was reading.*)

24 Nous **travaillions.** (*We were working.*)

25 Je **nageais.** (*I was swimming.*)

26 Vous **vous ennuyiez.** (*You were getting bored.*)

27 Tu **faisais** de la voile. (*You were sailing/used to sail.*)

28 Nous **riions.** (*We were laughing.*)

29 Il **neigeait.** (*It was snowing.*)

30 Je **conduisais.** (*I was driving.*)

31 **Autrefois je prenais le train.**

32 **Nous allions à l'école tous les jours.**

33 **Ils jouaient au golf le weekend.**

34 **Je faisais souvent des promenades.**

35 **D'habitude il rencontrait ses amis au café.**

36 **Vous vous dépêchiez tout le temps.**

37 **Le vendredi elle sortait avec ses amis.**

38 **Nous partions en vacances chaque été.**

39 **Tu mangeais toujours vite.**

40 **En général, les étudiants parlaient français en classe.**

41 **c.**

42 **f.**

43 **a.**

44 **e.**

45 **d.**

46 **b.**

47 **c.**

48 **d.**

49 **a.**

50 **b.**

Chapter 12

Comprehending the Passé Composé and the Pluperfect Tenses

. . . .

In This Chapter

▶ Making the passé composé with **avoir**

▶ Forming the passé composé with **être**

▶ Knowing how to say no in the passé composé

▶ Making the pluperfect

. . . .

*U*nlike the imperfect tense, which describes what was happening (see Chapter 11), the passé composé recounts events that have already taken place and at a specific time in the past. You use the passé composé to express a completed action in the past. For example, with this tense you can recount what you have done and accomplished, where you've been, and the people you've met yesterday, last week, last month, or even years ago.

Meanwhile, the pluperfect tense is closely related because it's also a compound past tense just like the passé composé. However, it describes events that have taken place even before the passé composé. The meaning of the pluperfect in English is *had*. For example, **Nous avions déjà mangé quand papa est rentré** means *We had already eaten when dad came home. Had eaten* is in the pluperfect and *came* is in the passé composé because one action happened before the other action.

This chapter shows you how to form the passé composé and pluperfect tenses and provides plenty of opportunities for you to practice them.

Forming the Passé Composé

The *passé composé,* as the name indicates, is a compound tense made up of an auxiliary verb and a past participle. The French language has only two auxiliaries: **avoir** (*to have*) and **être** (*to be*).

To form the passé composé, you first conjugate the auxiliaries in the present tense and then add the past participle. (Sounds simple enough, right?) To make it even easier, remember that most verbs take the auxiliary **avoir**. However, certain verbs, especially those that express motion, such as **aller** (*to go*), **partir** (*to leave*), and **venir** (*to come*) take **être.** I start with verbs that take **avoir** as their auxiliary.

avoir (*to have*)	
j'**ai**	nous **avons**
tu **as**	vous **avez**
il/elle/on **a**	ils/elles **ont**
J'**ai** trois enfants. (*I have three children.*)	

Regular verbs and the passé composé

To form the past participle of regular **-er** verbs, such as **parler** (*to speak*), simply drop the **r** and add an accent aigu to the **e**, like so: **é** (**parlé**). Now add this past participle to the auxiliary and you've formed the past tense.

The passé composé has three meanings in English. For example, **J'ai parlé** means *I spoke, I have spoken,* and *I did speak.* Even verbs with spelling changes (see Chapter 3), such as **jeter** (*to throw*), **acheter** (*to buy*), **essayer** (*to try*), and **espérer** (*to hope*), have a regular past participle. Simply drop the **r** from the infinitive and add accent aigu to the **e,** like so: **jeté, acheté, essayé,** and **espéré.**

For the regular **-ir** verbs, such as **finir** (*to finish*), simply drop the **-r** and voilà: **fini.** Finally, for the regular **-re** verbs, like **vendre** (*to sell*), drop the **-re** and add a **u,** to get **vendu.**

To form the passé composé, you take the present tense of the auxiliary verb and add the appropriate past participle. Check out the following tables that provide examples of three verbs in the passé composé, conjugated in their entirety. Note that each has **avoir** as its auxiliary.

parler (*to speak*)	
j'**ai parlé**	nous **avons parlé**
tu **as parlé**	vous **avez parlé**
il/elle/on **a parlé**	ils/elles **ont parlé**
Nous **avons parlé** aux enfants. (*We spoke to the children.*)	

finir (*to finish*)	
j'**ai fini**	nous **avons fini**
tu **as fini**	vous **avez fini**
il/elle/on **a fini**	ils/elles **ont fini**
Elle **a fini** ses devoirs. (*She finished her homework.*)	

vendre (*to sell*)	
j'**ai vendu**	nous **avons vendu**
tu **as vendu**	vous **avez vendu**
il/elle/on **a vendu**	ils/elles **ont vendu**
Les étudiants **ont vendu** leurs livres. (*The students sold their books.*)	

Now it's your turn. Put the following verbs in the passé composé. (Check out the sample problem if you need any clarification.)

Q. Nous _____ (nettoyer) la maison.

A. Nous **avons nettoyé** la maison. (*We cleaned the house.*)

1. Tu _____ (rendre) les livres.

2. Elle _____ (voyager).

3. Nous _____ (choisir).

4. Ils _____ (dîner).

5. Je _____ (étudier).

6. Vous _____ (réussir).

7. Ils _____ (vendre) leur voiture.

8. Tu _____ (perdre) tes clés.

9. Nous _____ (travailler).

10. Elle _____ (réfléchir).

Irregular verbs and the passé composé

Many French verbs have an irregular past participle. Usually, if a verb is irregular in the present tense (like the verbs presented in Chapter 4), then it also has an irregular past participle. However, irregular verbs that follow the same conjugation pattern as **partir** (*to leave*) have regular past participles. These verbs include **sortir** (*to go out*), **dormir** (*to sleep*), **mentir** (*to lie*), **servir** (*to serve*), and **aller** (*to go*). For the **-ir** verbs like **partir**, just drop the **r**, and for the verb **aller**, drop the **r** and add an accent aigu on the **e**. I group the verbs with an irregular past participle here according to their endings. The previous section explains that you form the past participle of regular **-re** verbs by dropping the **-re** and adding a **u**. Many irregular verbs (those ending in **-oir**, **-re**, or **-ir**) have a past participle that also ends in **u**. Table 12-1 lists the irregular verbs and their past participles that end in **u**.

Table 12-1	Irregular Verbs and Their Past Participles Ending in u
Infinitive	*Past Participle*
apercevoir (*to see, to perceive*)	**aperçu**
appartenir (*to belong to*)	**appartenu**
avoir (*to have*)	**eu**
battre (*to beat*)	**battu**
boire (*to drink*)	**bu**

(continued)

Table 12-1 *(continued)*

Infinitive	Past Participle
connaître (*to know*)	connu
convaincre (*to convince*)	convaincu
courir (*to run*)	couru
croire (*to believe*)	cru
décevoir (to disappoint)	déçu
devenir (*to become*)	devenu
devoir (*to owe, to have to*)	dû
falloir (*to be necessary, to have to*)	fallu
lire (*to read*)	lu
paraître (*to appear*)	paru
plaire (*to please*)	plu
pleuvoir (*to rain*)	plu
pouvoir (*to be able to*)	pu
recevoir (*to receive*)	reçu
revenir (*to come back*)	revenu
savoir (*to know*)	su
tenir (*to hold*)	tenu
venir (*to come*)	venu
vivre (*to live*)	vécu
voir (*to see*)	vu
vouloir (*to want*)	voulu

Some past participles end in **t**. Table 12-2 shows those verbs along with their past participles.

Table 12-2   Irregular Verbs and Their Past Participles Ending in t

Infinitive	Past Participle
conduire (*to drive*)	conduit
construire (*to construct, to build*)	construit
couvrir (*to cover*)	couvert
dire (*to say*)	dit
écrire (*to write*)	écrit
faire (*to do, to make*)	fait

Infinitive	Past Participle
inscrire (*to note, to write down*)	**inscrit**
offrir (*to offer*)	**offert**
ouvrir (*to open*)	**ouvert**
souffrir (*to suffer*)	**souffert**

Table 12-3 lists some irregular verbs whose past participles end in **s**. Note that you create the past participle the same way for any verb that ends in **-mettre** or **-prendre**.

Table 12-3	Irregular Verbs and Their Past Participles Ending in s
Infinitive	*Past Participle*
mettre (*to put, to place*)	**mis**
admettre (*to admit*)	**admis**
prendre (*to take*)	**pris**
apprendre (*to learn*)	**appris**

Some past participles of irregular verbs end in **i.** Table 12-4 shows the irregular verbs that have past participles ending in **i.**

Table 12-4	Irregular Verbs and Their Past Participles Ending in i
Infinitive	*Past Participle*
partir (*to leave*)	**parti**
rire (*to laugh*)	**ri**
sortir (*to go out*)	**sorti**
sourire (*to smile*)	**souri**
suivre (*to follow, to take a course*)	**suivi**

In addition to **avoir** (which you can see more on earlier in this section), three other irregular verbs have the following forms in the past participle. Table 12-5 lists these four irregular verbs and their past participles.

Table 12-5	Irregular Verbs and Their Past Participles
Infinitive	*Past Participle*
avoir (*to have*)	**eu**
être (*to be*)	**été**
mourir (*to die*)	**mort**
naître (*to be born*)	**né**

Try putting the following verbs in the passé composé. If you don't remember how to spell their past participles, refer to the tables in this chapter. Check out the sample problem.

Q. Elle _____ (offrir) des bonbons aux enfants.

A. Elle **a offert** des bonbons aux enfants. (*She offered candy to the children.*)

11. Nous _____ (conduire).

12. Ils _____ (courir).

13. Je _____ (lire).

14. Vous _____ (souffrir).

15. Tu _____ (sourire).

16. Elle _____ (apercevoir) le chien.

17. Nous _____ (voir) le Président.

18. Elles _____ (apprendre) le français.

19. Vous _____ (suivre) les cours.

20. Tu _____ (vivre) en France.

Making sure the past participle agrees with the preceding direct object

Throughout this section, I show you the way to form the past participles, but you need to know another important fact before you can spell them correctly. You need to make sure the past participles are in agreement with the preceding direct object if there is one. Depending on the direct object, you need to make the following changes to the past participle:

✔ If the preceding direct object is masculine singular, then leave the past participle alone.

✔ If the preceding direct object is feminine singular, add an **e**.

✔ If the preceding direct object is masculine plural, add an **s**.

✔ If the preceding direct object is feminine plural, add an **es**.

Check out the following examples to see how the past participle can change.

J'ai mis les fleurs dans le vase. (*I put the flowers in the vase.*)

Je **les** ai mi**ses** dans le vase. (*I put them in the vase.*)

To replace the direct object **les fleurs,** which is feminine plural, with the direct object pronoun **les,** which means *them,* place the direct object pronoun before the verb, and then the past participle **mis** agrees with **les** and therefore it is spelled **mises.** I provide one more example.

Il a vu Nicole. (*He saw Nicole.*)

Il **l'**a vue. (*He saw her.*)

Table 12-6 is a list of the direct object pronouns.

Table 12-6	Direct Object Pronouns
French Pronoun	*English Equivalent*
me	*me*
te	*you*
se	*himself/herself/oneself/themselves* (for pronominal verbs only)
le	*him/it*
la	*her/it*
nous	*us*
vous	*you*
les	*them*

Note: The pronominal pronouns *me, te, se, nous,* and *vous* can also be direct object pronouns. Check out Chapter 5 for more on pronominal verbs.

Drop the vowel of **me, te, se, le,** and **la** and add an apostrophe when the verb begins with a vowel or a mute **h.** In the passé composé when the auxiliary is **avoir,** this is always the case.

Ils m'ont prévenu(e). (*They warned me.*)

Je t'ai cherché(e). (*I looked for you.*)

Nous l'avons fini(e). (*We finished it.*)

Replace the direct object, which is underlined in each question, with a direct object pronoun. Make sure the past participle agrees with the preceding direct object pronoun; if it doesn't, make the appropriate changes, like in the following example.

O. Elle a aperçu <u>la foule</u>. (*She noticed the crowd.*)

A. Elle **l'**a aperçue. (*She noticed it.*)

21. Elle a appris <u>la leçon</u>.

_____

22. Nous avons pris <u>le train</u>.

_____

23. Ils ont fait <u>les devoirs</u>. (masculine, plural)

_____

24. J'ai vu <u>Hélène</u>.

_____

25. Vous avez récité <u>le poème</u>.

_____

26. Nous avons appelé <u>les enfants</u>. (masculine, plural)

_____

27. Il a reçu <u>les cartes</u>. (feminine, plural)

_____

28. Tu as écrit <u>la dissertation</u>.

_____

29. Ils ont compris <u>le journaliste</u>.

_____

30. Elle a rencontré <u>ses amis</u>. (masculine, plural)

_____

Creating the Passé Composé with Être

Some specific verbs, such as verbs of motion and verbs that aren't followed by a direct object, are intransitive and take the auxiliary **être.** (An _intransitive verb_ is one that isn't followed by a direct object. Check out Chapter 1 for more info.) You conjugate the verb **être** in the present tense and add the past participle of the verb you want.

être _(to be)_	
je **suis**	nous **sommes**
tu **es**	vous **êtes**
il/elle/on **est**	ils/elles **sont**
Vous **êtes** optimiste. (_You are optimistic._)	

To remember which verbs take **être** (_to be_), picture the house of **être** (see Figure 12-1). Picture a huge door, an elegant staircase, a bed, and a chair. Are you wondering how this visual aid can help you? Many of the verbs that take **être** are what I call "door" verbs. You can **go, come, return, enter, arrive,** and **pass** through the door in the house of **être.** What about the staircase? You can **go up, go down,** and if you aren't careful, you can **fall.** Now picture the bed. Way before hospitals, people were **born** in the house and **died** in the house. So these verbs take **être.** The last types of verbs belonging to this category are all pronominal verbs, which take **être** as their auxiliary. You form the passé composé of **être** verbs the same way as **avoir** verbs. You conjugate the verb **être** in the present tense followed by the past participle of the verbs.

Il est arrivé à 9 heures. (_He arrived at 9 o'clock._)

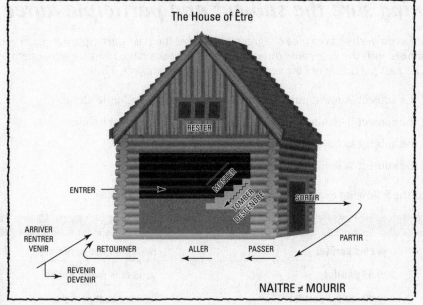

Figure 12-1:
The House of Être:
Remember that these verbs use être in the passé composé.

Table 12-7 shows the verbs that use **être** when forming the passé composé, along with their past participles.

Table 12-7	The House of Être: Forming the Passé Composé
Infinitive	*Past Participle*
aller (*to go*)	**allé**
arriver (*to arrive*)	**arrivé**
descendre* (*to go downstairs, to descend*)	**descendu**
devenir (*to become*)	**devenu**
entrer (*to enter*)	**entré**
monter* (*to go up stairs, to climb*)	**monté**
mourir (*to die*)	**mort**
naître (*to be born*)	**né**
partir (*to leave*)	**parti**
passer* (*to pass, to spend*)	**passé**
rentrer* (*to come back home*)	**rentré**
rester (*to stay*)	**resté**
retourner* (*to return*)	**retourné**
revenir (*to come back*)	**revenu**
sortir* (*to go out*)	**sorti**
tomber (*to fall*)	**tombé**
venir (*to come*)	**venu**

** These verbs can take either auxiliary, **avoir** or **être**. They take the auxiliary **avoir** when they're followed by a direct object. However, they take **être** when they aren't followed by a direct object.*

Making sure the subject and participle agree

Just like **avoir** verbs have rules of agreement where the past participle agrees in gender and number with the preceding direct object, **être** verbs have rules for agreement as well. The past participle of **être** verbs agrees with the subject. Thus,

 ✔ If the subject is masculine singular, leave the past participle alone.

 ✔ If the subject is feminine singular, add an **e** to the past participle.

 ✔ If the subject is masculine plural, add an **s**.

 ✔ If the subject is feminine plural, add an **es**.

Look at the following example conjugated in the passé composé.

partir (*to leave*)	
je **suis parti(e)**	nous **sommes partis(es)**
tu **es parti(e)**	vous **êtes parti(e)(s)(es)**
il/elle/on **est parti(e)**	ils/elles **sont partis(es)**
Nous **sommes partis** à midi. (*We left at noon.*)	

Put these verbs in the passé composé. Don't forget to conjugate the auxiliary **être** in the present and then add the past participle. Remember to make sure the past participle agrees with the subject.

Q. Elle _____ (monter) dans un taxi.

A. Elle **est montée** dans un taxi. (*She got in a taxi.*)

31. Nous _____ (aller) au cinéma.

32. Ils _____ (naître) en Europe.

33. Je _____ (tomber).

34. Vous _____ (descendre) du train.

35. Tu _____ (arriver) en retard.

36. Elle _____ (devenir) célèbre.

37. Il _____ (mourir) en 1969.

38. Nous _____ (rentrer) tôt.

39. Je _____ (rester) à la maison.

40. Ils _____ (venir) ensemble.

Forming the passé composé with pronominal verbs

All pronominal verbs take **être** as their auxiliary. However, they don't have the same rule of agreement as the nonpronominal **être** verbs. The past participle of pronominal verbs follows that same rule of agreement as the verbs taking **avoir** as their auxiliary. That is, the past participle agrees with the preceding direct object if the sentence has one. (Check out "Making sure the participle and direct object agree" earlier in this chapter for more info.)

In most sentences with pronominal verbs, the pronominal pronoun (which corresponds to the subject) is the preceding direct object. If this is the case, then you have agreement, which shows in the past participle, and you should follow these rules:

- ✔ If the pronominal pronoun is masculine singular, leave the past participle alone.

- ✔ If the pronominal pronoun is feminine singular, add an **e**.

- ✔ If the pronominal pronoun is masculine plural, add an **s**.

- ✔ If the pronominal pronoun is feminine plural, add an **es**.

The following example conjugates **se coucher** (*to go to bed*) in the passé composé.

se coucher (*to go to bed*)	
je **me suis couché(e)**	nous **nous sommes couchés(es)**
tu **t'es couché(e)**	vous **vous êtes couché(e)(s)(es)**
il/elle/on **s'est couché(e)**	ils/elles **se sont couchés(es)**
Nous **nous sommes couchés** à 10 heures. (*We went to bed at 10 o'clock.*)	

If the sentence has a direct object other than the pronominal pronoun, then the pronominal pronoun is indirect and you don't have agreement. Take the verb **se laver** (*to wash oneself*). When the verb isn't followed by a direct object, you have agreement with the pronominal pronoun. However, when the same verb is followed by a direct object, the pronominal pronoun is the indirect object and you don't have agreement. Check out Table 12-8 as an example.

Table 12-8	Se Laver (*to wash oneself*) with and without a Direct Object
Se Laver without a Direct Object	*Se Laver with a Direct Object*
Je **me suis lavé(e)**. (*I washed myself.*)	Je **me suis lavé** les cheveux. (*I washed my hair.*)
Tu **t'es lavé(e)**. (*You washed yourself.*)	Tu **t'es lavé** les cheveux. (*You washed your hair.*)
Il **s'est lavé**. (*He washed himself.*)	Il **s'est lavé** les cheveux. (*He washed his hair.*)

(continued)

Table 12-8 *(continued)*

Se Laver without a Direct Object	Se Laver with a Direct Object
Elle **s'est lavée.** (*She washed herself.*)	Elle **s'est lavé** les cheveux. (*She washed her hair.*)
Nous **nous sommes lavés(es).** (*We washed ourselves.*)	Nous **nous sommes lavé** les cheveux. (*We washed our hair.*)
Vous **vous êtes lavé(e)(s)(es).** (*You washed yourself [ves.]*)	Vous **vous êtes lavé** les cheveux. (*You washed your hair.*)
Ils **se sont lavés.** (*They washed themselves.*)	Ils **se sont lavé** les cheveux. (*They washed their hair.*)
Elles **se sont lavées.** (*They washed themselves.*)	Elles **se sont lavé** les cheveux. (*They washed their hair.*)

Some pronominal verbs have pronominal pronouns that are always indirect object pronouns. In this case, the past participle doesn't agree with the pronominal pronouns. Table 12-9 shows these verbs.

Table 12-9 Pronominal Verbs with Indirect Object Pronouns

Verb	Translation
s'acheter	*to buy for oneself or for each other*
s'écrire	*to write to each other*
se demander	*to wonder*
se dire	*to say to oneself or to each other*
se donner	*to give to oneself or to each other*
se parler	*to speak to each other*
se promettre	*to promise oneself or each other*
se rendre compte de	*to realize*
se rendre visite	*to visit each other*
se ressembler	*to look alike, to resemble each other*
se sourire	*to smile at each other*
se téléphoner	*to call each other*

Remember that the past participle and the indirect object pronouns have no agreement between them. This rule applies to verbs taking the auxiliary **avoir** as well as to pronominal verbs. Table 12-10 shows the indirect objects.

Table 12-10	Indirect Object Pronouns
French Pronoun	*English Equivalent*
me	to me
te	to you
se	to himself/to herself/to themselves (for pronominal verbs only)
lui	to him/to her
nous	to us
vous	to you
leur	to them

Note: *The pronominal pronouns* **me, te, se, nous,** *and* **vous** *can also be indirect object pronouns. Check out Chapter 5 for more on pronominal verbs.*

Je leur ai téléphoné. (*I called them.*)

Nous lui avons promis. (*We promised him/her.*)

Vous vous êtes dit au revoir. (*You said goodbye to each other.*)

Put the following pronominal verbs in the passé composé. Don't forget to make sure the past participle agrees with the pronominal pronoun when it's the direct object.

Q. Nous _____ (se rencontrer).

A. Nous **nous sommes rencontrés.** (*We met each other.*)

41. Ils _____ (se téléphoner).

42. Je _____ (s'habiller).

43. Elles _____ (se brosser) les dents.

44. Tu _____ (s'amuser).

45. Nous _____ (s'écrire).

46. Il _____ (se lever) tard.

47. Vous _____ (se parler).

48. Elle _____ (se maquiller).

49. Nous _____ (se dépêcher).

50. Ils _____ (se donner) des cadeaux.

Flexible Verbs: Using Either Avoir or Être

Certain verbs can take either auxiliary, **avoir** or **être,** in the passé composé. The way you can tell which one they take is in the way they're used. If they're followed by a direct object, then they take **avoir** as their auxiliary. If they aren't followed by a direct object, then they take **être** as their auxiliary.

Note that verbs such as **descendre, monter, passer, rentrer, retourner,** and **sortir** can take either auxiliary — **avoir** or **être** (see Table 12-7 earlier in this chapter). These verbs take **avoir** when they're followed by a direct object. In this case, they're transitive. They take **être** when they aren't followed by a direct object and they're intransitive. See the examples in Table 12-11.

Table 12-11	Verbs That Take Either Auxiliary (Avoir or Être)
Transitive (avoir)	*Intransitive (être)*
Elle **a passé** un examen. (*She took an exam.*)	Elle **est passée** par la bibliothèque. (*She passed by the library*).
Elle **a monté** la valise. (*She brought the suitcase up.*)	Elle **est montée** dans un taxi. (*She got in a taxi.*)
Elle **a descendu** les livres. (*She brought the books down.*)	Elle **est descendue** au sous-sol. (*She went down to the basement.*)
Elle **a sorti** le chien. (*She took out the dog.*)	Elle **est sortie** avec ses amis. (*She went out with her friends.*)
Elle **a rentré** la voiture. (*She put the car in.*)	Elle **est rentrée** à minuit. (*She came home at midnight.*)
Elle **a retourné** les crêpes. (*She turned over the crepes.*)	Elle **est retournée** à son livre. (*She returned to her book/reading.*)

Can you tell the difference between a transitive and an intransitive verb? Choose between **avoir** and **être** and put the following verbs in the passé composé.

0. Je _____ (sortir) avec mes amis.

A. Je **suis sorti** avec mes amis. (*I went out with my friends.*)

51. Nous _____ (passer) une semaine à la Martinique.

52. Il _____ (monter) dans sa chambre.

53. Tu _____ (sortir) ton livre.

54. Vous _____ (descendre) le linge.

55. Je _____ (rentrer) à l'heure.

56. Ils _____ (retourner) les cassettes vidéo.

57. Nous _____ (sortir) avec des amis.

58. Tu _____ (passer) par Paris.

59. Elle _____ (monter) le bébé dans sa chambre.

60. Vous _____ (rentrer) le chien.

Making the Passé Composé Negative

If you want to say that you didn't do something or you didn't go anywhere, you make the passé composé negative. Just place **ne** before the auxiliary, which is the conjugated verb, and **pas** after the auxiliary.

> **Je n'ai pas voyagé.** (*I didn't travel.*)
>
> **Nous n'avons pas lu le journal.** (*We didn't read the newspaper.*)

For pronominal verbs, the **ne** precedes not only the auxiliary but also the pronominal pronoun and the **pas** follows that auxiliary.

> **Tu ne t'es pas couché(e).** (*You didn't go to bed.*)
>
> **Nous ne nous sommes pas amusés.** (*We didn't have fun.*)

Now you try. Make the following sentences negative and then translate them.

Q. Ils sont sortis.

A. Ils **ne sont pas** sortis. *They did not go out.*

61. Ils se sont ennuyés.

_____

_____

62. Tu t'es habillé(e).

_____

_____

63. Nous avons appris la leçon.

_____

_____

64. Elle est partie.

_____

_____

65. Ils se sont souri.

_____

_____

66. Vous avez vu le film.

_____

_____

67. Je me suis brossé les cheveux.

_____

68. Nous sommes nés en Californie.

_____

69. Elles se sont rappelées leur jeunesse.

_____

70. Tu as parlé à tes parents.

_____

Forming the Pluperfect

You use the pluperfect to recount an action that happened even before the passé composé. It's not only a completed action in the past, but one that had taken place even before the passé composé. These two tenses are both past compound tenses.

You form the pluperfect just like the passé composé, except that you conjugate the auxiliaries **avoir** and **être** in the imperfect tense and add the past participle of the verb. The following shows the imperfect forms of **avoir** and **être,** followed by an example of how to form the pluperfect.

avoir (*to have*)	
j'**avais**	nous **avions**
tu **avais**	vous **aviez**
il/elle/on **avait**	ils/elles **avaient**
Nous **avions** déjà **mangé** quand tu es arrivé. (*We had already eaten when you arrived.*)	

être (*to be*)	
j'**étais**	nous **étions**
tu **étais**	vous **étiez**
il/elle/on **était**	ils/elles **étaient**
Ils **étaient partis** quand nous avons téléphoné. (*They had left when we called.*)	

Je suis allé au théâtre hier, mais j'avais acheté mon billet le mois dernier. (*I went to the theater yesterday, but I had bought my ticket last month.*)

You also use the pluperfect to express regret with the condition **si** (*if only*). You use the pluperfect after a **si** clause in a hypothetical sentence with the past conditional tense in the result clause (see Chapter 18).

Si j'étais arrivé plutôt. (*If only I had arrived earlier.*)

Si nous avions su. (*If only we had known.*)

S'il avait réussi, à ses examens, il serait allé en Europe. (*If he had passed his exams, he would have gone to Europe.*)

Put the following verbs in the pluperfect. Check out the example if you need assistance.

0. Le professeur _____ (rendre) les examens.

A. Le professeur **avait rendu** les examens. (*The professor had given back the exams.*)

71. Papa _____ (rentrer) tard.

72. Les enfants _____ (finir) leurs devoirs.

73. Je _____ (suivre) tous mes cours.

74. Nous _____ (recevoir) notre diplôme.

75. Elle _____ (voyager).

76. Vous _____ (travailler) toute votre vie.

77. Il _____ (écrire) sa thèse.

78. Tu _____ (aller) en Afrique.

79. Nous _____ (se réveiller) de bonne heure.

80. Mes parents _____ (élever) quatre enfants.

Answer Key

This section contains the answers to the practice problems in this chapter. Compare your answers to the correct ones. Are you a passé composé wiz? Remember that the passé composé has three meanings in English. For example, **J'ai choisi le vin rouge** means *I chose, I have chosen,* and *I did choose the red wine.* In this Answer Key, however, I provide only the most common translation.

1 Tu **as rendu** les livres. (*You gave back the books.*)

2 Elle **a voyagé.** (*She travelled.*)

3 Nous **avons choisi.** (*We chose.*)

4 Ils **ont dîné.** (*They dined.*)

5 J'**ai étudié.** (*I studied.*)

6 Vous **avez réussi.** (*You have succeeded.*)

7 Ils **ont vendu** leur voiture. (*They sold their car.*)

8 Tu **as perdu** tes clés. (*You lost your keys.*)

9 Nous **avons travaillé.** (*We worked.*)

10 Elle **a réfléchi.** (*She reflected.*)

11 Nous **avons conduit.** (*We drove.*)

12 Ils **ont couru.** (*They ran.*)

13 J'**ai lu.** (*I read.*)

14 Vous **avez souffert.** (*You [have] suffered.*)

15 Tu **as souri.** (*You smiled.*)

16 Elle **a aperçu** le chien. (*She noticed the dog.*)

17 Nous **avons vu** le Président. (*We saw the President.*)

18 Elles **ont appris** le français. (*They learned French.*)

19 Vous **avez suivi** les cours. (*You took courses.*)

20 Tu **as vécu** en France. (*You lived in France.*)

21 **Elle l'a apprise.** (*She learned it.*)

22 **Nous l'avons pris.** (*We took it.*)

23 **Ils les ont faits.** (*They did it.*)

24 **Je l'ai vue.** (*I saw her.*)

25 **Vous l'avez récité.** (*You recited it.*)

26 **Nous les avons appelés.** (*We called them.*)

27 **Il les a reçues.** (*He received them.*)

28 **Tu l'as écrite.** (*You wrote it.*)

29 **Ils l'ont compris.** (*They understood him.*)

30 **Elle les a rencontrés.** (*She met them.*)

31 Nous **sommes allés** au cinéma. (*We went to the movies.*)

32 Ils **sont nés** en Europe. (*They were born in Europe.*)

33 Je **suis tombée.** (*I fell.*)

34 Vous **êtes descendu** du train. (*You got off the train.*)

35 Tu **es arrivée** en retard. (*You arrived late.*)

36 Elle **est devenue** célèbre. (*She became famous.*)

37 Il **est mort** en 1969. (*He died in 1969.*)

38 Nous **sommes rentrés** tôt. (*We came home early.*)

39 Je **suis restée** à la maison. (*I stayed in the house.*)

40 Ils **sont venus** ensemble. (*They came together.*)

41 Ils **se sont téléphoné.** (*They called each other.*)

42 Je **me suis habillé(e).** (*I got dressed.*)

43 Elles **se sont brossé** les dents. (*They brushed their teeth.*)

44 Tu **t'es amusé(e).** (*You had fun.*)

45 Nous **nous sommes écrit.** (*We wrote to each other.*)

46 Il **s'est levé** tard. (*He got up late.*)

47 Vous **vous êtes parlé.** (*You spoke to each other.*)

48 Elle **s'est maquillée.** (*She put on makeup.*)

49 Nous **nous sommes dépêchés.** (*We hurried.*)

50 Ils **se sont donné** des cadeaux. (*They gave each other presents.*)

Nous **avons passé** une semaine à la Martinique. (*We spent a week in Martinique.*)

Il **est monté** dans sa chambre. (*He went up to his room.*)

Tu **as sorti** ton livre. (*You took out your book.*)

Vous **avez descendu** le linge. (*You brought the laundry down[stairs].*)

Je **suis rentrée** toujours à l'heure. (*I always came home on time.*)

Ils **ont retourné** les cassettes vidéo. (*They returned the videos.*)

Nous **sommes sortis** avec des amis. (*We went out with friends.*)

Tu **es passée** par Paris. (*You passed by Paris.*)

Elle **a monté** le bébé dans sa chambre. (*She brought the baby up to her room.*)

Vous **avez rentré** le chien. (*You brought the dog in.*)

Ils **ne se sont pas ennuyés.** *They did not get bored.*

Tu **ne t'es pas habillée.** *You did not get dressed.*

Nous **n'avons pas appris** la leçon. *We did not learn the lesson.*

Elle **n'est pas partie.** *She did not leave.*

Ils **ne se sont pas souri.** *They did not smile at each other.*

Vous **n'avez pas vu** le film. *You did not see the film.*

Je **ne me suis pas brossé** les cheveux. *I did not brush my hair.*

Nous **ne sommes pas nés** en Californie. *We were not born in California.*

Elles **ne se sont pas rappelées** leur jeunesse. *They did not remember their youth.*

Tu **n'as pas parlé** à tes parents. *You did not speak to your parents.*

Papa **était rentré** tard. (*Dad had come home late.*)

Les enfants **avaient fini** leurs devoirs. (*The children had finished their homework.*)

J'**avais suivi** tous mes cours. (*I had taken all my courses.*)

Nous **avions reçu** notre diplôme. (*We had received our diploma.*)

Elle **avait voyagé.** (*She had travelled.*)

Vous **aviez travaillé** toute votre vie. (*You had worked your whole life.*)

Il **avait écrit** sa thèse. (*He had written his thesis.*)

Tu **étais allé** en Afrique. (*You had gone to Africa.*)

Nous **nous étions réveillés** de bonne heure. (*We had woken up early.*)

Mes parents **avaient élévé** quatre enfants. (*My parents had raised four children.*)

Chapter 13

Contrasting the Imperfect with the Passé Composé

• •

In This Chapter
▶ Knowing the differences between the imperfect and the passé composé
▶ Choosing when to use each tense

• •

*W*hen you recount past events, you often describe the circumstances in which the events took place as well as tell what happened using specific actions. This chapter guides you in distinguishing between the two tenses — the imperfect and the passé composé. (For more on forming the imperfect and the passé composé, see Chapters 11 and 12.)

Identifying the Main Differences between the Two Tenses

The choice between the passé composé and the imperfect depends on the context of what you're saying. At times, the choice between these two tenses is subjective and depends on the way you view the events. So when do you use the imperfect versus the passé composé?

You use the imperfect to provide background information, such as descriptions of scenery, weather, physical appearance, and mental state. You also use it to describe events that have occurred an unspecified number of times as well as ongoing and habitual actions. The translation of the imperfect in English is *used to do something, would do something,* or *was doing something.*

On the other hand, you use the passé composé for completed actions in the past, actions that occurred at a specific moment in time and a specific number of times, and changes or interruptions of a state or actions.

Table 13-1 serves as a guide and provides example sentences for each use.

Table 13-1	Differences between the Imperfect and Passé Composé		
When to Use Imperfect	*Example*	*When to Use Passé Composé*	*Example*
Habitual or continuous action	**Je lisais.** (*I was reading.*)	Change or interruption in the action	**Je lisais quand tu es entré.** (*I was reading when you entered.*)

(continued)

Table 13-1 (continued)

When to Use Imperfect	Example	When to Use Passé Composé	Example
Physical description and mental state	**Elle portait sa nouvelle robe et elle se sentait belle.** (*She was wearing her new dress and was feeling beautiful.*)	Physical description and mental state are the result of a specific action	**Parce qu'il pleuvait, elle a porté son imperméable.** (*Because it was raining, she wore her raincoat.*)
Description of weather	**Il neigeait et il faisait très froid.** (*It was snowing and it was very cold.*)	Change in the weather or the weather at a specific moment	**Il a neigé ce matin.** (*It snowed this morning.*)
An event that has taken place an unspecified number of times	**Quand j'étais à Paris, je prenais le métro.** (*When I was in Paris, I used to/would take the subway.*)	An event that has taken place a specific number of times	**Quand j'étais à Paris, j'ai pris le métro trois fois.** (*When I was in Paris, I took the subway three times.*)
Ongoing simultaneous actions	**Maman préparait le déjeuner et papa tondait la pelouse.** (*Mom was preparing lunch and Dad was mowing the lawn.*)	Actions completed at a specific time in the past	**A midi, maman a préparé le déjeuner et papa a tondu la pelouse.** (*At noon, Mom prepared lunch and Dad mowed the lawn.*)

Try to distinguish between these two tenses. In the following sentences, put the verb in parentheses in the imperfect or the passé composé.

Q. En général, ils _____ (dîner) assez tard.

A. En général, ils **dînaient** assez tard. (*In general, they would eat fairly late.*)

1. Je _____ (se doucher) quand tu me _____ (appeler).

2. Nous _____ (aller) au théâtre cinq fois.

3. Benjamin _____ (jouer) au tennis pendant que Mélanie _____ (nager).

4. Il _____ (pleuvoir) mais il _____ (faire) très doux.

5. Quand il _____ (être) petit, il _____ (mettre) toujours ses chaussures de travers.

6. Dans la forêt, il y _____ (avoir) un silence profond.

7. Je _____ (corriger) les examens pendant que tu _____ (faire) tes devoirs.

8. Le professeur _____ (expliquer) le subjonctif trois fois.

9. Ils _____ (travailler) quand ils _____ (entendre) des sirènes.

10. Chaque été, nous _____ (aller) à la plage.

Selecting the Right Tense: Imperfect or Passé Composé?

When speaking in the past, you need to know which tense is the correct one to use. Are you discussing something that happened only one time or are you referring to something that happened habitually? This section can help you make the right choice by pointing out helpful key words that can point you in the right direction. This section also looks at certain verbs that are used more in the imperfect as well as pointers about understanding the context so that you can choose the right tense.

Relying on helpful key words

Although the choice of the imperfect or the passé composé depends on the context of the narration as well as the perspective of the speaker or author, certain key words may help you to choose more accurately between these two tenses. This section looks more closely at those key words.

Because the imperfect tense is one of description, habitual action, and nonspecific time, certain key words express general or continuous time with which you use the imperfect. On the other hand, expressions that express precise and specific time or specific number of times indicate a completed action, which is expressed by the passé composé.

> **J'allais à l'école tous les jours**. (*I would go to school every day.*)
>
> **Hier, je suis allé à l'école**. (*Yesterday, I went to school.*)

In the first sentence, **tous les jours** (*every day*) indicates a general time; therefore, the verb is in the imperfect tense. In the second sentence, **hier** (*yesterday*) indicates a specific time; therefore the verb is in the passé composé.

Table 13-2 shows some key words that can help you determine whether you need to use the imperfect or the passé composé.

Table 13-2	Choosing between the Imperfect and Passé Composé
Key Words That Indicate Imperfect Tense	*Key Words That Indicate Passé Composé*
autrefois (*in the past*)	**ce matin** (*this morning*)
chaque année (*each year*) **chaque fois** (*each time*) **chaque jour** (*each day*) **chaque mois** (*each month*) **chaque semaine** (*each week*)	**hier** (*yesterday*)
d'habitude/habituellement (*usually*)	**l'année dernière** (*last year*)

(continued)

Table 13-2 (continued)

Key Words That Indicate Imperfect Tense	Key Words That Indicate Passé Composé
généralement/en général (*generally*)	**la semaine dernière** (*last week*)
souvent (*often*)	**quand** (*when*) — this verb indicates the passé composé only when the ongoing action is interrupted
toujours (*always*)	**soudain/soudainement** (*suddenly*)
tous les jours (*every day*)	**tout d'un coup** (*all of a sudden*)

With these practice exercises, look at the verb in parentheses. Determine whether you need to conjugate it in the imperfect or passé composé. Use the key words as your guide.

Q. L'année dernière, ma soeur _____ (obtenir) son diplôme.

A. L'année dernière, ma soeur **a obtenu** son diplôme. (*Last year, my sister got her diploma.*)

11. Je le _____ (voir) chaque fois que je _____ (aller) au cours.

12. En général, nous _____ (partir) en vacances en juin.

13. Hier, ils _____ (faire) les courses.

14. Les enfants _____ (jouer) dans le parc quand tout d'un coup il _____ (commencer) à pleuvoir.

15. Autrefois mes grands-parents _____ (habiter) en Champagne.

16. Papa _____ (travailler) souvent le samedi.

17. Tu _____ (dormir) quand je _____ (rentrer).

18. Je _____ (se promener) d'habitude au jardin de Luxemburg.

19. La semaine dernière nous _____ (recevoir) une contravention.

20. Ils _____ (boire) toujours du vin au dîner.

Eyeing verbs usually used with the imperfect

In Chapter 11, you discover that the imperfect describes physical and mental states. You can use some verbs for this type of description, so they're usually in the imperfect tense. Check out the following examples in Table 13-3.

Table 13-3	Descriptive Verbs in the Imperfect
Infinitive	*Example in the Imperfect*
adorer (*to adore*)	**Elle adorait les pêches.** (*She adored peaches.*)
aimer (*to like, to love*)	**J'aimais les promenades.** (*I loved the walks.*)

Infinitive	Example in the Imperfect
avoir (*to have*)	**Il y avait des nuages.** (*There were clouds.*)
croire (*to believe*)	**Vous croyiez que nous étions déçus.** (*You believed that we were disappointed.*)
détester (*to hate*)	**Ils détestaient partir.** (*They hated to leave.*)
espérer (*to hope*)	**Tu espérais réussir.** (*You hoped to succeed.*)
être (*to be*)	**Il était en retard.** (*He was late.*)
penser (*to think*)	**Nous pensions que tu ne venais pas.** (*We thought that you were not coming.*)
préférer (*to prefer*)	**Je préférais le jazz.** (*I preferred/used to prefer jazz.*)

Looking at verbs that have different meanings in imperfect and passé composé

Certain verbs have different connotations depending on whether they're in the imperfect or the passé composé. In the passé composé, these verbs have more of an emphasis on something that you've accomplished, whereas in the imperfect, they emphasize more of a generality or an attempt to do something that probably didn't materialize or happen. Table 13-4 shows you some examples of these types of verbs.

Table 13-4	Different Meanings: Imperfect versus Passé Composé	
Infinitive	Imperfect	Passé Composé
croire (*to believe*)	**Tu croyais que je partirais.** (*You thought that I would leave.*)	**Tu as cru que je partirais.** (*You concluded that I would leave.*)
devoir (*to have to*)	**Il devait travailler.** (*He was supposed to work.*)	**Il a dû travailler.** (*He had to work.*)
falloir (*to have to*) This verb is used only in the third person singular **il,** but it can have multiple meanings in English.	**Il fallait partir.** (*I/We/They should have left*).	**Il a fallu partir.** (*I/We/They had to leave.*)
pouvoir (*to be able to*)	**Je pouvais faire mes devoirs.** (*I could/was capable of doing my homework.*)	**J'ai pu faire mes devoirs.** (*I succeeded in doing my homework.*)
savoir (*to know*)	**Elle savait que j'étais du retour.** (*She knew that I was back.*)	**Elle a su que j'étais du retour.** (*She discovered/found out that I was back.*)
vouloir (*to want*)	**Nous voulions voyager.** (*We wanted to travel.*)	**Nous avons voulu voyager.** (*We decided to travel.*)

You also use the imperfect tense with the following constructions in order to express ongoing actions in the past: **être en train de** (*to be in the middle of something*) and **venir de** + infinitive (*had just done something*).

> **Il était en train de conduire quand il a vu l'accident.** (*He was [in the middle of] driving when he saw the accident*).
>
> **Je venais de jouer au tennis alors j'avais mal au bras.** (*I had just played tennis so my arm was sore/hurting.*)

Translate the following sentences and put the verbs in the imperfect or the passé composé. For some sentences, more than one verb can be used. Refer to Table 13-4.

Q. I thought that you were married.

A. **Je croyais que tu étais marié.**

21. They had to pay a fine (une amende).

_____

22. Sarah was supposed to write a composition.

_____

23. We had to sell the house.

_____

24. You decided to register for classes.

_____

25. I knew that he was ill.

_____

26. Mathieu succeeded in winning the medal.

_____

27. We thought you were leaving.

_____

28. They found out the truth.

_____

29. My parents wanted to go to Paris.

_____

30. I had to stay with the kids.

_____

Understanding the context

Although certain rules guide you in choosing between the imperfect and the passé composé, sometimes the choice also depends on the context of the narration as well as on the speaker's or author's point of view. Along with these two tenses, you can also add the pluperfect (see Chapter 12 on how to form the pluperfect), which expresses a completed action in the past that had happened even before the passé composé. Remember that the meaning of the pluperfect in English is *had*.

J'ai trouvé le livre que j'avais perdu. (*I found the book that I had lost.*)

In the following paragraph, decide which past tenses are more accurate for each blank. Choose from the pluperfect, the imperfect, and the passé composé.

Q. Il _____ (faire) beau et je _____ (décider) de me promener dans le parc. Pendant que je _____ (se promener), il _____ (commencer) à pleuvoir.

A. Il **faisait** beau et j'**ai décidé** de me promener dans le parc. Pendant que je **me promenais,** il **a commencé** à pleuvoir. (*It was nice out and I decided to take a walk in the park. While I was walking, it began to rain.*)

Hélene [31]_____(naître) dans une petite ville au nord de

France. Sa famille et elle [32]_____ (habiter) une maison à

trois chambres que son grand-perè [33]_____ (construire)

vingt ans avant. Son père [34]_____ (travailler) au

centre-ville et sa mère [35]_____ (s'occuper) de son frère et

d'elle aussi bien que de ses grands-parents. Elle [36]_____

(aller) à l'école à pied avec tous les enfants du quartier. Ils

[37]_____ (porter) des uniformes bleus avec des cols de

dentelles blanches. Un jour, quand elle [38]_____ (rentrer)

à la maison, son père [39]_____ (annoncer) qu'ils

partiraient pour les États-Unis. En deux mois, tout

[40]_____ (être) prêt pour le grand déménagement. Le jour

de leur départ, tous ses amis [41]_____ (venir) lui rendre

visite pour lui dire au revoir. Hélene [42]_____ (se sentir)

triste de quitter sa patrie, mais elle [43]_____ (être)

impatiente de voir son nouveau pays.

Answer Key

This section contains the answers to all the practice exercises in this chapter. Review your answers to see how you did.

1. Je **me douchais** quand tu m'**as appelé**. (*I was taking a shower when you called me.*)

2. Nous **sommes allés** au théâtre cinq fois. (*We went to the theater five times.*)

3. Benjamin **jouait** au tennis pendant que Mélanie **nageait.** (*Benjamin was playing tennis while Mélanie was swimming.*)

4. Il **pleuvait** mais il **faisait** très doux. (*It was raining but it was very mild.*)

5. Quand il **était** petit, il **mettait** toujours ses chaussures de travers. (*When he was young, he would always put on his shoes the wrong way.*)

6. Dans la forêt, il y **avait** un silence profond. (*In the forest, there was a profound silence.*)

7. Je **corrigeais** les examens pendant que tu **faisais** tes devoirs. (*I was correcting the exams while you were doing your homework.*)

8. Le professeur **a expliqué** le subjonctif trois fois. (*The professor explained the subjunctive three times.*)

9. Ils **travaillaient** quand ils **ont entendu** des sirènes. (*They were working when they heard sirens.*)

10. Chaque été, nous **allions** à la plage. (*Every summer, we would go to the beach.*)

11. Je le **voyais** chaque fois que j'**allais** au cours. (*I would see him every time I would go to class.*)

12. En général, nous **partions** en vacances en juin. (*In general, we would leave for vacation in June.*)

13. Hier, ils **ont fait** les courses. (*Yesterday, they ran errands.*)

14. Les enfants **jouaient** dans le parc quand tout d'un coup il **a commencé** à pleuvoir. (*The children were playing in the park when all of a sudden it began to rain.*)

15. Autrefois mes grands-parents **habitaient** en Champagne. (*In the past my grandparents used to live in Champagne.*)

16. Papa **travaillait** souvent le samedi. (*Dad would often work on Saturdays.*)

17. Tu **dormais** quand je **suis rentré**. (*You were sleeping when I came home.*)

18. Je **me promenais** d'habitude au jardin de Luxemburg. (*I would usually go for a walk/stroll in the Luxemburg Garden.*)

19. La semaine dernière nous **avons reçu** une contravention. (*Last week we received a ticket.*)

20. Ils **buvaient** toujours du vin au dîner. (*They would always drink some wine at dinner.*)

21. **Ils ont dû payer une amende.**

22. **Sarah devait écrire une composition.**

23 **Il a fallu vendre la maison.** Or, **Nous avons dû vendre la maison.**

24 **Tu as voulu t'inscrire aux cours.**

25 **Je savais qu'il était malade.**

26 **Mathieu a pu gagner la médaille.**

27 **Nous croyions que tu partais.**

28 **Ils ont su la vérité.**

29 **Mes parents voulaient aller à Paris.**

30 **J'ai dû rester avec les enfants.**

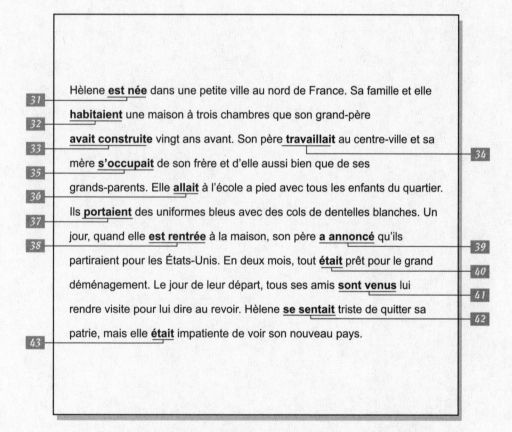

31 Hèlene **est née** dans une petite ville au nord de France. Sa famille et elle

32 **habitaient** une maison à trois chambres que son grand-père

33 **avait construite** vingt ans avant. Son père **travaillait** au centre-ville et sa **34**

35 mère **s'occupait** de son frère et d'elle aussi bien que de ses

36 grands-parents. Elle **allait** à l'école a pied avec tous les enfants du quartier.

37 Ils **portaient** des uniformes bleus avec des cols de dentelles blanches. Un

38 jour, quand elle **est rentrée** à la maison, son père **a annoncé** qu'ils **39**

partiraient pour les États-Unis. En deux mois, tout **était** prêt pour le grand **40**

déménagement. Le jour de leur départ, tous ses amis **sont venus** lui **41**

rendre visite pour lui dire au revoir. Hèlene **se sentait** triste de quitter sa **42**

43 patrie, mais elle **était** impatiente de voir son nouveau pays.

(Helen was born in a small town in the north of France. Her family and she lived in a three bedroom house that her grandfather had built twenty years before. Her father was working in the center of town and her mother was taking care of her brother and her as well as of her grandparents. She would go to school on foot with all the children of the neighborhood. They would wear blue uniforms with white lace collars. One day, when she came home, her father announced that they would leave for the United States. In two months, everything was ready for the big move. The day of their departure, all her friends came to visit her to say good bye. Helen felt sad leaving her homeland, but she waited with impatience to see her new country.)

Chapter 14

Deciphering the Literary Tenses: The Passé Simple and Passé Antérieur

● ●

In This Chapter

▶ Conjugating the passé simple

▶ Forming the passé antérieur

● ●

French has some tenses that are reserved for writing only. The passé simple and the passé antérieur, or past anterior, are two such tenses. You only need to recognize them in case you ever curl up with your favorite French novel or short story.

The passé simple is a literary tense that expresses a completed action in the past. In fact, it has the same meaning as the passé composé, which is a compound tense. Meanwhile, the passé antérieur is the past of the passé simple. You use it when one action in the past has to happen before another action takes place in the past. This chapter does have a short section on it just so that you can identify it when you see it.

Because they're both literary tenses, you don't use them in everyday conversation. This chapter briefly looks at the passé simple and passé antérieur and helps you identify and conjugate them in case you do encounter them.

Creating the Passé Simple

As the name indicates, the passé simple is a simple verb, which means that the verb is conjugated by itself without an auxiliary. If you have never seen the passé simple before, it can seem very odd (especially the plural endings). This section helps you recognize it. And don't worry about using it too much in your own writing. You can use the passé composé instead to express a completed action in the past. Check out Chapter 13 for more on the passé composé. This section shows you how to conjugate the passé simple for regular and irregular verbs.

Regular verbs

The passé simple of regular verbs is fairly easy to form. Just drop the **-er, -ir,** and **-re** of the infinitives and add the endings. However, **-er** verbs have different endings than **-ir** and **-re** verbs. The following charts show you the different endings.

Regular -er Verb Endings for the Passé Simple	
je -**ai**	nous -**âmes**
tu -**as**	vous -**âtes**
il/elle/on -**a**	ils/elles -**èrent**

parler (*to speak*)	
je parl**ai**	nous parl**âmes**
tu parl**as**	vous parl**âtes**
il/elle/on parl**a**	ils/elles parl**èrent**
Il **parla** de la politique française. (*He spoke about French politics.*)	

Regular -ir and -re Verb Endings for the Passé Simple	
je -**is**	nous -**îmes**
tu -**is**	vous -**îtes**
il/elle/on -**it**	ils/elles -**irent**

finir (*to finish*)	
je fin**is**	nous fin**îmes**
tu fin**is**	vous fin**îtes**
il/elle fin**it**	ils/elles fin**irent**
Mes grands-parents **finirent** la construction de leur maison avant la guerre. (*My grandparents finished building their house before the war.*)	

vendre (*to sell*)	
je vend**is**	nous vend**îmes**
tu vend**is**	vous vend**îtes**
il/elle/on vend**it**	ils/elles vend**irent**
La France **vendit** la Louisiane aux États-Unis en 1803. (*France sold Louisiana to the United States in 1803.*)	

Most irregular verbs

You form the passé simple of most irregular verbs by taking their past participles and adding endings. If the past participle of a verb ends in **u**, add the following endings: **-s, -s, -t, -ûmes, -ûtes, -rent.**

boire (*to drink*)	
je bu**s**	nous b**ûmes**
tu bu**s**	vous b**ûtes**
il/elle/on bu**t**	ils/elles bu**rent**
Nous **bûmes** un Dom Perignon pour nos cinquante ans de mariage. (*We drank Dom Perignon champagne for our 50th wedding anniversary.*)	

You also use these same endings for **avoir,** whose past participle ends in **u.**

avoir (*to have*)	
j'eu**s**	nous eu**mes**
tu eu**s**	vous eu**tes**
il/elle/on eu**t**	ils/elles eu**rent**
Vous **eûtes** votre diplôme avant la manifestation des étudiants. (*You got your degree before the students' protest.*)	

The passé simple of **être** is irregular, although the endings are the same as **avoir.**

être (*to be*)	
je fu**s**	nous f**ûmes**
tu fu**s**	vous f**ûtes**
il/elle/on fu**t**	ils/elles fu**rent**
Il **fut** Président de la République Française en 1945. (*He was President of the French Republic in 1945.*)	

Table 14-1 lists some verbs whose past participles end in **u** and thus follow the same pattern as **boire** (*to drink*).

Table 14-1	Verbs with Past Participles That End in u
Infinitive	*Past Participle Stem*
boire (*to drink*)	**bu-**
connaître (*to know*)	**connu-**
courir (*to run*)	**couru-**
croire (*to believe*)	**cru-**
devoir (*to owe, to have to*)	**dû-**
falloir (*to have to, to must*)*	**fallu-**
lire (*to read*)	**lu-**
paraître (*to appear, to seem*)	**paru-**

(continued)

Table 14-1 *(continued)*

Infinitive	Past Participle Stem
plaire (*to please*)	**plu-**
pleuvoir (*to rain*)*	**plu-**
pouvoir (*to be able to*)	**pu-**
recevoir (*to receive*)	**reçu-**
savoir (*to know*)	**su-**
vivre (*to live*)	**vécu-**
vouloir (*to want to*)	**voulu-**

** These verbs are used in the third person singular (**il**) only.*

Irregular stem verbs with regular endings

Some verbs have an irregular stem but regular endings: **-is, -is, -it, -îmes, -îtes,** and **-irent. Dire** (*to say*) is a good example.

dire (*to say*)	
je d**is**	nous d**îmes**
tu d**is**	vous d**îtes**
il/elle/on d**it**	ils/elles d**irent**
Elle **dit** au revoir à ses amis avant de partir. (*She told her friends goodbye before leaving.*)	

Table 14-2 lists some verbs similar to **dire.**

Table 14-2	Verbs with Irregular Stems and Regular Endings
Infinitive	Stem
craindre (*to fear*)	**craign-**
dire (*to say*)	**d-**
écrire (*to write*)	**écriv-**
faire (*to do, to make*)	**f-**
mettre (*to put, to place*)	**m-**
naître (*to be born*)	**naqu-**
prendre (*to take*)	**pr-**
rire (*to laugh*)	**r-**
voir (*to see*)	**v-**

Completely irregular

The passé simple of the verbs **venir** (*to come*) and **tenir** (*to hold*) and all their compounds are irregular and have different endings. The endings are as follows: **-ins, -ins, -int, -înmes, -întes,** and **-inrent.**

venir (*to come*)	
je v**ins**	nous v**înmes**
tu v**ins**	vous v**întes**
il/elle/on v**int**	ils/elles v**inrent**
Ils **vinrent** avant le coucher du soleil. (*They came before sunset.*)	

Put the following verbs in the passé simple.

0. Nous _____ (avoir) de la chance.

A. Nous **eûmes** de la chance. (*We were lucky.*)

1. Il _____ (naître) le 3 décembre, 1816.

2. Les enfants _____ (craindre) les histoires d'épouvante.

3. Vous _____ (voir) des tableaux au musée.

4. Vincent Van Gogh _____ (envoyer) beaucoup de lettres à son frère Théo.

5. Gaugin _____ (passer) beaucoup de temps à Tahiti.

6. Nous _____ (faire) des costumes pour Mardi Gras.

7. Je _____ (recevoir) des cadeaux pour mon anniversaire.

8. Mon grand-père _____ (finir) ses études en 1923.

9. Il _____ (être) stupéfait.

10. Elle _____ (vivre) quarante ans en France.

Creating the Passé Antérieur

The passé antérieur is a compound tense, and it expresses an action that has taken place even before the passé simple. The passé antérieur is also a literary tense, and you don't use it in conversational French. You need only to recognize it when you come across it while reading your favorite French author(s). Like the passé simple, you see it mostly in the third person singular and third person plural. Form it by putting the auxiliaries **avoir** and **être** in the passé simple and adding the past participle of any verb of your choice. Remember to follow the same rules of agreement of the past participle with the passé antérieur as you do with the passé composé or with any comound past tense. (Check out Chapter 12 for the lowdown on the rules of agreement.)

parler (*to speak*)	
j'**eus parlé**	nous **eûmes parlé**
tu **eus parlé**	vous **eûtes parlé**
il/elle/on **eut parlé**	ils/elles **eurent parlé**
Il **eut parlé** au peuple à la radio avant d'apparaître à la télévision. (*He had spoken to the people on the radio before appearing on television.*)	

partir (*to leave*)	
je **fus parti(e)**	nous **fûmes partis(es)**
tu **fus parti(e)**	vous **fûtes parti(e)(s)(es)**
il/elle/on **fut parti(e)**	ils/elles **furent partis(es)**
Ils **furent partis** avant l'ouragan. (*They had left before the hurricane.*)	

Because the passé antérieur expresses an action that has taken place before the action of the passé simple, you generally use it after the following conjunctions: **quand** (*when*), **lorsque** (*when*), **après que** (*after*), **dès que** (*as soon as*), and **à peine . . . que** (*hardly*). With the expression **à peine . . . que,** you have to invert the subject and the conjugated verb. This is similar to what you do in English with this expression. Look at the following example and its translation in English.

> **À peine eut-il fini sa pièce, qu'il la présenta au roi.** (*Hardly had he finished his play, when he presented it to the king.*)

> **Quand les étudiants eurent manifesté, les ouvriers les suivirent.** (*When the students protested/had protested, the workers followed them.*)

Choose between the passé simple and the passé antérieur forms of the verbs in parentheses and conjugate them.

Q. Lorsque son père _____ (laisser) ses clés, Sébastien les _____ (prendre).

A. Lorsque son père **eut laissé** ses clés, Sébastien **les prit.** (*When his father had left the keys, Sébastien took them.*)

11. A peine qu'il _____ (sortir), que le téléphone _____ (sonner).

12. Lorsque le patron _____ (surveiller) les employés, ils _____ (travailler) attentivement.

13. Après qu'ils _____ (finir) leur travail, ils _____ (être) payés.

14. Quand nous _____ (décider) de voyager, nous _____ (choisir) l'Asie.

15. Dès qu'elle _____ (finir) ses études, elle _____ (trouver) du travail.

Answer Key

This section contains the correct answers to the practice problems in this chapter.

1 Il **naquit** le 3 décembre, 1816. (*He was born on December 3, 1816.*)

2 Les enfants **craignirent** les histoires d'épouvante. (*The children feared the horror stories.*)

3 Vous **vîtes** des tableaux au musée. (*You saw paintings at the museum.*)

4 Vincent Van Gogh **envoya** beaucoup de lettres à son frère Théo. (*Van Gogh sent many letters to his brother Théo.*)

5 Gaugin **passa** beaucoup de temps à Tahiti. (*Gaugin spent a lot of time in Tahiti.*)

6 Nous **fîmes** des costumes pour Mardi Gras. (*We made costumes for Mardi Gras.*)

7 Je **reçus** des cadeaux pour mon anniversaire. (*I received gifts for my birthday.*)

8 Mon grand-père **finit** ses études en 1923. (*My grandfather finished his studies in 1923.*)

9 Il **fut** stupéfait. (*He was astonished.*)

10 Elle **vécut** quarante ans en France. (*She lived in France for forty years.*)

11 A peine **fut-il sorti**, que le téléphone **sonna.** (*Hardly had he left, when the telephone rang.*)

12 Lorsque le patron **eut surveillé** les employés, ils **travaillèrent** attentivement. (*When the boss had kept a watch on the employees, they worked attentively.*)

13 Après qu'ils **eurent fini** leur travail, ils **furent** payés. (*After they had finished their work, they were paid.*)

14 Quand nous **eûmes décidé** de voyager, nous **choisîmes** l'Asie. (*When we had decided to travel, we chose Asia.*)

15 Dès qu'elle **eut fini** ses études, elle **trouva** du travail. (*As soon as she had finished her studies, she found a job.*)

Part IV
Looking Ahead: The Future and the Conditional Tenses

The 5th Wave   By Rich Tennant

SAGE

Fenn

LAVENDE

THYME   ROSEMARY

"I told him to study some French verbs before our trip to Paris, and he's been sitting in the garden ever since."

In this part . . .

After a long winter, do you look forward to spring? After an exhausting week at work, do you look forward to the weekend? If so, you're not alone. But how do you look forward to things, like your weekend, your vacation, or to a celebration? With the future tense of course.

This part shows you how to form the future tense so you can express anything you can imagine in the future. In addition to forming the future tense, I also show you how to use it in French, which is important because you use the future tense a bit differently in French than in English following certain expressions. I also explain the future perfect tense, which you use when you want to state that one future action has to happen before another future action can occur, or that you will have to finish something by a certain time.

In addition to the future and future perfect, I show you how to form and use the conditional and past conditional tenses. You can order anything you want to eat or drink in a French restaurant with the conditional tense and show your good manners at the same time.

Chapter 15

Moving Forward with the Future Tense

In This Chapter

▶ Forming the regular and irregular forms of the future tense

▶ Knowing the differences between the future tense in English and in French

▶ Expressing yourself in the future tense

Imagine you're sitting in a café with your best friend and she asks whether you've ever been to Bora Bora. What a coincidence. You've never been there, but you're planning on going next month. Do you know which verb tense you use to describe your trip next month?

In order to describe your trip to Bora Bora next month, you use the future tense. With this tense you can describe events that will occur either at a specific time or an unspecified time in the future. In this chapter, you can discover how to form the future tense and how to use it with various expressions.

Forming the Future of Regular Verbs

Do you want to tell your sister about your upcoming doctor's visit? Or perhaps you want to tell your brother about the French test you're dreading that you have to take next week. You need to use the future tense, which is one of the simplest tenses to form.

Creating the future tense for regular **-er, -ir,** and **-re** verbs is a piece of cake. All you have to do is take the infinitive verb, which serves as the stem, and simply add the appropriate endings. Remember that the future stem of all verbs, be they regular or irregular, always ends in **-r.** So for **-er** and **-ir** verbs, just add the endings. For **-re** verbs, drop the **e** and then add the appropriate endings, which I show in the following examples. *Note:* Even some irregular verbs (those that have an irregular conjugation in the present tense) are regular in the future because they have a regular stem in the future (just take their infinitives and add the endings to form the future).

Future Tense Verb Endings	
je **-ai**	nous **-ons**
tu **-as**	vous **-ez**
il/elle/on **-a**	ils/elles **-ont**

Do these future endings look familiar? If you're familiar with the present conjugation of **avoir** (*to have*), you may notice a similarity.

The following are the three categories of regular verbs — **-er, -ir,** and **-re** — in the future tense.

parler (*to speak*)	
je parler**ai**	nous parler**ons**
tu parler**as**	vous parler**ez**
il/elle/on parler**a**	ils/elles parler**ont**
Je parlerai à l'agent de voyage demain. (*I will speak to the travel agent tomorrow.*)	

finir (*to finish*)	
je finir**ai**	nous finir**ons**
tu finir**as**	vous finir**ez**
il/elle/on finir**a**	ils/elles finir**ont**
Ils **finiront** leurs études l'année prochaine. (*They will finish their studies next year.*)	

vendre (*to sell*)	
je vendr**ai**	nous vendr**ons**
tu vendr**as**	vous vendr**ez**
il/elle/on vendr**a**	ils/elles vendr**ont**
Nous **vendrons** nos livres à la fin du semestre. (*We will sell our books at the end of the semester.*)	

Put these verbs in the future tense.

Q. Tu _____ (étudier).

A. Tu **étudieras**. (*You will study.*)

1. Les enfants _____ (jouer).

2. Il _____ (apprendre).

3. Vous _____ (comprendre).

4. Je _____ (travailler).

5. Nous _____ (partir).

6. Elle _____ (réussir).

7. Tu _____ (lire).

8. Vous _____ (boire).

9. Les étudiants _____ (répondre).

10. Nous _____ (arriver).

Forming the Future of Spelling-Change Verbs

Some **-er** verbs have a mute or silent **e** in the infinitive. When you conjugate these types of verbs in the present tense, some spelling changes are required in order to pronounce the mute **e.** You either add an accent grave to the **e,** like so **(è),** or you double the consonant after the mute **e.** (See Chapter 3 for a list of these types of verbs.) The same types of changes occur to these verbs in the future tense. In order to pronounce the mute **e** in the infinitive, add an accent grave to the **e** (see Table 15-1) or double the consonant after the mute **e** (see Table 15-2). Now add the future endings, which are always the same.

Verbs whose infinitive form ends in **-yer** change to **-ier** before the endings; I show you examples of these verbs in Table 15-3. (The only exception is the verb **envoyer** [*to send*], whose future stem is **enverr-.**)

Table 15-1	Adding an Accent Grave (è) to Spelling-Change Verbs in the Future Tense
Verb	*Future Tense Stem*
acheter (*to buy*)	**achèter-**
amener (*to bring*)	**amèner-**
mener (*to lead*)	**mèner-**
(se) lever (*to rise/to stand up*)	**(se) lèver-**
(se) promener (*to go for a walk/a stroll*)	**(se) promèner-**

Table 15-2	Doubling the Consonant of Spelling-Change Verbs in the Future Tense
Verb	*Future Tense Stem*
épeler (*to spell*)	**epeller-**
jeter (*to throw*)	**jetter-**
(s') appeler (*to call/to call oneself/to be named*)	**(s') appeller-**

Table 15-3	Changing -yer to -ier with Spelling-Change Verbs in the Future Tense
Verb	*Future Tense Stem*
employer (*to use*)	**emploier-**
essayer (*to try*)	**essaier-**
nettoyer (*to clean*)	**nettoier-**

J'achèterai mon billet la semaine prochaine. (*I will buy my ticket next week.*)

Elle appellera son chien. (*She will call her dog.*)

Nous nettoierons notre chambre. (*We will clean our room.*)

The following verbs don't have a stem change in the future tense. In other words, don't change the accents in the infinitive for **espérer** (*to hope*), **préférer** (*to prefer*), and **répéter** (*to repeat*).

Tu répéteras après le professeur. (*You will repeat after the professor.*)

Put these verbs in the future tense and then translate the sentences.

0. Je _____ (épeler) le nom du pays. _____

A. J'**épellerai** le nom du pays. *I will spell the name of the country.*

11. Nous _____ (essayer) la mousse au chocolat.

_____

12. Ils _____ (amener) leurs amis.

_____

13. Vous _____ (jeter) la balle.

_____

14. Je _____ (appeler) mon ami.

_____

15. Tu _____ (nettoyer) ta chambre.

_____

16. Elle _____ (acheter) le jouet.

_____

17. Nous _____ (préférer) le thé.

_____

18. Elles _____ (mener) le groupe.

_____

19. Tu _____ (espérer) voyager.

_____

20. Vous _____ (employer) l'ordinateur.

_____

Forming the Future of Irregular Verbs

Some verbs have an irregular future stem. However, the endings remain the same. Table 15-4 lists the verbs with the irregular future tense stem.

Table 15-4	Irregular Future Tense Verbs
Irregular Verb	**Future Tense Stem**
aller (*to go*)	**ir-**
avoir (*to have*)	**aur-**
courir (*to run*)	**courr-**
devenir (*to become*)	**deviendr-**
devoir (*to owe, to have to*)	**devr-**
envoyer (*to send*)	**enverr-**
être (*to be*)	**ser-**
faire (*to do, to make*)	**fer-**
falloir (*to have to, to must*)	**faudr-**
mourir (*to die*)	**mourr-**
pleuvoir (*to rain*)	**pleuvr-**
pouvoir (*to be able to*)	**pourr-**
recevoir (*to receive*)	**recevr-**
retenir (*to retain, to keep*)	**retiendr-**
revenir (*to come back*)	**reviendr-**
savoir (*to know*)	**saur-**
tenir (*to hold*)	**tiendr-**
valoir (*to be worth*)	**vaudr-**
venir (*to come*)	**viendr-**
voir (*to see*)	**verr-**
vouloir (*to want to*)	**voudr-**

J'irai à la plage. (*I will go to the beach.*)

Elle saura la réponse bientôt. (*She will know the answer soon.*)

Put the following verbs in the future tense and translate them.

Q. Il _____ (pleuvoir) demain.

A. Il **pleuvra** demain. *It will rain tomorrow.*

21. Vous _____ (aller) au cinéma.

_____

22. Tu _____ (venir) ce soir.

_____

23. Ils _____ (voir) le film.

_____

24. Je _____ (pouvoir) sortir.

_____

25. Nous _____ (faire) le marché.

_____

Identifying the Differences between English and French when Using the Future Tense

You use the future tense a bit differently in French than in English. In French, you use the future with expressions that imply a future action, as in the expressions *as soon as* and *when*. For example, in English you say, *When I go to France, I will speak French.* However, you aren't in France yet and therefore this implies a future action. The French say, *When I will go to France, I will speak French.* Table 15-5 is a short table with these expressions.

Table 15-5	Expressions Followed by the Future
French Expression	*English Translation*
aussitôt que	*as soon as*
dès que	*as soon as*
lorsque	*when*
quand	*when*
tant que	*as long as*

Aussitôt que papa rentrera, nous dînerons. (*As soon as dad comes [will come] home, we will have dinner.*)

Translate the following sentences. Remember that the future tense is used in both clauses in French.

Q. As long as it doesn't rain, we will go to the beach.

A. **Tant qu'il ne pleuvra pas, nous irons à la plage.**

26. As soon as we have dinner, we will go to the movies.

_____

27. When they go to Rome, they will visit the Coliseum.

_____

28. I will travel as soon as I have enough money.

_____

29. When we wake up, we will have breakfast.

_____

30. She will have a glass of wine when she finishes these exercises.

_____

Expressing Yourself and Using References: Future Style

After you become comfortable creating the simple future tense, you'll become familiar with some expressions and when to use them. These expressions allow you to form complete sentences in order to describe future events. Table 15-6 lists some time expressions, which provide more specific information as to when in the future the event will take place. You can place them either in the beginning or at the end of the sentence.

Table 15-6	Important Expressions to Use with the Future Tense
French Expression	*English Translation*
demain	*tomorrow*
demain matin	*tomorrow morning*
demain après-midi	*tomorrow afternoon*
demain soir	*tomorrow evening*
la semaine prochaine	*next week*
le mois prochain	*next month*
l'année prochaine	*next year*
lundi prochain	*next Monday*
plus tard	*later*
cet après-midi	*this afternoon*
ce soir	*this evening*
cet été	*this summer*

Ils passeront un examen demain. (*They will take the test tomorrow.*)

Translate the following sentences into French by using the future tense.

O. I will see my friends next Monday.

A. **Je verrai mes amis lundi prochain.**

31. We will travel to Europe this summer.

_____

32. I will play tennis next week.

_____

33. My in-laws will be arriving later.

_____

34. The professors will attend a conference next month.

_____

35. My friends and I will go to the movies Saturday evening.

_____

Now translate the following sentences from French to English by using the future tense.

O. Je partirai demain matin.

A. *I will leave tomorrow morning.*

36. Ils étudieront pour l'examen final.

_____

37. Michelle se réveillera à 7 heures demain matin.

_____

38. Nous nagerons cet après-midi.

_____

39. Vous vous verrez la semaine prochaine.

_____

40. Il achètera une nouvelle voiture.

_____

Answer Key

In this section you can find all the answers to the practice exercises in this chapter. How did you do?

1 Les enfants **joueront.** (*The children will play.*)

2 Il **apprendra.** (*He will learn.*)

3 Vous **comprendrez.** (*You will understand.*)

4 Je **travaillerai.** (*I will work.*)

5 Nous **partirons.** (*We will leave.*)

6 Elle **réussira.** (*She will succeed.*)

7 Tu **liras.** (*You will read.*)

8 Vous **boirez.** (*You will drink.*)

9 Les étudiants **répondront.** (*The students will answer.*)

10 Nous **arriverons.** (*We will arrive.*)

11 Nous **essaierons** la mousse au chocolat. *We will try the chocolate mousse.*

12 Ils **amèneront** leurs amis. *They will bring their friends.*

13 Vous **jetterez** la balle. *You will throw the ball.*

14 J'**appellerai** mon ami. *I will call my friend.*

15 Tu **nettoieras** ta chambre. *You will clean your room.*

16 Elle **achètera** le jouet. *She will buy the toy.*

17 Nous **préférerons** le thé. *We will prefer tea.*

18 Elles **mèneront** le groupe. *They will lead the group.*

19 Tu **espéreras** voyager. *You will hope to travel.*

20 Vous **emploierez** l'ordinateur. *You will use the computer.*

21 Vous **irez** au cinéma. *You will go to the movies.*

22 Tu **viendras** ce soir. *You will come this evening.*

23 Ils **verront** le film. *They will see the film.*

24 Je **pourrai** sortir. *I will be able to go out.*

25 Nous **ferons** le marché. *We will do the shopping.*

26 Aussitôt que nous dînerons, nous irons au cinéma.

27 Quand ils iront à Rome, ils visiteront le Colisée.

28 Je voyagerai dès que j'aurai assez d'argent.

29 Lorsque nous nous réveillerons, nous prendrons le petit-déjeuner.

30 Elle aura un verre de vin quand elle finira ces exercices.

31 Nous voyagerons en Europe cet été.

32 Je jouerai au tennis la semaine prochaine.

33 Mes beaux-parents arriveront plus tard.

34 Les professeurs assisteront à une conférence le mois prochain.

35 Mes amis et moi iront au cinéma samedi soir.

36 *They will study for the final exam.*

37 *Michelle will wake up at 7 o'clock tomorrow morning.*

38 *We will go swimming this afternoon.*

39 *You will see each other next week.*

40 *He will buy a new car.*

Chapter 16

Completing a Future Action with the Future Perfect

In This Chapter

▶ Creating the future perfect tense

▶ Knowing the expressions that require the use of the future perfect

In today's world, when everything has to be done yesterday, do you ever say to yourself "I will have this or that done by a certain time," such as before you leave the office or by Friday? If so, you use the future perfect tense.

The future perfect tense is a compound tense requiring an auxiliary and a past participle. You use it to describe events that will have taken place before another future action. You can also use the future perfect alone to express that a future action will have been completed by a certain time in the future. The meaning of this tense in English is *will have done something*. You can also use the future perfect to express a probability or a supposition. For example, **Paul n'est pas venu à l'école hier. Il aura été malade** means *Paul did not come to school yesterday. He probably was/must have been ill.*

Like the simple future tense (see Chapter 15), you use the future perfect with expressions that imply a future action, such as *when* and *as soon as*. In this chapter, you discover how to form the future perfect tense and how to correctly use it.

Forming the Future Perfect

The future perfect tense is a compound tense, and it follows the same pattern as all other past compound tenses in French. You need one of the two auxiliaries, **avoir** (*to have*) or **être** (*to be*), followed by the past participle of any verb you want.

You form the future perfect by putting the auxiliaries in the future tense and adding the past participle of the verb of your choice. Remember that the choice of the auxiliary depends on the verb. Most verbs take the auxiliary **avoir,** and some take **être.** (For a list of these verbs and for the formation of the past participles, see Chapter 12.)

First, you need to know how to conjugate **avoir** and **être** in the future tense. After you conjugate the auxiliary, you add the past participle.

avoir (*to have*)	
j'**aurai**	nous **aurons**
tu **auras**	vous **aurez**
il/elle/on **aura**	ils/elles **auront**
Ils **auront** les résultats bientôt. (*They will have the results soon.*)	

être (*to be*)	
je **serai**	nous **serons**
tu **seras**	vous **serez**
il/elle/on **sera**	ils/elles **seront**
Nous **serons** à l'heure. (*We will be on time.*)	

The following tables show three examples — the verbs **finir** (*to finish*), **arriver** (*to arrive*), and **se réveiller** (*to wake up*). **Finir** takes the auxiliary **avoir, arriver** takes **être,** and **se réveiller** also takes **être.**

For pronominal verbs, place the pronominal pronoun in front of the auxiliary **être,** which is followed by the past participle of the verb. All pronominal verbs are conjugated with the auxiliary **être.**

finir (*to finish*)	
j'**aurai fini**	nous **aurons fini**
tu **auras fini**	vous **aurez fini**
il/elle/on **aura fini**	ils/elles **auront fini**
Ils **auront fini** avant le weekend. (*They will have finished before the weekend.*)	

arriver (*to arrive*)	
je **serai arrivé(e)**	nous **serons arrivés(es)**
tu **seras arrivé(e)**	vous **serez arrivé(s)(e)(es)**
il/elle/on **sera arrivé(e)**	ils/elles **seront arrivés(es)**
Nous **serons arrivés** avant le 5 août. (*We will have arrived before the 5th of August.*)	

se réveiller (*to wake up*)	
je me **serai réveillé(e)**	nous nous **serons réveillés(es)**
tu te **seras réveillé(e)**	vous vous **serez réveillé (s)(e)(es)**
il/elle/on se **sera réveillé(e)**	ils/elles se **seront réveillés(es)**
Je **me serai réveillé(e)** de bonne heure pour préparer le petit-déjeuner. (*I will have awakened early to prepare breakfast.*)	

Put the following verbs in the future perfect and then translate the sentences.

Q. Je _____ (finir) mes exercices.

A. J'**aurai fini** mes exercices. *I will have finished my exercises.*

1. Ils _____ (avoir) un accident.

   _____

2. Elle _____ (prendre) le vol d'avant.

   _____

3. Tu _____ (ne pas manger) toute la journée.

   _____

4. Vous _____ (partir) tôt.

   _____

5. Il lui _____ (envoyer) des fleurs.

   _____

6. Elle _____ (appeler) la police.

   _____

7. Ils _____ (oublier) de fermer à clé.

   _____

8. Tu _____ (voir) la Joconde.

   _____

9. Vous _____ (gagner) la loterie.

   _____

10. Il _____ (rentrer).

    _____

To put the future perfect in the negative, simply place the **ne** before the auxiliary and place **pas** or any other negative word after the auxiliary. For pronominal verbs, the **ne** precedes the pronominal pronoun and the **pas** or another negative word follows the auxiliary.

> **Il n'aura pas fini sa composition avant la classe.** (*He will not have finished his composition before class.*)
>
> **Tu ne te seras pas levé avant sept heures.** (*You will not have gotten up by seven o'clock.*)

Put these verbs in the future perfect tense and then translate the sentences.

O. Nous _____ (ne pas se rencontrer) avant samedi.

A. Nous **ne nous serons pas rencontrés** avant samedi. *We will not have met each other before Saturday.*

11. Il _____ (partir) avant huit heures.

_____

12. Nous _____ (ne pas manger) avant de sortir.

_____

13. Les enfants _____ (rentrer) après avoir joué au foot.

_____

14. Dans une semaine, tu _____ (recevoir) ton diplôme.

_____

15. Tu _____ (se réveiller) avant notre départ.

_____

16. Mes parents _____ (ne pas arriver) avant dix heures.

_____

17. Dans trois jours nous _____ (partir) pour l'Australie.

_____

18. Je _____ (poster) les cartes postales avant la fin de la journée.

_____

19. Avant de quitter le pays, Eric _____ (vendre) sa voiture.

_____

20. Tu _____ (ne pas rester) après minuit.

_____

Using the Future Perfect Correctly

Like the future tense (see Chapter 15), you can use the future perfect with expressions that imply a future action, as in the expressions *as soon as* and *when*. However, doing so is very different from English, which uses the present or present perfect tense. Check out the following example: In English, you say *As soon as I finish my courses, I will receive my diploma.* You haven't finished your courses yet, so this statement implies a future action. In French, you can either use the future simple tense in both clauses (*As soon as I will finish my courses, I will receive my diploma.*) or because one action (the fact that I will have to finish my courses) has to happen before another action can take place (I will receive my diploma), you use the future perfect followed by the future (*As soon as I will have finished my courses, I will receive my diploma*).

Dès que je finirai mes cours, je recevrai mon diplôme. (*As soon as I will finish my courses, I will receive my diploma.*)

Dès que j'aurai fini mes cours, je recevrai mon diplôme. (*As soon as I will have finished my courses, I will receive my diploma.*)

You can also use the future or future perfect after the expressions **après que** (*after*), **tant que** (*as long as*), or **une fois que** (*once*) if future action is implied. Table 16-1 lists some common French expressions. If you see one of these expressions, you may need to use the future perfect tense if the future is implied.

Table 16-1	Common Future Perfect Expressions
French Expression	*English Translation*
après que	after
aussitôt que	as soon as
dès que	as soon as
lorsque	when
quand	when
tant que	as long as
une fois que	once

Après que mes invités seront arrivés, je servirai l'apéritif. (*After my guests will have arrived, I will serve the aperitif.*)

You can also use the future perfect to express or even explain a probability.

Caroline n'est pas chez elle, elle aura travaillé tard. (*Caroline is not at home, she must have had to work late.*)

Choose between the future and the future perfect. Remember to put the action that has to come first in the future perfect and the action that comes second in the simple future.

0. Une fois que nous _____ (faire) nos devoirs, nous _____ (aller) voir un film.

A. Une fois que nous **aurons fait** nos devoirs, nous **irons** voir un film. (*Once we will have done our homework, we will go see a movie.*)

21. Je te _____ (payer) aussitôt que je _____ (toucher) mon chèque.

22. Après qu'il _____ (trouver) un emploi, sa femme _____ (ne plus travailler).

23. Lorsque que l'entrepreneur _____ (construire) notre maison, nous _____ (déménager).

24. Nous _____ (sortir) après qu'Alexandre _____ (s'habiller).

25. Une fois que je _____ (acheter) les billets, nous _____ (pouvoir) entrer.

26. Quand je _____ (finir) mes études, mes parents me _____ (donner) un cadeau.

27. Vous _____ (envoyer) votre curriculum vitae quand tu le _____ (rédiger).

28. Tu _____ (faire) le tour du monde lorsque tu _____ (gagner) à la loterie.

29. Aussitôt que vous _____ (se lever), je vous _____ (préparer) quelque chose à manger.

30. Une fois qu'elle _____ (prendre) des médicaments, elle _____ (se sentir) mieux.

Answer Key

This section includes the answers to the practice problems in this chapter. Compare your answers to see how you did.

1 Ils **auront eu** un accident. *They probably had/must have had an accident.*

2 Elle **aura pris** le vol d'avant. *She probably took/must have taken an earlier flight.*

3 Tu **n'auras pas mangé** toute la journée. *You will not have eaten/probably have not eaten all day.*

4 Vous **serez parti** tôt. *You will probably have left/must have left early.*

5 Il lui **aura envoyé** des fleurs. *He will have sent/probably sent her/him flowers.*

6 Elle **aura appelé** la police. *She will have called/probably called/must have called the police.*

7 Ils **auront oublié** de fermer à clé. *They probably forgot/must have forgotten to lock the door.*

8 Tu **auras vu** la Joconde. *You will have seen/probably saw/must have seen the Mona Lisa.*

9 Vous **aurez gagné** la loterie. *You probably won/must have won the lottery.*

10 Il **sera rentré.** *He will have come back home/probably came/must have come home.*

11 Il **sera parti** avant huit heures. *He will have left by eight o'clock.*

12 Nous **n'aurons pas mangé** avant de sortir. *We will not have eaten before leaving.*

13 Les enfants **seront rentrés** après avoir joué au foot. *The children will have come home after having played soccer.*

14 Dans une semaine, tu **auras reçu** ton diplôme. *In a week, you will have received your diploma (will have graduated).*

15 Tu **te seras réveillé(e)** avant notre départ. *You will have awakened before our departure.*

16 Mes parents **ne seront pas arrivés** avant dix heures. *My parents will not have arrived before/by ten o'clock.*

17 Dans trois jours nous **serons partis** pour l'Australie. *In three days, we will have left for Australia.*

18 J'**aurai posté** les cartes postales avant la fin de la journée. *I will have mailed the postcards before the end of the day.*

19 Avant de quitter le pays, Eric **aura vendu** sa voiture. *Before leaving the country, Eric will have sold his car.*

20 Tu **ne seras pas resté(e)** après minuit. *You will not have stayed after midnight.*

21 Je te **paierai** aussitôt que j'**aurai touché** mon chèque. (*I will pay you as soon as I will have cashed my check.*)

22 Après qu'il **aura trouvé** un emploi, sa femme **ne travaillera plus.** (*After he will have found a job, his wife will no longer work.*)

23 Lorsque que l'entrepreneur **aura construit** notre maison, nous **déménagerons.** (*When the contractor will have built our house, we will move.*)

24 Nous **sortirons** après qu'Alexandre **se sera habillé.** (*We will go out after Alexandre will have gotten dressed.*)

25 Une fois que j'**aurai acheté** les billets, nous **pourrons** entrer. (*Once I will have bought the tickets, we will be able to enter.*)

26 Quand j'**aurai fini** mes études, mes parents me **donneront** un cadeau. (*When I will have finished my studies, my parents will give me a gift.*)

27 Vous **enverrez** votre curriculum vitae quand vous l'**aurez rédigé.** (*You will send your curriculum vitae [résumé] when you will have written it up.*)

28 Tu **feras** le tour du monde lorsque tu **auras gagné** à la loterie. (*You will take a trip around the world when you will have won the lottery.*)

29 Aussitôt que vous **vous serez levé,** je vous **préparerai** quelque chose à manger. (*As soon as you will have gotten up, I will prepare you something to eat.*)

30 Une fois qu'elle **aura pris** des médicaments, elle **se sentira** mieux. (*Once she will have taken medication, she will feel better.*)

Chapter 17

Could-ing and Would-ing with the Present Conditional Tense

· ·

In This Chapter

▶ Creating the conditional tense

▶ Trying the conditional

· ·

*Y*ou likely use the present conditional tense all the time, whether you realize it or not. Perhaps you and your friends sit around and talk about not what you *do* (present tense), *did do* (past tense), or *will do* (future tense) but about what you *would do* (conditional tense). Examples in English include sentences like *I would go out with him, We would go to the movies if anything good were playing, You would tell her what you think,* and *They would throw a great party.*

So, the conditional is a mood that expresses a possibility, a supposition, or a wish. You also use it to make polite requests or suggestions, as in *Would you allow me to accompany you?* or *I would choose the yellow dress.* The conditional has two tenses: present and past. This chapter concentrates on the present conditional; see Chapter 18 for more on the past conditional. As you can tell from the examples, the conditional tense is translated as *would* in English. (But don't confuse the conditional tense with the imperfect tense that I talk about in Chapter 11. The imperfect can express the *would* of the past, as in *When I was young, I would go fishing with my grandfather,* meaning that I *used to go* fishing with my grandfather.)

At first, you may be able to get by without the present conditional in French. But this tense makes you more polite, makes your writing more interesting, and spices up your conversation. Read through this chapter and master the ability to tell the world what you *would do.*

Forming the Conditional

The conditional tense allows you to express your opinions, likes, and dislikes more politely, and to make suggestions without seeming too imposing. You may even call it the diplomatic tense. Furthermore, you use the conditional tense in hypothetical sentences as in *If it were not raining, we would go to the beach.*

You form the conditional by taking the infinitive of most verbs (the infinitive provides the stem) and adding endings. If you read Chapter 15, you see that you form the future tense the same way. The conditional and the future tenses share a stem, but the endings are different. The endings of the future tense are derived from the verb **avoir** (*to have*), whereas the endings for the conditional match the endings for the imperfect tense (see the following table). The conditional tense is a composite of the future and the imperfect; it has the same stem as the future tense and the endings of the imperfect tense. (If you need more information on the future tense, see Chapter 15; for details on the imperfect tense, see Chapter 11.)

Imperfect and Conditional Verb Endings	
je -**ais**	nous -**ions**
tu -**ais**	vous -**iez**
il/elle/on -**ait**	ils/elles -**aient**

The conditional stem always ends in **r;** therefore, remember to drop the **e** from -**re** verbs. Check out the following examples on how to conjugate regular verbs in the present conditional tense.

parler (*to speak*)	
je parler**ais**	nous parler**ions**
tu parler**ais**	vous parler**iez**
il/elle/on parler**ait**	ils/elles parler**aient**
Il parlerait au directeur. (*He would speak to the director.*)	

finir (*to finish*)	
je finir**ais**	nous finir**ions**
tu finir**ais**	vous finir**iez**
il/elle/on finir**ait**	ils/elles finir**aient**
Nous finirions avant huit heures. (*We would finish before eight o'clock.*)	

vendre (*to sell*)	
je vendr**ais**	nous vendr**ions**
tu vendr**ais**	vous vendr**iez**
il/elle/on vendr**ait**	ils/elles vendr**aient**
Je vendrais ma voiture. (*I would sell my car.*)	

Now you can practice forming the conditional tense. Put the following verbs in the present conditional.

Q. Je (demander) des renseignements.

A. Je **demanderais** des renseignements. (*I would ask for information.*)

1. Vous _____ (voyager).

2. Sarah _____ (écrire) des poèmes.

3. Nous _____ (rendre) les vidéos.

4. M. et Mme Nadal _____ (choisir) du champagne.

5. Tu _____ (s'inscrire) à l'université.

6. Julien _____ (obéir) au conseiller.

7. Je _____ (poser) des questions.

8. Mlle Cottin, _____ (aimer)-vous du café?

9. Amélie _____ (préférer) la vanille au chocolat.

10. Mes amis et moi _____ (sortir) ce soir.

Considering spelling-change -er verbs

With some **-er** infinitives, you can add either an accent grave (see Table 17-1) or double the consonant (see Table 17-2) in order to form the conditional stem (as well as the future tense). Also, verbs whose infinitive form ends in **-yer** change to **-ier** before adding the endings (see Table 17-3). (The only exception is the verb **envoyer** [*to send*], whose future and conditional stem is **enverr-.**) Check out the following tables for lists of these verbs.

Table 17-1	Adding the Accent Grave (è) to Spelling-Change Verbs in the Conditional Tense
Verb	*Conditional Tense Stem*
acheter (*to buy*)	**achèter-**
amener (*to bring*)	**amèner-**
mener (*to lead*)	**mèner-**

Table 17-2	Doubling the Consonant of Spelling-Change Verbs in the Conditional Tense
Verb	*Conditional Tense Stem*
épeler (*to spell*)	**épeller-**
jeter (*to throw*)	**jetter-**
(s') appeler (*to call* [*oneself*], *to name*)	**(s') appeller-**

Table 17-3	Changing -yer to -ier with Spelling-Change Verbs in the Conditional Tense
Verb	*Conditional Tense Stem*
employer (*to use*)	**emploier-**
essayer (*to try*)	**essaier-**
nettoyer (*to clean*)	**nettoier-**

Tu essaierais les escargots. (*You would try the snails.*)

The following verbs don't have a stem change in the conditional tense: **préférer** (*to prefer*), **espérer** (*to hope*), and **répéter** (*to repeat*).

Nous préférerions le vin blanc. (*We would prefer the white wine.*)

Conjugate the infinitive into the present conditional tense in the following practice problems.

Q. Il _____ (amener) sa petite amie.

A. Il **amènerait** sa petite amie. (*He would bring his girlfriend.*)

11. Nous _____ (acheter) des disques compacts.

12. Tu _____ (nettoyer) ton appartement.

13. Les étudiants _____ (répéter) le dialogue.

14. Vous _____ (épeler) des mots difficiles.

15. Les enfants _____ (jeter) des cailloux.

16. Nous _____ (espérer) rester.

17. Elle _____ (employer) l'ordinateur.

18. Vous _____ (amener) vos parents.

19. Marc _____ (acheter) des baguettes.

20. Je _____ (mener) la discussion.

Creating the conditional with irregular verbs

Some verbs have an irregular stem. Despite this irregularity, however, you still form the conditional the same way by adding the same endings. Table 17-4 shows these irregular verbs in alphabetical order with the irregular stems and the verbs' English translations.

Table 17-4	Irregular Conditional Tense Verbs
Irregular Verb	*Conditional Tense Stem*
aller (*to go*)	ir-
avoir (*to have*)	aur-
courir (*to run*)	courr-
devenir (*to become*)	deviendr-
devoir (*to owe, to have to*)	devr-
envoyer (*to send*)	enverr-

Irregular Verb	Conditional Tense Stem
être (*to be*)	**ser-**
faire (*to do, to make*)	**fer-**
falloir (*to have to, must*)	**faudr-**
mourir (*to die*)	**mourr-**
pleuvoir (*to rain*)	**pleuvr-**
pouvoir (*to be able to*)	**pourr-**
recevoir (*to receive*)	**recevr-**
retenir (*to retain, to keep*)	**retiendr-**
revenir (*to come back*)	**reviendr-**
savoir (*to know*)	**saur-**
tenir (*to hold*)	**tiendr-**
valoir (*to be worth*)	**vaudr-**
venir (*to come*)	**viendr-**
voir (*to see*)	**verr-**
vouloir (*to want*)	**voudr-**

Nous tiendrions le drapeau. (*We would hold the flag.*)

Form the conditional tense of the verbs in parentheses.

Q. Je _____ (être) ravi de vous voir.

A. Je **serais** ravi de vous voir. (*I would be delighted to see you.*)

21. _____ (pouvoir)-vous m'aider?

22. Je _____ (acheter) des vêtements.

23. Mathieu, tu _____ (devoir) être prudent.

24. Nous _____ (faire) la cuisine.

Using the Conditional

The conditional tense is very versatile — you use it on a daily basis. The conditional tense helps you avoid some faux pas and shows your good manners. You use the conditional in order to be polite, to make suggestions, or to hypothesize. In this section, I show you how to use the conditional step by step. I also provide problems for you to practice these concepts.

Being polite, expressing a wish, and offering suggestions

First and foremost, you use the conditional tense to make polite requests or suggestions. The most common verbs that are used this way are **vouloir** (*to want to*), **aimer** (*to like, to love*), **pouvoir** (*to be able to*), and **devoir** (*to owe, to have to*). For example, if you're at a restaurant or a café and you're ordering, using the conditional is much more polite than the present tense.

Je voudrais/j'aimerais un Orangina. (*I would like an Orangina.*)

Pourriez-vous me prêter votre stylo? (*Could you lend me your pen?*)

For offering suggestions, use the verb **devoir** (*to have to*) in the conditional followed by the infinitive. **Devoir** in the conditional means *should* in English.

Tu devrais faire attention. (*You should pay attention.*)

Try being polite or making suggestions by using the present conditional tense. Translate the following sentences into French. You can use either **est-ce que** or inversion. (In the Answer Key, I use inversion whenever possible.)

Q. Could they accompany us?

A. **Est-ce qu'ils pourraient nous accompagner?** Or, **Pourraient-ils nous accompagner?**

25. Would you like some coffee? _____

26. They should not smoke. _____

27. Could you help me? _____

28. She should stay in bed. _____

Wondering if: The hypothetical

You also use the conditional in the second hypothetical sentence's result clause when you're using the imperfect in the **si** (*if*) clause. In other words,

Si + imperfect yields the present conditional in the result clause.

The following examples show how to use the conditional with a hypothetical sentence.

S'il pleuvait, je porterais un imperméable. (*If it were raining, I **would** wear a raincoat.*)

Si nous avions du temps, nous partirions ce weekend. (*If we had/were to have time, we **would** leave or get away this weekend.*)

You can switch the two clauses by starting your sentence with the result clause and following it with the **si** clause. What you can't do is switch the verb tenses.

> **Ils réussiraient aux examens, s'ils étudiaient.** (*They **would** pass the exams if they studied/were to study.*)

Now it's your turn to practice some hypothetical sentences. I fill in the imperfect tense after the **si** clause, and you fill in the conditional tense in the result clause.

Q. S'il faisait beau, nous _____ (pouvoir) pique-niquer.

A. S'il faisait beau, nous **pourrions** pique-niquer. (*If it were nice out, we would be able to have a picnic.*)

29. Si tu n'étais pas en retard, tu _____ (ne pas manquer) le train.

30. Vous _____ (voir) l'exposition si vous alliez au musée.

31. S'ils pouvaient voyager, où _____ (aller)-ils?

32. S'il neigeait, les enfants _____ (faire) un bonhomme de neige.

33. Je _____ (être) décu si je ratais mon bac.

Conditional with indirect discourse

The last way you can use the conditional tense is in an *indirect discourse,* such as when the main verb is in the past tense, and then you use the conditional to express the future. In indirect discourse one person repeats or cites the words of another. For example: *Marc said that he would come to the opera.* **Marc a dit qu'il viendrait à l'opéra.**

> **Ils ont admis qu'ils ne sauraient pas quoi faire.** (*They admitted that they would not know what to do.*)

The following sentences are in indirect discourse. Put the verb in parentheses in the conditional.

Q. Mélanie a dit qu'elle _____ (venir) sa maison.

A. Mélanie a dit qu'elle **vendrait** sa maison. (*Melanie said that she would sell her house.*)

34. Olivier m'a dit qu'il _____ (venir) me voir dimanche.

35. Ils ont affirmé qu'ils _____ (pouvoir) réparer la voiture.

36. Céline a expliqué qu'elle _____ (suivre) des cours de finance.

37. Les enfants avaient annoncé qu'ils _____ (jouer) dans le parc.

38. Sébastien a declaré qu'il _____ (partir) bientôt.

Answer Key

In this section, you can find the answers to the exercises in this chapter. Compare your answers to the correct ones.

1 Vous **voyageriez**. (*You would travel.*)

2 Sarah **écrirait** des poèmes. (*Sarah would write poems.*)

3 Nous **rendrions** les vidéos. (*We would give back the videos.*)

4 M. et Mme Nadal **choisiraient** du champagne. (*Mr. and Mrs. Nadal would choose champagne.*)

5 Tu **t'inscrirais** à l'université. (*You would register at the university.*)

6 Julien **obéirait** au conseiller. (*Julien would obey the counselor.*)

7 Je **poserais** des questions. (*I would ask questions.*)

8 Mlle Cottin, **aimeriez**-vous du café? (*Miss Cottin, would you like some coffee?*)

9 Amélie **préférerait** la vanille au chocolat. (*Amélie would prefer vanilla to chocolate.*)

10 Mes amis et moi **sortirions** ce soir. (*My friends and I would go out this evening.*)

11 Nous **achèterions** des disques compacts. (*We would buy CDs.*)

12 Tu **nettoierais** ton appartement. (*You would clean your apartment.*)

13 Les étudiants **répéteraient** le dialogue. (*The students would repeat the dialog.*)

14 Vous **épelleriez** des mots difficiles. (*You would spell difficult words.*)

15 Les enfants **jetteraient** des cailloux. (*The children would throw pebbles.*)

16 Nous **espérerions** rester. (*We would hope to stay.*)

17 Elle **emploierait** l'ordinateur. (*She would use the computer.*)

18 Vous **amèneriez** vos parents. (*You would bring your parents.*)

19 Marc **achèterait** des baguettes. (*Marc would buy some baguettes.*)

20 Je **mènerais** la discussion. (*I would lead the discussion.*)

21 **Pourriez**-vous m'aider? (*Would you be able to help me?*)

22 J'**achèterais** des vêtements. (*I would buy clothes.*)

23 Mathieu, tu **devrais** être prudent. (*Mathieu, you should be careful.*)

24 Nous **ferions** la cuisine. (*We would cook.*)

25 **Voudriez-vous du café?** Or, **Voudrais-tu du café?**

26 **Ils ne devraient pas fumer.**

27 **Pourriez-vous m'aider?** Or, **Pourrais-tu m'aider?**

28 **Elle devrait rester au lit.**

29 Si tu n'étais pas en retard, tu **ne manquerais pas** le train. (*If you were not late, you would not miss the train.*)

30 Vous **verriez** l'exposition si vous alliez au musée. (*You would see the exhibit if you were to go to the museum.*)

31 S'ils pouvaient voyager, où **iraient**-ils? (*If they could/were able to travel, where would they go?*)

32 S'il neigeait, les enfants **feraient** un bonhomme de neige. (*If it were snowing, the children would make a snowman.*)

33 Je **serais** déçu si je ratais mon bac. (*I would be disappointed if I were to fail my bac* [*baccalaureate*].)

34 Olivier m'a dit qu'il **viendrait** me voir dimanche. (*Olivier told me that he would come see me on Sunday.*)

35 Ils ont affirmé qu'ils **pourraient** réparer la voiture. (*They affirmed that they would be able to repair the car.*)

36 Céline a expliqué qu'elle **suivrait** des cours de finance. (*Céline explained that she would take courses in finance.*)

37 Les enfants avaient annoncé qu'ils **joueraient** dans le parc. (*The children had announced that they would play in the park.*)

38 Sébastien a declaré qu'il **partirait** bientôt. (*Sébastien declared that he would leave soon.*)

Chapter 18

Trying the Past Conditional Tense: Could Have and Would Have

....

In This Chapter
▶ Forming the past conditional tense
▶ Using the past conditional

....

You use the past conditional tense in all those situations when you could just kick your-self because you should have said this or should have done that. For example, you may say *I should have locked the door* when a thief takes your car stereo or *I should not have locked the door* when you lock your keys inside your car. You may tell your friend *you should have gone out with him* or you may say *she shouldn't have said that* if you're trying to make someone feel better. In all those instances, you're using the past conditional tense.

The past conditional often expresses a missed opportunity in the past, an uncertainty, or a regret. For example, **Elle aurait voulu voyager mais elle n'avait pas assez d'argent** means *She would have liked to travel but she didn't have enough money.* In English, the past conditional is translated as *would have done something.* Furthermore, in English it's used to express what *would have* or *would not have* occurred if something had happened or had not happened.

In this chapter, I show you how to form the past conditional tense and then how to use it. I offer plenty of exercises so that you can practice these concepts.

Creating the Past Conditional

You form the past conditional by putting the auxiliaries **avoir** (*to have*) and **être** (*to be*) in the conditional tense and adding the past participle of the verbs. Check out the following tables that conjugate the auxiliaries in the conditional form.

avoir (*to have*)	
j'**aurais**	nous **aurions**
tu **aurais**	vous **auriez**
il/elle/on **aurait**	ils/elles **auraient**

être (*to be*)	
je **serais**	nous **serions**
tu **serais**	vous **seriez**
il/elle/on **serait**	ils/elles **seraient**

The verbs **étudier** (*to study*) and **partir** (*to leave*) serve as examples of the two types of auxiliaries: **avoir** and **être. Étudier** takes the auxiliary **avoir,** and **partir** takes **être.** The past participle of verbs taking **être** as their auxiliary agrees with the subject. Therefore, if the subject is feminine singular, add an **e,** if it's masculine plural, add an **s,** and if it's feminine plural, add an **es.** If you aren't sure about the past participle of verbs, look at Chapter 12.

étudier (*to study*)	
j'**aurais étudié**	nous **aurions étudié**
tu **aurais étudié**	vous **auriez étudié**
il/elle/on **aurait étudié**	ils/elles **auraient étudié**
Elle **aurait étudié.** (*She would have studied.*)	

partir (*to leave*)	
je **serais parti(e)**	nous **serions partis(es)**
tu **serais parti(e)**	vous **seriez parti(e)(s)(es)**
il/elle/on **serait parti(e)**	ils/elles **seraient partis(es)**
Nous **serions partis.** (*We would have left.*)	

Nous aurions voulu vous aider. (*We would have liked to help you.*)

Ils seraient arrivés. (*They would have arrived.*)

For pronominal verbs, place the pronominal pronoun in front of the auxiliary **être,** which is followed by the past participle of the verb. Remember that all pronominal verbs are conjugated with the auxiliary **être,** which is conjugated in the conditional.

se lever (*to get up*)	
je **me serais levé(e)**	nous **nous serions levés(es)**
tu **te serais levé(e)**	vous **vous seriez levé(e)(s)(es)**
il/elle/on **se serait levé(e)**	ils/elles **se seraient levés(es)**
Vous **vous seriez levés.** (*You would have gotten up.*)	

To make the past conditional negative, place **ne** in front of the auxiliary and **pas** after the auxiliary. For pronominal verbs, place **ne** in front of the pronominal pronoun and the **pas** after the auxiliary.

Je n'aurais pas fini. (*I would not have finished.*)

Benjamin ne se serait pas réveillé. (*Benjamin would not have woken up.*)

To ask a question using inversion with past tenses, you simply invert the subject and the auxiliary.

Serions-nous arrivés à l'heure? (*Would we have arrived on time?*)

Te serais-tu amusé? (*Would you have had fun?*)

Now it's your turn. Put the verbs in parentheses in the past conditional.

Q. Corinne _____ (devoir) téléphoner.

A. Corinne **aurait dû** téléphoner. (*Corinne should have called.*)

1. Antoine _____ (payer) par chèque.

2. Vous _____ (préférer) partir tôt.

3. Mélanie et Alexandre _____ (se souvenir) de leur jeunesse.

4. Tu _____ (rester) toute la journée.

5. Sarah _____ (pouvoir) te présenter à ses amis.

6. Je _____ (apprendre) le russe.

7. Étienne _____ (recevoir) la médaille.

8. Nous _____ (se voir).

9. Les parents de Sophie _____ (être) déçus.

10. Aurore _____ (aimer) les rencontrer au café.

Correctly Using the Past Conditional

The past conditional expresses a missed opportunity or a regret. You can use the past conditional in a simple sentence or in a more complex sentence with two or more clauses. For example, you can say **J'aurais dû étudier plus** (*I should have studied more*), or you can say **Si j'avais eu temps, j'aurais étudié plus** (*If I had had the time, I would have studied more*).

Before you correctly use the past conditional in a complex sentence, you need to understand how you use it in a hypothetical sentence. A *hypothetical sentence* expresses a supposition, a condition, or a possibility introduced by the conjunction *if* or **si.** A hypothetical sentence has two clauses — a subordinate clause introduced by **si** and a result clause or a main clause. The tenses of these clauses vary depending on which hypothetical sentence you use. Here's what you need to know about the three hypothetical sentences:

✔ In the first hypothetical sentence, you use the present after **si,** and you can use the present, the immediate future, the simple future, or even the imperative form in the result clause. Use the tense that makes the most sense for what you want to say.

✔ In the second hypothetical sentence, you use the imperfect after **si,** and you use the present conditional in the result clause. (See Chapter 17.)

✔ In the third hypothetical sentence, you use the pluperfect after **si,** and you use the past conditional in the result clause. This sentence is the most common use of the past conditional. If the **si** clause uses the pluperfect (see Chapter 12 for more on forming the pluperfect), then you use the past conditional in the result clause.

Table 18-1 puts the hypothetical sentences all together.

Table 18-1	Hypothetical Sentences		
Tense in the Si Clause	*If or Subordinate Clause*	*Tense in the Result Clause*	*Result or Main Clause*
Present	**S'il pleut . . .** *If it rains . . .*	Present	**. . . je porte un imperméable.** *. . . I wear a raincoat.*
Present	**S'il pleut . . .** *If it rains . . .*	Simple future	**. . . je porterai un imperméable.** *. . . I will wear a raincoat.*
Present	**S'il pleut . . .** *If it rains . . .*	Immediate future	**. . . je vais porter un imperméable.** *. . . I am going to wear a raincoat.*
Present	**S'il pleut . . .** *If it rains . . .*	Imperative	**. . . porte ton imperméable.** *. . . wear your raincoat.*
Imperfect	**S'il pleuvait . . .** *If it were to rain . . .*	Present conditional	**. . . je porterais un imperméable.** *. . . I would wear my raincoat.*
Pluperfect	**S'il avait plu . . .** *If it had rained . . .*	Past conditional	**. . . J'aurais porté un imperméable.** *. . . I would have worn my raincoat.*

You may begin a sentence with the result clause, followed by the subordinate or **si** clause. However, you can't switch the tenses, which means that the present (except for the first example sentence, in which both clauses can be in the present tense), the imperfect, and the pluperfect are always placed in the **si** clause and the future, conditional, and past conditional are always placed in the result clause.

> **Si tu avais fini tes devoirs, tu serais allé jouer.** (*If you had finished your homework, you would have gone to play.*)

As with the other two hypothetical sentences, you may begin your sentence with the result clause, followed by the **si** clause. However, you can't switch the tenses. In other words, you always put the pluperfect in the **si** clause and the past conditional in the result clause.

> **Nous serions arrivés plus tôt s'il n'y avait pas eu d'embouteillages.** (*We would have arrived earlier if there hadn't been any traffic jams.*)

Fill in these hypothetical sentences. Remember to place the past conditional in the result clause.

0. S'il n'avait pas plu, nous _____ (aller) à la plage.

A. S'il n'avait pas plu, nous **serions allés** à la plage. (*If it hadn't rained, we would have gone to the beach.*)

11. Si tu avais regardé la carte, tu _____ (suivre) la bonne route.

12. S'il n'avait pas fait de vent, je _____ (rester) à la plage.

13. Ils _____ (ne pas aller) en classe, s'ils avaient su que le professeur était absent.

14. Je _____ (se dépêcher) si j'avais été en retard.

15. Si Anne n'avait pas étudié, elle _____ (ne pas réussir) à l'examen.

16. Est-ce que vous _____ (être) moins fatigué si vous aviez travaillé plus près de chez vous?

17. Nous _____ (venir) si tu nous avais dit.

18. Si Sébastien s'était inscrit à ce cours, il _____ (recevoir) trois unités de valeur.

19. Si tu t'étais levé tôt, tu _____ (éviter) la circulation.

20. Les enfants _____ (jouer) dehors s'il n'avait pas fait si froid.

I want to provide you with some more practice problems so that you have a firm grasp on the three hypothetical sentences. In the following exercise, match the lettered logical result clause with the numbered **si** clause by putting the correct letter in each blank.

0. Si vous n'étiez pas venu

A. **g.** Si vous n'étiez pas venu, vous auriez manqué une bonne soirée. (*If you hadn't come, you would have missed a good party.*)

21. _____ Si tu avais pris des leçons de musique   **a.** je me promènerais.

22. _____ Si on veut   **b.** nous aurions rencontré tes parents.

23. _____ Si Audrey avait de la chance   **c.** ils seraient arrivés dans une demi heure.

24. _____ S'il faisait beau   **d.** tu ne glisserais pas.

25. _____ Si j'ai le temps   **e.** tu aurais joué beaucoup mieux.

26. _____ Si nous étions venus   **f.** elle trouverait un appartement pas trop cher.

27. _____ S'ils avaient pris le métro   **g.** vous auriez manqué une bonne soirée.

28. _____ Si tu marchais prudemment   **h.** on peut.

29. _____ Si Caroline vient avec nous   **i.** elle s'assiéra à côté de toi.

30. _____ Si vous étiez resté chez vous   **j.** je viendrai avec vous.

What? More practice? Yes, I want to make sure that you understand this concept. In the following sentences, all three hypothetical sentences are included. In each sentence, one of the verbs is filled in for you. It's up to you to fill in the second verb. Refer to Table 18-1 and conjugate the verbs in parentheses in the required tense.

0. J'aurais fini mes devoirs, si je _____ (commencer) plus tôt.

A. J'aurais fini mes devoirs, si j'**avais commencé** plus tôt. (*I would have finished my homework if I had begun earlier.*)

31. Si Eric lisait le journal, il _____ (savoir) ce qui se passait dans le monde.

32. Nous _____ (pouvoir) voyager, si nous prenons notre retraite.

33. Si mes parents avaient habité plus près, je les _____ (voir) plus souvent.

34. S'il faisait du vent, vous _____ (ne pas aller) à la plage.

35. Si vous aviez été fatigués, vous _____ (devoir) vous reposer.

36. Si tu étais malade, tu _____ (prendre) des médicaments.

37. Les enfants _____ (être) heureux s'ils gagnaient le match.

38. S'il avait eu des œufs, il _____ (faire) une omelette.

39. Audrey _____ (travailler), si elle finit ses études.

40. Si je gagnais à la loterie, je _____ (faire) le tour du monde.

Answer Key

This section provides the correct answers for all the problems in this chapter. Please review and compare them to your answers.

1 Antoine **aurait payé** par chèque. (*Antoine would have paid by check.*)

2 Vous **auriez préféré** partir tôt. (*You would have preferred to leave early.*)

3 Mélanie et Alexandre **se seraient souvenus** de leur jeunesse. (*Mélanie and Alexandre would have remembered their youth.*)

4 Tu **serais resté** toute la journée. (*You would have stayed the whole day.*)

5 Sarah **aurait pu** te présenter à ses amis. (*Sarah could have introduced you to her friends.*)

6 J'**aurais appris** le russe. (*I would have learned Russian.*)

7 Étienne **aurait reçu** la médaille. (*Étienne would have won the medal.*)

8 Nous **nous serions vus.** (*We would have seen each other.*)

9 Les parents de Sophie **auraient été** déçus. (*Sophie's parents would have been disappointed.*)

10 Aurore **aurait aimé** les rencontrer au café. (*Aurore would have liked to meet them at the café.*)

11 Si tu avais regardé la carte, tu **aurais suivi** la bonne route. (*If you had looked at the map, you would have followed the right route.*)

12 S'il n'avait pas fait de vent, je **serais resté** à la plage. (*If it had not been windy, I would have stayed at the beach.*)

13 Ils **ne seraient pas allés** en classe, s'ils avaient su que le professeur était absent. (*They would not have gone to class if they had known that the professor was absent.*)

14 Je **me serais dépêché** si j'avais été en retard. (*I would have hurried if I had been late.*)

15 Si Anne n'avait pas étudié, elle **n'aurait pas réussi** à l'examen. (*If Anne had not studied, she would not have passed the exam.*)

16 Est-ce que vous **auriez été** moins fatigué si vous aviez travaillé plus près de chez vous? (*Would you have been less tired if you had worked closer to home?*)

17 Nous **serions venus** si tu nous avais dit. (*We would have come if you had told us.*)

18 Si Sébastien s'était inscrit à ce cours, il **aurait reçu** trois unités de valeur. (*If Sébastien had registered for this course, he would have received three credits.*)

19 Si tu t'étais levé tôt, tu **aurais évité** la circulation. (*If you had gotten up early, you would have avoided the traffic.*)

20 Les enfants **auraient joué** dehors s'il n'avait pas fait si froid. (*The children would have played outside if it hadn't been so cold.*)

21 **e.** Si tu avais pris des leçons de musique, tu aurais joué beaucoup mieux. (*If you had taken music lessons, you would have played much better.*)

22 **h.** Si on veut, on peut. (*If one wants, one can.*)

23 **f.** Si Audrey avait de la chance, elle trouverait un appartement pas trop cher. (*If Audrey were lucky, she would find an apartment that's not too expensive.*)

24 **a.** S'il faisait beau, je me promènerais. (*If it were nice out, I would take a walk.*)

25 **j.** Si j'ai le temps, je viendrai avec vous. (*If I have time, I will come with you.*)

26 **b.** Si nous étions venus, nous aurions rencontré tes parents. (*If we had come, we would have met your parents.*)

27 **c.** S'ils avaient pris le métro, ils seraient arrivés dans une demi heure. (*If they had taken the subway, they would have arrived in a half an hour.*)

28 **d.** Si tu marchais prudemment, tu ne glisserais pas. (*If you were to walk carefully, you would not slip.*)

29 **i.** Si Caroline vient avec nous, elle s'assiéra à côté de toi. (*If Caroline comes with us, she will sit next to you.*)

30 **g.** Si vous étiez resté chez vous, vous auriez manqué une bonne soirée. (*If you had stayed home, you would have missed a good party.*)

31 Si Eric lisait le journal, il **saurait** ce qui se passait dans le monde. (*If Eric were to read the newspaper, he would know what was happening in the world.*)

32 Nous **pourrons** voyager, si nous prenons notre retraite. (*We will be able to travel if we take our retirement.*)

33 Si mes parents avaient habité plus près, je les **aurais vus** plus souvent. (*If my parents had lived closer, I would have seen them more often.*)

34 S'il faisait du vent, vous **n'iriez pas** à la plage. (*If it were windy, you would not go to the beach.*)

35 Si vous aviez été fatigués, vous **auriez dû** vous reposer. (*If you had been tired, you should have rested.*)

36 Si tu étais malade, tu **prendrais** des médicaments. (*If you were ill, you would take some medication.*)

37 Les enfants **seraient** heureux s'ils gagnaient le match. (*The children would be happy if they were to win the game.*)

38 S'il avait eu des œufs, il **aurait fait** une omelette. (*If he had had eggs, he would have made an omelette.*)

39 Audrey **travaillera**, si elle finit ses études. (*Audrey will work if she finishes her studies.*)

40 Si je gagnais la loterie, je **ferais** le tour du monde. (*If I were to win the lottery, I would travel all over the world.*)

Part V
Considering Your Mood: Subjunctive or Not

The 5th Wave   By Rich Tennant

©RICHTENNANT

"Honey, can you look in the phrase book and tell me how 'scrambled' is pronounced in French?"

In this part . . .

The mood of a verb indicates the writer or speaker's point of view regarding the events. The indicative — including the present, past, and future — expresses facts as well as objective observations. It expresses what is happening, has happened, or will happen. Meanwhile the subjunctive mood expresses what you want to happen, command to happen, or doubt will happen. Chapter 19 looks at conjugating the present subjunctive, Chapter 20 focuses on using the present subjunctive, and Chapter 21 shows you how to conjugate and use the past subjunctive.

Chapter 19

Creating the Present Subjunctive

• •

In This Chapter

▶ Working with regular verbs

▶ Forming the subjunctive with "irregular" verbs

▶ Taking a stab with stem changers

▶ Trying out true irregular verbs

• •

*U*nlike the indicative mood, which expresses an objective reality, the subjunctive mood expresses the speaker's or writer's subjective points of view, emotions, fears, and doubts. To use the subjunctive, you place it in the subordinate clause introduced by **que** (*that*) when a verb or verbal expression in the main clause expresses emotion, will, wish, command, doubt, or subjectivity. When the verb in the main clause expresses a fact or an objective observation, then you use the indicative instead of the subjunctive.

This chapter looks at how you conjugate good ol' regular verbs, verbs that are irregular in other tenses but regular in the subjunctive, stem-changing verbs, and true irregular verbs. After you know how to form the present subjunctive, you can check out Chapter 20, which shows you how to *use* the present subjunctive. Because French doesn't have a future subjunctive, the present subjunctive expresses the future as well as the present and can be translated in English in the tense that makes the most sense.

Forming the Present Subjunctive with Regular Verbs

The subjunctive isn't a difficult tense to form. All you need is to be familiar with the present indicative conjugation of the verbs be they regular verbs, spelling-change verbs, or even some irregular verbs. (Check out Chapters 2, 3, and 4 for the present indicative of verbs.) In this section, I start off with forming the present subjunctive of regular verbs.

You form the present subjunctive the same way, whether the verb is regular or not and whether it has a stem change or not. To form the present subjunctive, start from the third person plural of the indicative, the **ils/elles** form, drop the **-ent** to form the stem, and add the following endings: **-e, -es, -e, -ions, -iez,** or **-ent.**

Present Subjunctive Verb Endings	
je **-e**	nous **-ions**
tu **-es**	vous **-iez**
il/elle/on **-e**	ils/elles **-ent**

The verbs **parler** (*to speak*), **finir** (*to finish*), and **vendre** (*to sell*) serve as examples of the three categories of regular verbs. You create the stem for each with the **ils/elles** form of the indicative, like so:

- ✔ **Parler** (*to speak*) becomes **ils/elles parlent** in the third person plural indicative. Delete the **-ent** from this form to create the stem, and you get **parl-**.

- ✔ **Finir** (*to finish*) becomes **ils/elles finissent** in the third person plural indicative. Delete the **-ent** from this form to create the stem, and you get **finiss-**.

- ✔ **Vendre** (*to sell*) becomes **ils/elles vendent** in the third person plural indicative. Delete the **-ent** from this form to create the stem, and you get **vend-**.

parler (*to speak*)	
que je **parle**	que nous **parlions**
que tu **parles**	que vous **parliez**
qu'il/elle/on **parle**	qu'ils/elles **parlent**
Il est essentiel que nous **parlions** au directeur. (*It is essential that we speak to the director.*)	

finir (*to finish*)	
que je **finisse**	que nous **finissions**
que tu **finisses**	que vous **finissiez**
qu'il/elle/on **finisse**	qui'ils/elles **finissent**
Il est possible que je **finisse** à 5 heures. (*It's possible that I will finish at 5 o'clock.*)	

vendre (*to sell*)	
que je **vende**	que nous **vendions**
que tu **vendes**	que vous **vendiez**
qu'il/elle/on **vende**	qu'ils/elles **vendent**
Mes parents veulent que je **vende** ma voiture. (*My parents want me to sell my car.*)	

Il doute que je nous arrivions avant midi. (*He doubts that we will arrive before noon.*)

Nous sommes surpris que tu vendes ta maison. (*We are surprised that you are selling your house.*)

As strange as it looks and sounds, you do add the extra **-i** to regular verbs whose **nous** form already ends in **-ions** and **vous** form already ends in **-iez** in the present indicative. These verbs include **étudier** (*to study*), **rire** (*to laugh*), and **sourire** (*to smile*). I conjugate **étudier** in the following table. The stem (from **ils étudient**, the third person plural indicative) is **étudi-**.

étudier (*to study*)	
que j'étudie	que nous étudiions
que tu étudies	que vous étudiiez
qu'il/elle/on étudie	qu'ils/elles étudient
Il est important que nous **étudiions**. (*It is important that we study.*)	

Now take time to conjugate the following regular verbs into the present subjunctive.

Q. Il faut que nous _____ (regarder) les nouvelles.

A. Il faut que nous **regardions** les nouvelles. (*It is necessary that we watch the news.*)

1. Mon professeur exige que je _____ (choisir) un sujet de thèse.

2. Je suis ravi que tu _____ (aimer) mon cadeau.

3. Nous sommes heureux qu'ils _____ (réussir) à l'école.

4. Il est regrettable que nous _____ (ne pas habiter) plus près de la ville.

5. Il faut qu'elle _____ (rendre) les CD.

6. Ils sont surpris que je _____ (chanter) bien.

7. Il est étonnant que les enfants _____ (grandir) si vite.

8. Tu ne crois pas que le train _____ (arriver) à l'heure?

9. Maman veut que nous _____ (obéir) à nos grands-parents.

10. Il est dommage que tu _____ (perdre) patience.

Typically Irregular, but Regular in the Subjunctive

Most irregular verbs follow the same pattern in the subjunctive as the regular verbs. You simply take their third person plural form (**ils/elles**) and add the same endings: **-e, -es, -e, -ions, -iez,** and **-ent.**

Check out Table 19-1 as an example of several irregular verbs that follow the regular conjugation in the present subjunctive.

Table 19-1	Typically Irregular Verbs but Regular in the Subjunctive	
Infinitive	*Ils Form in the Present Indicative*	*Subjunctive Stem*
conduire (*to drive*)	**ils conduisent**	**conduis-**
connaître (*to know*)	**ils connaissent**	**connaiss-**
craindre (*to fear*)	**ils craignent**	**craign-**
dire (*to say*)	**ils disent**	**dis-**
dormir (*to sleep*)	**ils dorment**	**dorm-**
écrire (*to write*)	**ils écrivent**	**écriv-**
lire (*to read*)	**ils lisent**	**lis-**
mettre (*to put, to place*)	**ils mettent**	**mett**
offrir (*to offer*)	**ils offrent**	**offr-**
partir (*to leave*)	**ils partent**	**part-**
servir (*to serve*)	**ils servent**	**serv-**
sortir (*to go out*)	**ils sortent**	**sort-**
suivre (*to follow, to take a course*)	**ils suivent**	**suiv-**
vivre (*to live*)	**ils vivent**	**viv-**

> **Il est important que les enfants lisent tous les jours.** (*It is important that children read every day.*)

Conjugate the following verbs in parentheses in the present subjunctive.

Q. Je doute qu'elle _____ (dire) des mensonges.

A. Je doute qu'elle **dise** des mensonges. (*I doubt that she's telling lies.*)

11. Mes parents sont inquiets que je _____ (craindre) les ascenseurs.

12. Eric est fâché que ses amis _____ (partir) en vacances sans lui.

13. Il est important que nous _____ (vivre) en paix.

14. Je veux que tu _____ (mettre) ta ceinture de sécurité.

15. Il est nécessaire que tous les étudiants _____ (suivre) cinq cours par semestre.

16. Il est essentiel que nous _____ (dormir) bien.

17. Croyez-vous que ce journaliste _____ (écrire) bien?

18. Il est douteux qu'ils _____ (servir) du vin.

19. Je suis surpris que vous _____ (connaître) mon oncle.

20. Papa n'aime pas que nous _____ (sortir) si tard.

Looking At Stem Changers

Certain verbs in French have one stem for all the singular and third person plural subjects and another stem for the **nous** and **vous** forms. These verbs are often referred to as *boot* verbs because when you draw around the subject pronouns, the singular and third person plural form the shape of a boot, whereas the **nous** and **vous** forms are left outside of the boot. Remember that these verbs have the same stem changes in the present indicative as well as the present subjunctive.

Certain verbs have two different stems: one for the singular (**je, tu, il/elle/on**) and third person plural (**ils/elles**) and another for the **nous** and **vous** forms. The stem of the subjunctive form of these verbs is also derived from the third person plural **ils/elles,** and the endings are the same as the regular verbs in the subjunctive (see "Forming the Present Subjunctive with Regular Verbs" earlier in this chapter). The way to remember these verbs is to refer to their present indicative, where they also have this type of stem difference.

Check out the following examples that conjugate **boire** (*to drink*) in both the present indicative and the present subjunctive so that you can compare them.

boire (*to drink*) in the present indicative	
je **bois**	nous **buvons**
tu **bois**	vous **buvez**
il/elle/on **boit**	ils/elles **boivent**
Nous **buvons** beaucoup de lait. (*We drink a lot of milk.*)	

boire (*to drink*) in the present subjunctive	
que je **boive**	que nous **buvions**
que tu **boives**	que vous **buviez**
qu'il/elle/on **boive**	qu'ils/elles **boivent**
Il est bon que nous **buvions** beaucoup de lait. (*It is good that we drink a lot of milk.*)	

The following verbs also have two stems, just like **boire. Prendre** (*to take*) (and all its compounds) forms its stem from the present indicative of the **ils** form, **ils prennent.** Delete the **-ent** and use **prenn-** as the stem for the **je, tu, il/elle/on,** and **ils/elles** forms. Use **pren-** for **nous** and **vous.**

prendre (*to take*)	
que je **prenne**	que nous **prenions**
que tu **prennes**	que vous **preniez**
qu'il/elle/on **prenne**	qu'ils/elles **prennent**
Il est nécessaire que tu **prennes** ton passeport. (*It is necessary that you take your passport.*)	

You conjugate the following verbs just like **prendre: apprendre** (*to learn*), **comprendre** (*to understand*), **entreprendre** (*to undertake*), **reprendre** (*to retake, to resume*), and **surprendre** (*to surprise*).

Another verb that has a stem change in the present subjunctive is **venir** (*to come*). I conjugate it in the following example, using the stem **vienn-** from **ils viennent,** the present indicative, for the **je, tu, il/elle/on,** and **ils/elles** forms. Use **ven-** for **nous** and **vous.**

venir (*to come*)	
que je **vienne**	que nous **venions**
que tu **viennes**	que vous **veniez**
qu'il/elle/on **vienne**	qu'ils/elles **viennent**
Nous sommes heureux que vous **veniez**. (*We are happy that you're coming.*)	

All compounds of **venir** are conjugated the same way. These include **devenir** (*to become*), **intervenir** (*to intervene*), **parvenir** (*to reach, to succeed*), **revenir** (*to return*), and **se souvenir** (*to remember*). Also, you conjugate similar verbs, like **tenir** (*to hold*) and its compounds, the same way. These include **appartenir** (*to belong*), **contenir** (*to contain*), **maintenir** (*to maintain*), **obtenir** (*to obtain*), **retenir** (*to retain*), and **soutenir** (*to support*).

Recevoir (*to receive*) is another verb that has a stem change in the present subjunctive. Its stems include **reçoiv-** for the **je, tu, il/elle/on,** and **ils/elles** forms and **recev-** for **nous** and **vous.**

recevoir (*to receive*)	
que je **reçoive**	que nous **recevions**
que tu **reçoives**	que vous **receviez**
qu'il/elle/on **reçoive**	qu'ils/elles **reçoivent**
Il est possible qu'ils **reçoivent** la coupe. (*It is possible that they receive the cup.*)	

Verbs that are conjugated like **recevoir** include **apercevoir** (*to see, to notice*), **concevoir** (*to conceive*), **décevoir** (*to disappoint*), and **percevoir** (*to perceive, to comprehend*).

Another verb that has a stem change in the present subjunctive is **croire** (*to believe*). Check out the following example that conjugates it. Remember that the stem for **je, tu, il/elle/on,** and **ils/elles** forms is **croi-** and for the **nous** and **vous** forms **croy-.**

croire (*to believe*)	
que je **croie**	que nous **croyions**
que tu **croies**	que vous **croyiez**
qu'il/elle/on **croie**	qu'ils/elles **croient**
Je doute qu'elle **croie** tout ce qu'il dit. (*I doubt that she believes all he says.*)	

Voir (*to see*) is conjugated like **croire.**

Another verb that has a stem change in the present subjunctive is **devoir** (*to owe, to have to*). Check out the following example to conjugate it. Stems of this verb are **doiv-** for the **je, tu, il/elle/on,** and **ils/elles** forms and **dev-** for **nous** and **vous.**

devoir (*ought to, must, to owe*)	
que je **doive**	que nous **devions**
que tu **doives**	que vous **deviez**
qu'il/elle/on **doive**	qu'ils/elles **doivent**
Je ne crois pas que tu **doives** payer maintenant. (*I don't believe that you have to pay now.*)	

All verbs ending in **-yer** are two-stem verbs as well. Like all the verbs that I've mentioned in this section thus far, the subjunctive tense is derived from the **ils** form of the present indicative. However, with the two-stem verbs, the **nous** and **vous** forms have a different stem. The verb **essayer** (*to try*) serves as an example. The stems for this verb are as follows: **essai-** for the **je, tu, il/elle/on,** and **ils/elles** forms and **essay-** for **nous** and **vous.**

essayer (*to try*)	
que j'**essaie**	que nous **essayions**
que tu **essaies**	que vous **essayiez**
qu'il/elle/on **essaie**	qu'ils/elles **essaient**
Je veux que tu **essaies** de venir. (*I want you to try to come.*)	

Try conjugating some of these verbs. Follow the example and put the infinitives in the third person plural indicative (**ils/elles**) and then in the subjunctive of the indicated subject pronouns.

0. Infinitive: vivre

Present indicative: ils _____

Present subjunctive: que tu _____, que vous _____

A. ils **vivent,** que tu **vives,** que vous **viviez**

21. Infinitive: apercevoir

Present indicative: ils _____

Present subjunctive: que je _____, qu'ils _____

22. Infinitive: nettoyer

Present indicative: ils _____

Present subjunctive: qu'il _____, que nous _____

23. Infinitive: venir

Present indicative: ils _____

Present subjunctive: que tu _____, qu'elle _____

24. Infinitive: prendre

Present indicative: ils _____

Present subjunctive: qu'il _____, que vous _____

25. Infinitive: se souvenir

Present indicative: ils _____

Present subjunctive: que je _____, que nous _____

26. Infinitive: essayer

Present indicative: ils _____

Present subjunctive: que tu _____, que nous _____

27. Infinitive: boire

Present indicative: ils _____

Present subjunctive: qu'elle _____, que vous _____

28. Infinitive: voir

Present indicative: ils _____

Present subjunctive: que je _____, qu'elles _____

29. Infinitive: apprendre

Present indicative: ils _____

Present subjunctive: qu'il _____, que nous _____

30. Infinitive: devoir

Present indicative: ils _____

Present subjunctive: que je _____, que vous _____

Eyeing the Irregulars

Some verbs are completely irregular in the present subjunctive. The stem of the subjunctive isn't derived from the third person plural (**ils/elles**) the way the rest of the verbs' stems are. However, even these irregular verbs have the same endings in the subjunctive as the regular verbs: **-e, -es, -e, -ions, -iez,** and **-ent.** Check out the following verbs:

aller (*to go*)	
que j'**aille**	que nous **allions**
que tu **ailles**	que vous **alliez**
qu'il/elle/on **aille**	qu'ils/elles **aillent**
Il faut que j'**aille** au magasin. (*I have to go to the store.*)	

faire (*to do, to make*)	
que je **fasse**	que nous **fassions**
que tu **fasses**	que vous **fassiez**
qu'il/elle/on **fasse**	qu'ils/elles **fassent**
Je préfère que tu **fasses** la vaisselle. (*I prefer that you do the dishes.*)	

pouvoir (*to be able to*)	
que je **puisse**	que nous **puissions**
que tu **puisses**	que vous **puissiez**
qu'il/elle/on **puisse**	qu'ils/elles **puissent**
Nous sommes contents qu'ils **puissent** venir. (*We are happy that they can come.*)	

savoir (*to know*)	
que je **sache**	que nous **sachions**
que tu **saches**	que vous **sachiez**
qu'il/elle/on **sache**	qu'ils/elles **sachent**
Il est important que tu **saches** conduire. (*It's important that you know how to drive.*)	

vouloir (*to want*)	
que je **veuille**	que nous **voulions**
que tu **veuilles**	que vous **vouliez**
qu'il/elle/on **veuille**	qu'ils/elles **veuillent**
C'est impressionnant qu'elle **veuille** piloter un avion. (*It is impressive that she wants to pilot a plane.*)	

French has only two irregular verbs that don't have the same endings in the subjunctive as all other verbs. Can you guess which ones? Yes, you're right if you guessed **avoir** (*to have*) and **être** (*to be*).

avoir (to have)	
que j'**aie**	que nous **ayons**
que tu **aies**	que vous **ayez**
qu'il/elle/on **ait**	qu'ils/elles **aient**
Il est nécessaire que nous **ayons** de la patience. (*It is necessary that we have patience.*)	

être (to be)	
que je **sois**	que nous **soyons**
que tu **sois**	que vous **soyez**
qu'il/elle/on **soit**	qu'ils/elles **soient**
Les parents veulent que leurs enfants **soient** sages. (*The parents want their children to behave.*)	

The following two verbs exist only in the third person singular, the **il** form: **pleuvoir** (*to rain*) and **falloir** (*to be necessary*).

- ✔ **qu'il pleuve** (*that it rains/will rain*)
- ✔ **qu'il faille** (*that it is/will be necessary*)

Follow the example and put the infinitives of the irregular verbs in parentheses in the subjunctive of the indicated subject pronoun.

0. Faire: que tu _____, qu'ils _____

A. que tu **fasses**, qu'ils **fassent**

31. Pouvoir: que je _____, que nous _____

32. Être: qu'elle _____, que vous _____

33. Vouloir: que tu _____, qu'elles _____

34. Savoir: qu'on _____, que nous _____

35. Avoir: que j'_____, que vous _____

36. Faire: qu'il _____, que nous _____

37. Pouvoir: que tu _____, qu'ils _____

38. Être: que je _____, qu'elles _____

39. Vouloir: que je _____, que nous _____

40. Faire: que tu _____, qu'elles _____

Answer Key

This section contains the answers to the exercises that you encounter in this chapter. Review your answers and compare them to the correct ones. Keep in mind that the present subjunctive can also express the future as well as the present because there is no future subjunctive.

1 Mon professeur exige que je **choisisse** un sujet de thèse. (*My professor requires that I choose a thesis topic.*)

2 Je suis ravi que tu **aimes** mon cadeau. (*I am delighted that you like my gift.*)

3 Nous sommes heureux qu'ils **réussissent** à l'école. (*We are happy that they succeed/are succeeding in school.*)

4 Il est regrettable que nous **n'habitions pas** plus près de la ville. (*It is regrettable that we don't live closer to the city.*)

5 Il faut qu'elle **rende** les CD. (*It is necessary that she give back the CDs.*)

6 Ils sont surpris que je **chante** bien. (*They are surprised that I sing well.*)

7 Il est étonnant que les enfants **grandissent** si vite. (*It is surprising that the children grow up so fast.*)

8 Tu ne crois pas que le train **arrive** à l'heure? (*You don't believe that the train is arriving on time?*)

9 Maman veut que nous **obéissions** à nos grands-parents. (*Mom wants us to obey our grandparents.*)

10 Il est dommage que tu **perdes** patience. (*It is too bad that you lose/are losing patience.*)

11 Mes parents sont inquiets que je **craigne** les ascenseurs. (*My parents are worried that I fear elevators.*)

12 Eric est fâché que ses amis **partent** en vacances sans lui. (*Eric is angry that his friends are leaving for vacation without him.*)

13 Il est important que nous **vivions** en paix. (*It is important that we live in peace.*)

14 Je veux que tu **mettes** ta ceinture de sécurité. (*I want you to put on your seat belt.*)

15 Il est nécessaire que tous les étudiants **suivent** cinq cours par semestre. (*It is necessary that all the students take five courses a semester.*)

16 Il est essentiel que nous **dormions** bien. (*It is essential that we sleep well.*)

17 Croyez-vous que ce journaliste **écrive** bien? (*Do you believe that this journalist writes well?*)

18 Il est douteux qu'ils **servent** du vin. (*It is doubtful that they serve/will serve wine.*)

19 Je suis surpris que vous **connaissiez** mon oncle. (*I am surprised that you know my uncle.*)

20 Papa n'aime pas que nous **sortions** si tard. (*Dad doesn't like that we go out so late.*)

21 Present indicative: ils **aperçoivent**

Present subjunctive: que **j'aperçoive**, qu'ils **aperçoivent**

22 Present indicative: ils **nettoient**

Present subjunctive: qu'il **nettoie**, que nous **nettoyions**

23 Present indicative: ils **viennent**

Present subjunctive: que tu **viennes**, qu'elle **vienne**

24 Present indicative: ils **prennent**

Present subjunctive: qu'il **prenne**, que vous **preniez**

25 Present indicative: ils **se souviennent**

Present subjunctive: que je **me souvienne**, que nous **nous souvenions**

26 Present indicative: ils **essaient**

Present subjunctive: que tu **essaies**, que nous **essayions**

27 Present indicative: ils **boivent**

Present subjunctive: qu'elle **boive**, que vous **buviez**

28 Present indicative: ils **voient**

Present subjunctive: que je **voie**, qu'elles **voient**

29 Present indicative: ils **apprennent**

Present subjunctive: qu'il **apprenne**, que nous **apprenions**

30 Present indicative: ils **doivent**

Present subjunctive: que je **doive**, que vous **deviez**

31 que je **puisse**, que nous **puissions**

32 qu'elle **soit**, que vous **soyez**

33 que tu **veuilles**, qu'elles **veuillent**

34 qu'on **sache**, que nous **sachions**

35 que j'**aie**, que vous **ayez**

36 qu'il **fasse**, que nous **fassions**

37 que tu **puisses**, qu'ils **puissent**

38 que je **sois**, qu'elles **soient**

39 que je **veuille**, que nous **voulions**

40 que tu **fasses**, qu'elles **fassent**

Chapter 20

Knowing How to Use the Present Subjunctive

In This Chapter

▶ Expressing wishes and preferences

▶ Showing emotion or judgment

▶ Doubting and being subjective

▶ Adding idiomatic expressions to your conversation

*I*n Chapter 19, I show you how to form the present subjunctive. In this chapter, I show you how to use it. The subjunctive is used much more often in French than in English. In fact, English has retained very little of its subjunctive tense. You can find it in such sentences as *They ask that she drive carefully* or *I request that you be on time.* But enough about English. You already know how to speak it, right?

You use the present subjunctive in the subordinate clause when three key criteria are present in a sentence. If you're missing any of these elements, then don't use the subjunctive. The three criteria are

✔ Two clauses linked by **que** (*that*).

✔ Two different subjects for each of the two clauses. (If the subject of both clauses is the same, then you use the infinitive.)

✔ A verb, verbal expression, or impersonal expression in the main clause that's in the indicative and expresses doubt, subjectivity, emotion, volition, or command.

If any of these elements is missing, then you need to use either the infinitive or the indicative instead of the subjunctive.

Except for some idiomatic expressions, you never use the subjunctive by itself. In other words, you can't start a sentence in the subjunctive. Because no future subjunctive exists, you use the present subjunctive to express an action in the subordinate clause that takes place after an action in the main clause. Also, the present subjunctive is used when the verb in the subordinate clause is simultaneous to — meaning it happens at the same time as — the verb in the main clause.

You may be asking yourself how you know whether a certain verb or verbal expression in the main clause requires the subjunctive in the subordinate clause. This chapter looks more closely at that issue so that you'll be confident every time you have to make that choice.

Expressing Wish, Will, Preference, and Command

In order to guide you in using the subjunctive correctly, I separate the verbs and verbal expressions that require the use of the subjunctive into different categories. You use the subjunctive in the subordinate clause when the verb or verbal expression in the main clause expresses wish, will, preference and command. Table 20-1 lists verbs that express just that.

Table 20-1	Verbs That Express Wish, Will, Preference, and Command
French Phrase	*English Translation*
accepter que	to accept that
admettre que	to admit that
adorer que	to love that, to adore that
aimer (mieux) que	to like that, to prefer that
apprécier que	to appreciate that
s'attendre à ce que	to expect that
commander que	to order that, to command that
demander que	to ask that
désirer que	to desire that, to wish that
détester que	to hate that
empêcher que	to prevent that
éxiger que	to demand that, to require that
interdire que	to forbid that
s'opposer à ce que	to oppose that
ordonner que	to order that
permettre que	to allow that
préférer que	to prefer that
proposer que	to propose that
recommander que	to recommend that
refuser que	to refuse that
regretter que	to regret that
souhaiter que	to wish that
suggérer que	to suggest that
tenir à ce que	to insist that
vouloir (bien) que	to want/would like that

Je veux que tu sois gentil. (_I want you to be nice;_ Literally: _I want that you be nice._)

Put the subjunctive in the subordinate clause. Notice that the clauses have different subjects.

Q. Le juge recommande que l'accusé _____ (dire) la vérité.

A. Le juge recommande que l'accusé **dise** la vérité. (_The judge recommends that the defendant tell the truth._)

1. Les professeurs proposent que nous _____ (lire) attentivement.

2. Tu tiens à ce que je _____ (venir) avec toi.

3. Le pilote ordonne que nous _____ (attacher) notre ceinture de sécurité.

4. Le médecin n'aime pas que ses patients _____ (toucher) l'équipement médical.

5. La loi empêche que l'on _____ (jeter) les ordures dans la rue.

6. J'apprécie que tu me _____ (comprendre).

7. Alexandre préfère que nous _____ (voyager) ensemble.

8. Mes parents refusent que je _____ (prendre) la voiture.

9. Céline propose qu'on _____ (aller) au cinéma.

10. Nous souhaitons que nos amis _____ (avoir) de bonnes notes.

Showing Emotion or Judgment

Another important category of verbs and verbal expressions is the one that expresses emotion as well as judgment. Take a look at Table 20-2 for a list of these verbs and verbal expressions.

Table 20-2	Phrases That Show Emotion or Judgment
French Phrase	_English Translation_
avoir honte que	_to be ashamed that_
avoir peur que	_to be afraid that_
craindre que	_to fear that_
déplorer que	_to deplore that_
être choqué que	_to be shocked that_
être content que	_to be happy/content that_

(continued)

Table 20-2 (continued)

French Phrase	English Translation
être déçu que	to be disappointed that
être désolé que	to be sorry that
être embarrassé que	to be embarrassed that
être ému que	to be moved that
être enchanté que	to be enchanted that
être étonné que	to be surprised that
être fâché que	to be angry that
être fier que	to be proud that
être furieux que	to be furious that
être gêné que	to be bothered/embarrassed that
être heureux que	to be happy that
être horrifié que	to be horrified that
être inquiet que	to be worried that
être malheureux que	to be unhappy that
être mécontent que	to be unhappy that
être navré que	to be very sorry that
être ravi que	to be delighted that
être stupéfait que	to be astonished that
être surpris que	to be surprised that
être triste que	to be sad that
se réjouir que	to be delighted that

Nous sommes heureux que vous veniez nous voir. (*We are happy that you're coming to see us.*)

Put the subjunctive in the subordinate clause. Notice that the clauses have different subjects.

Q. Il est mécontent que ses amis _____ (aller) au cinéma sans lui.

A. Il est mécontent que ses amis **aillent** au cinéma sans lui. (*He is unhappy that his friends go/will go to the movies without him.*)

11. Je suis ravi que vous _____ (pouvoir) venir.

12. Nous sommes surpris que tu _____ (ne pas avoir) d'argent.

13. Le professeur est furieux que les étudiants _____ (ne pas faire) attention.

14. Mme Castel est triste que son fils _____ (vivre) dans un tel état.

15. Les enfants sont déçus qu'il _____ (pleuvoir).

Expressing Doubt or Uncertainty

You also use the subjunctive when the verbs or verbal expressions in the main clause express doubt or uncertainty. However when the element of doubt or uncertainty no longer exists, then you use the indicative. Check out Table 20-3.

You use the verbs in Table 20-3 a bit differently than the ones in the previous two sections. The difference lies in the way you're using the verb: positively, negatively, or interrogatively. When you use the following verbs or expressions interrogatively or negatively in the main clause, you follow them with the subjunctive in the subordinate clause. When you use them affirmatively, you follow them with the indicative.

Croyez-vous qu'elle dise la vérité? (Subjunctive) (*Do you believe that she's telling the truth?*)

Vous ne croyez pas qu'elle dise la vérité. (Subjunctive) (*You don't believe that she's telling the truth.*)

Vous croyez qu'elle dit la vérité. (Indicative) (*You believe that she's telling the truth.*)

Table 20-3	Phrases That Express Doubt or Uncertainty	
Affirmative (Indicative)	*Interrogative (Subjunctive)*	*Negative (Subjunctive)*
croire que (*to believe that*)	Croire que?	ne pas croire que
trouver que (*to find that*)	Trouver que?	ne pas trouver que
penser que (*to think that*)	Penser que?	ne pas penser que
être sûr que (*to be sure that*)	Être sûr que?	ne pas être sûr que
être certain que (*to be certain that*)	Être certain que?	ne pas être certain que
il est vrai que (*it is true that*)	Est-il vrai que?	Il n'est pas vrai que
il est clair que (*it is clear that*)	Est-il clair que?	Il n'est pas clair que
il est probable que (*it is probable that*)	Est-il probable que?	Il n'est pas probable que
il est évident que (*it is evident that*)	Est-il évident que?	Il n'est pas évident que

The verb **douter que** (*to doubt that*) and the expression **il est douteux que** (*it is doubtful that*) follow a different pattern than the verbs and phrases in Table 20-3. You use the subjunctive in the subordinate clause when this verb and expression are used in the affirmative or in the interrogative because they imply doubt. However, in the negative, the element of doubt no longer exists and you use the indicative.

Tu doutes qu'il soit malade. (Subjunctive) (*You doubt that he's ill.*)

Now it's your turn. Choose between the present indicative and the subjunctive of the verbs in parentheses. Refer to the list of verbs and verbal expressions in Table 20-3 as a guide.

0. Il est vrai que nous _____ (vouloir) voyager.

A. Il est vrai que nous **voulons** voyager. (*It's true that we want to travel.*)

16. Êtes-vous sûr qu'il _____ (ne pas suivre) de cours?

17. Ne trouves-tu pas qu'il _____ (faire) froid?

18. Il est évident que tu _____ (savoir) parler français.

19. Je ne doute pas que mon équipe favori _____ (aller) gagner.

20. Il n'est pas clair que les droits humains _____ (être) respectés.

Showing Opinion, Necessity, and Possibility

The subjunctive is a mood of subjectivity. As such, any expression that expresses an opinion will be followed by the subjunctive. Expressions of necessity like **il faut que** (*it is necessary that*) as well as possibility like **il est possible que** (*it is possible that*) are also followed by the subjunctive. Table 20-4 lists these expressions.

Table 20-4	Phrases That Show Opinion, Necessity, and Possibility
French Phrase	*English Translation*
il est absurde que	*it is absurd that*
il est bizarre que	*it is strange/bizarre that*
il est bon que	*it is good that*
il est curieux que	*it is curious that*
il est essentiel que	*it is essential that*
il est étonnant que	*it is surprising that*
il est étrange que	*it is strange that*
il est important que	*it is important that*
il est impossible que	*it is impossible that*
il est indispensable que	*it is indispensable that*
il est injuste que	*it is unjust that*
il est inutile que	*it is useless that*
il est juste que	*it is just that*
il est naturel que	*it is natural that*

French Phrase	English Translation
il est nécessaire que	*it is necessary that*
il est normal que	*it is normal that*
il est possible que	*it is possible that*
il est regrettable que	*it is regrettable that*
il est ridicule que	*it is ridiculous that*
il est souhaitable que	*it is preferable/desirable that*
il est surprenant que	*it is surprising that*
il est utile que	*it is useful that*
il est dommage que	*it is too bad that*
il faut que	*it is necessary that*
il se peut que	*it may be that*
il vaut mieux que	*it is better that*

In all the expressions in Table 20-4, you can replace the **il est** (*it is*) with **c'est** (*it is*), except for the last three: **il faut que, il se peut que,** and **il vaut mieux que.**

> **Il se peut qu'il pleuve demain.** (*It may be that it will rain tomorrow.*)

Put the verb in parentheses in the present subjunctive.

Q. C'est utile que tu _____ (s'y connaître) en informatique.

A. C'est utile que tu **t'y connaisses** en informatique. (*It is useful that you know about computers.*)

21. Il vaut mieux que nous _____ (aller) nous coucher tôt ce soir.

22. Il est possible que mes beaux-parents _____ (prendre) leur retraite.

23. Il est nécessaire qu'Anne _____ (décrire) ses expériences.

24. C'est souhaitable que nous _____ (éviter) la circulation.

25. Il faut que je _____ (s'en aller).

Expressing Condition, Time, Concession, and Consequence

You also use the subjunctive after certain conjunctions, mainly the ones that express a condition or a concession. These conjunctions require the same criteria as the verbs or verbal expressions I mention in the previous sections. First, the subject in the main clause must be different from the subject of the subordinate clause. If the subject is the same, then use a preposition followed by the infinitive form of the verb. Second, these conjunctions must be followed by **que** (*that*).

The conjunctions listed in Table 20-5 connect two clauses. You use the subjunctive in the subordinate clause when the sentence has two different subjects. If the sentence has only one subject, these conjunctions become prepositions followed with an infinitive. Note that in such cases the **que** (*that*) is dropped, and most of the prepositions require **de** to introduce the infinitive.

Note: The translations in Table 20-5 apply to both the two subject clauses and single subject clauses.

Table 20-5   Using Subjunctive: Conjunctions or Prepositions?

Two Subject Clauses	Single Subject Clauses	Translation
à condition que	à condition de	*provided that*
*à moins que	à moins de	*unless*
afin que	afin de	*so that, in order that (to)*
*avant que	avant de	*before*
*de crainte que	de crainte de	*for fear (that)*
*de peur que	de peur de	*for fear (that)*
en attendant que	en attendant de	*while, until*
pour que	pour	*so that, in order that (to)*
sans que	sans	*without*

*See the following paragraph for more information on these conjunctions.

The conjunctions in Table 20-5 that have the asterisk before them can take the expletive **ne** before the subjunctive. And I know I said that **ne** is an expletive, but it's not a dirty word! In grammar, an expletive is a nonessential word or phrase that you don't need in the sentence in order to understand it. The expletive **ne** has no meaning, and you don't have to use it, but I highly recommend it because it's commonly used before the subjunctive after certain conjunctions even in casual conversations. Most importantly, you need to know that it doesn't make the verb negative. In order to make a verb negative, you put the **ne** before the conjugated verb and the **pas** or another negative expression after the verb.

> **Dépêchons-nous avant qu'il (ne) pleuve.** (*Let's hurry up before it rains.*)
>
> **Il étudie beaucoup de crainte que l'examen (ne) soit trop difficile.** (*He's studying a lot for fear that the exam is too difficult.*)

Note that you must always follow the conjunctions in Table 20-6 with a verb in the subjunctive, even when the clause has no change of subject. These conjunctions can never be prepositions.

Table 20-6   Conjunctions That Must Always Be Followed by the Subjunctive

Conjunction	English Translation
bien que	*although*
jusqu'à ce que	*until*

Conjunction	English Translation
pourvu que	*provided that*
quoique	*although*
quoi que	*whatever, no matter what*

Il jouera au match pourvu qu'il se sente bien. (*He will play in the game provided that he feels well.*)

Link these two clauses together by using a conjunction followed by the subjunctive or a preposition followed by the infinitive. Remember, the choice depends on the subject. If the sentence has one subject (the subjects in the two clauses are the same), use the preposition followed by an infinitive to link the sentences. If the sentence has two subjects (the subjects are different in each clause), use a conjunction followed by a verb in the subjunctive.

Q. Ils font des économies. (afin que/afin de) Ils peuvent aller en vacances.

A. Ils font des économies **afin de pouvoir** aller en vacances. (*They are saving money in order to be able to go on vacation.*)

26. Je te dis cela. (pour que/pour) Tu le sais.

_____

37. Nous ferons nos bagages. (avant que/avant de) Nous partons.

_____

38. Viens chez moi. (à moins que/à moins de) Tu as d'autres choses à faire.

_____

29. Le cambrioleur s'échappe. (de crainte que/de crainte de) La police vient.

_____

30. Mélanie va voyager. (à condition que/à condition de) Elle a de l'argent.

_____

Considering Indefinite, Doubtful, and Subjective Antecedents

An *antecedent* can be a noun, a pronoun, a concept, or a clause that comes before a relative pronoun and to which the relative pronoun refers. If you have a subordinate clause that refers to a concept (or antecedent) in the main clause, you may need to use the subjunctive. If the concept in the main clause is doubtful, indefinite, or subjective, you put the verb in the subordinate clause in the subjunctive. You also use the subjunctive after expressions such as **le seul** (*the only*), **l'unique** (*the unique*), **le premier** (*the first*), and **le dernier** (*the last*) in order to stress the rarity or the uniqueness of the antecedent. However, if you use these expressions to refer to factual or objective situations, then use the indicative in the subordinate clause.

C'est le meilleur professeur qui soit! (*He's the best professor ever there is!*) This is an exaggeration and therefore the verb is in the subjunctive.

Nous cherchons un hôtel qui ne soit pas trop cher. (*We are looking for a hotel that is not too expensive.*) This statement doesn't mean that we're never going to find a hotel that's reasonably priced. However, the mere fact that we're *looking for* an inexpensive hotel dictates the use of the subjunctive. When the verb **chercher** (*to look for*) is used affirmatively in the main clause, then put the verb in the subordinate clause in the subjunctive.

Connais-tu quelqu'un qui puisse s'occuper de mes enfants? (*Do you know anyone who can take care of my children?*) This question is the same type of concept as the previous two examples. Because you're asking if someone knows someone who can take care of the children, this warrants the use of the subjunctive in the subordinate clause.

However, when the main clause refers to a definite, concluded, or factual person or thing, you use the indicative in the subordinate clause.

C'est la plus mauvaise note que j'ai ce semestre. (*It's the worst grade that I have this semester.*) Even though this statement is superlative (the worst), it's factual rather than subjective. Therefore, you use the indicative.

Nous avons trouvé un hôtel qui n'est pas trop cher. (*We found a hotel that is not too expensive.*) We already found the hotel; therefore this is factual, and the verb in the subordinate clause is in the indicative and not the subjunctive.

Look at the antecedents and decide whether you would use the subjunctive or the indicative in the subordinate clause, and then correctly conjugate the verb.

Q. Le directeur cherche un assistant qui _____ (pouvoir) gérer sa compagnie.

A. Le directeur cherche un assistant qui **puisse** gérer sa compagnie. (*The director is looking for an assistant who can manage his company.*)

31. Y a-t-il un restaurant qui _____ (servir) des spécialités françaises?

32. Je connais quelqu'un qui _____ (être) très fort en mathématiques.

33. C'est le plus beau tableau que je _____ (voir) à l'exposition.

34. Elle veut trouver une femme de ménage qui _____ (faire) aussi la cuisine.

35. C'est la plus grande valise que _____ (vendre) ce magasin.

Looking at Idiomatic Expressions and Commands

You probably already know at least one idiomatic expression in French that takes the subjunctive. Have you heard this: **Vive la France!** (*Long live France!*)? Well, the verb is in the subjunctive. As in this phrase, you can use the subjunctive alone, without the requirement of a main clause, when it's part of an idiomatic expression. Take a look at the following idiomatic expressions.

Vive la France! (*Long live France!*)

Soit! (*So be it!*)

Ainsi soit-il! (*Amen!*)

Que je sache. (*As far as I know.*)

You also use the subjunctive as a command in the third person singular or plural preceded by the relative pronoun **que** (*that*).

Qu'il sorte! (*Have him leave!* Literally: *That he leave!*)

Qu'elle se taise! (*Have her be quiet!*)

Qu'ils reviennent! (*Have them come back!*)

Translate the following sentences into French.

Q. Have them eat!

A. **Qu'ils mangent.**

36. Long live love!

_____

_____

37. Have him speak!

_____

_____

38. Have them drink!

_____

_____

39. As far as she knows.

_____

_____

40. Have her sing!

_____

_____

Answer Key

In this section, you can find the correct answers to the practice problems in this chapter. Closely review your answers and compare them to the correct ones.

1 Les professeurs proposent que nous **lisions** attentivement. (*The professors propose that we read attentively.*)

2 Tu tiens à ce que je **vienne** avec toi. (*You insist that I come with you.*)

3 Le pilote ordonne que nous **attachions** notre ceinture de sécurité. (*The pilot orders that we fasten our seat belts.*)

4 Le médecin n'aime pas que ses patients **touchent** l'équipement médical. (*The doctor doesn't like that the patients touch the medical equipment.*)

5 La loi empêche que l'on **jette** les ordures dans la rue. (*The law prevents that one throw garbage in the street.*)

6 J'apprécie que tu me **comprennes.** (*I appreciate that you understand me.*)

7 Alexandre préfère que nous **voyagions** ensemble. (*Alexandre prefers that we travel together.*)

8 Mes parents refusent que je **prenne** la voiture. (*My parents refuse that I take the car.*)

9 Céline propose qu'on **aille** au cinéma. (*Céline proposes that we go to the movies.*)

10 Nous souhaitons que nos amis **aient** de bonnes notes. (*We wish that our friends have good grades.*)

11 Je suis ravi que vous **puissiez** venir. (*I am delighted that you can come.*)

12 Nous sommes surpris que tu **n'aies pas** d'argent. (*We are surprised that you don't have any money.*)

13 Le professeur est furieux que les étudiants **ne fassent pas** attention. (*The professor is furious that the students are not paying attention.*)

14 Mme Castel est triste que son fils **vive** dans un tel état. (*Mme Castel is sad that her son lives in such a state/condition.*)

15 Les enfants sont déçus qu'il **pleuve.** (*The children are disappointed that it is raining.*)

16 Êtes-vous sûr qu'il **ne suive pas** de cours? (*Are you sure that he is not taking any courses?*)

17 Ne trouves-tu pas qu'il **fasse** froid? (*Don't you find that it's cold?*)

18 Il est évident que tu **sais** parler français. (*It's evident that you know how to speak French.*)

19 Je ne doute pas que mon équipe favori **va** gagner. (*I don't doubt that my favorite team is going to win.*)

20 Il n'est pas clair que les droits humains **soient** respectés. (*It is not clear that human rights are respected.*)

21 Il vaut mieux que nous **allions** nous coucher tôt ce soir. (*It is better that we go to bed early this evening.*)

22 Il est possible que mes beaux-parents **prennent** leur retraite. (*It is possible that my in-laws take their retirement.*)

23 Il est nécessaire qu'Anne **décrive** ses expériences. (*It is necessary that Anne describe her experiences.*)

24 C'est souhaitable que nous **évitions** la circulation. (*It is preferable that we avoid the traffic.*)

25 Il faut que je **m'en aille.** (*It is necessary that I leave* or *I have to leave.*)

26 Je te dis cela **pour que** tu le **saches.** (*I am telling you this so that you know it.*)

27 Nous ferons nos bagages **avant de partir.** (*We will pack before leaving.*)

28 Viens chez moi **à moins d'avoir** d'autres choses à faire. (*Come to my house unless you have other things to do.*)

29 Le cambrioleur s'échappe **de crainte que** la police (ne) **vienne.** (*The burglar escapes for fear that the police will come.*)

30 Mélanie va voyager **à condition d'avoir** de l'argent. (*Mélanie is going to travel provided that she has money.*)

31 Y a-t-il un restaurant qui **serve** des spécialités françaises? (*Is there a restaurant that serves French specialities?*)

32 Je connais quelqu'un qui **est** très fort en mathématiques. (*I know someone who is very good/ strong in Math.*)

33 C'est le plus beau tableau que je **voie** à l'exposition. (*It is the most beautiful painting that I see in the exhibit.*)

34 Elle veut trouver une femme de ménage qui **fasse** aussi la cuisine. (*She wants to find a cleaning woman who also cooks.*)

35 C'est la plus grande valise que **vend** ce magasin. (*It's the biggest suitcase that this store sells.*)

36 **Vive l'amour!**

37 **Qu'il parle!**

38 **Qu'ils boivent!**

39 **Qu'elle sache.**

40 **Qu'elle chante!**

Chapter 21

Forming and Using the Past Subjunctive

. . . .

In This Chapter
▶ Creating the past subjunctive
▶ Using the past subjunctive
▶ Choosing between the present and past subjunctive

. . . .

*I*n French you use the past subjunctive much more often than in English. It's a compound tense and is used to express a completed action in the past. The choice between the present and past subjunctive depends on the time relationship between the main clause and the subordinate clause.

You use the past subjunctive, also known as the *perfect subjunctive,* in oral as well as written French. It follows the same rules as the present subjunctive that I talk about in Chapters 19 and 20. Use the past subjunctive when the action of the verb in the subordinate clause takes place before the action of the main verb. That sounds tricky, but you can see an example of this in this sentence: **Je suis triste que mon ami ne soit pas venu à ma boom hier** means *I am sad that my friend did not come to my party yesterday.* In this chapter I first show you how to form the past subjunctive and then how to correctly use it.

Forming the Past Subjunctive

Like all past tenses in French, the past subjunctive needs an auxiliary and a past participle of a verb of your choice. Remember that French has two auxiliaries — **avoir** (*to have*) and **être** (*to be*). To form the past subjunctive, you put these two auxiliaries in the present subjunctive and add the past participle. For a list of verbs taking these auxiliaries as well as a list of past participles, see Chapter 12.

The past subjunctive follows the same rules of agreement as any other compound past tense. If the auxiliary of the verb is **être**, then the past participle agrees with the subject. If the auxiliary of the verb is **avoir**, then the past participle agrees with the preceding direct object if the sentence has one. If the sentence doesn't have a preceding direct object, then the past participle doesn't change.

All pronominal verbs take the auxiliary **être**, but they follow the same rule of agreement as those taking the auxiliary **avoir**. The past participle agrees with the preceding direct object if the sentence has one. In the following examples, I conjugate an **avoir** verb (**voir**), an **être** verb (**partir**), and a pronominal verb (**se lever**) in the past subjunctive tense.

voir (*to see*)	
que j'**aie vu**	que nous **ayons vu**
que tu **aies vu**	que vous **ayez vu**
qu'il/elle/on **ait vu**	qu'ils/elles **aient vu**
C'est le meilleur film que j'**aie vu.** (*It's the best film that I've seen.*)	

partir (*to leave*)	
que je **sois parti(e)**	que nous **soyons partis(es)**
que tu **sois parti(e)**	que vous **soyez parti(s)(e)(es)**
qu'il/elle/on **soit parti(e)**	qu'ils/elles **soient partis(es)**
Il est triste que tu **sois parti.** (*He's sad that you left.*)	

se lever (*to get up*)	
que je **me sois levé(e)**	que nous **nous soyons levés(es)**
que tu **te sois levé(e)**	que vous **vous soyez levé(s)(e)(es)**
qu'il/elle/on **se sois levé(e)**	qu'ils/elles **se soient levés(es)**
Il est surprenant que vous **vous soyez leve** si tôt. (*It is surprising that you got up so early.*)	

Put the verbs in parentheses in the past subjunctive.

O. . . . que tu _____ (faire)

A. . . . que tu **aies fait**

1. . . . que nous _____ (venir)

2. . . . qu'ils _____ (chercher)

3. . . . que tu _____ (tomber)

4. . . . que vous _____ (demander)

5. . . . qu'elle _____ (rester)

Using the Past Subjunctive

The past subjunctive is like any other past tense. You use it in the subordinate clause; it follows the same rules as the present subjunctive. The verb or verbal expression in the main clause must express a wish, will, command, emotion, doubt, or a subjective point of view in order for the verb in the subordinate clause to be in the subjunctive. Remember: Use the past subjunctive when the action of the verb in the subordinate clause comes before the action of the verb in the main clause.

The choice between the present and past subjunctive doesn't depend on the tense of the verb in the main clause. The verb in the main clause can be in the present, past, future, or even the conditional.

> **Mon grand-père était surpris que je ne sois pas allé le voir.** (*My grandfather was surprised that I did not go to see him.*)

Try putting the verbs in parentheses in the past subjunctive. Check out the sample practice problem if you need help.

Q. Elle aurait préféré que nous _____ (téléphoner)

A. Elle aurait préféré que nous **ayons téléphoné.** (*She would have preferred that we called.*)

6. C'est dommage que ton chien _____ (mourir).

7. Croyez-vous qu'ils _____ (ne pas prendre) de vacances depuis trois ans?

8. Nous sommes ravis que notre fille _____ (recevoir) son diplôme.

9. J'étais surpris que tu _____ (ne pas téléphoner).

10. Je regrette qu'ils _____ (finir) avant sept heures.

Distinguishing between the Present and Past Subjunctive

You choose either the present or past subjunctive based on the time relationship of the action of the verb in the subordinate clause with the verb in the main clause.

Use the present subjunctive when the action of the verb in the subordinate clause occurs at the same time or after the action of the main verb.

> **Je suis triste que tu partes.** (*I am sad that you are leaving.*)
>
> **J'étais triste que tu partes.** (*I was sad that you were leaving.*)
>
> **Je serai triste que tu partes.** (*I will be sad that you will be leaving.*)

Use the past subjunctive when the action of the subordinate verb occurs before the action of the main verb.

> **Je suis triste que tu sois parti.** (*I am sad that you left.*)
>
> **J'étais triste que tu sois parti.** (*I was sad that you left.*)
>
> **Je serai triste que tu sois parti.** (*I will be sad that you left.*)

Decide between the present and past subjunctive in the following practice problems. Remember that if the action of the verb in the subordinate clause occurs at the same time or after the action of the main verb, you use the present subjunctive. But if the action of the subordinate verb occurs before the action of the main verb, use the past subjunctive.

Q. Bien qu'il _____ (essayer) d'ouvrir la porte, il n'a pas pu.

A. Bien qu'il **ait essayé** d'ouvrir la porte, il n'a pas pu. (*Even though he tried to open the door, he was not able to.*)

11. Je suis content que tu _____ (venir) hier soir.

12. Il faut que tu le _____ (faire) maintenant.

13. Bien que maman _____ (préparer) un grand repas, personne n'avait faim.

14. Tout le monde regrette que vous _____ (être) licencié.

15. Je lirai en attendant que tu _____ (s'habiller).

16. C'est le meilleur film que je jamais _____ (voir).

17. Nos parents nous laisseront sortir pourvu que nous _____ (amener) notre soeur.

18. J'aurais voulu que tu _____ (finir) tes études avant de te marier.

19. Il est nécessaire que nous _____ (apprendre) le subjonctif.

20. Il vaut mieux que vous lui _____ (téléphoner) avant de le voir.

Answer Key

This section contains the answers to the practice problems in this chapter. Compare your answers to the correct answers. (I don't provide translations for problems 1–5 because they're only verb conjugations and aren't complete sentences.)

1 . . . que nous **soyons venus(es)**

2 . . . qu'ils **aient cherché**

3 . . . que tu **sois tombé(e)**

4 . . . que vous **ayez demandé**

5 . . . qu'elle **soit restée**

6 C'est dommage que ton chien **soit mort.** (*It is too bad that your dog died.*)

7 Croyez-vous qu'ils **n'aient pas pris** de vacances depuis trois ans? (*Do you believe that they did not take a vacation for three years?*)

8 Nous sommes ravis que notre fille **ait reçu** son diplôme. (*We are delighted that our daughter received her diploma.*)

9 J'étais surpris que tu **n'aies pas téléphoné.** (*I was surprised that you didn't call.*)

10 Je regrette qu'ils **n'aient pas fini** avant sept heures. (*I regret that they did not finish before seven o'clock.*)

11 Je suis content que tu **sois venu(e)** hier soir. (*I am happy that you came yesterday evening.*)

12 Il faut que tu le **fasses** maintenant. (*It is necessary that you do it now.*)

13 Bien que maman **ait préparé** un grand repas, personne n'avait faim. (*Even though mom prepared a big meal, no one was hungry.*)

14 Tout le monde regrette que vous **ayez été** licencié. (*Everyone regrets that you were laid off.*)

15 Je lirai en attendant que tu **t'habilles.** (*I will read while waiting that you get dressed.*)

16 C'est le meilleur film que j'**aie jamais vu.** (*It's the best film that I ever saw.*)

17 Nos parents nous laisseront sortir pourvu que nous **amenions** notre soeur. (*Our parents will allow us to go out provided that we bring our sister.*)

18 J'aurais voulu que tu **aies fini** tes études avant de te marier. (*I would have liked that you had finished your studies before getting married.*)

19 Il est nécessaire que nous **apprenions** le subjonctif. (*It is necessary that we learn the subjunctive.*)

20 Il vaut mieux que vous lui **téléphoniez** avant de le voir. (*It is better that you call him before seeing him.*)

Part VI
The Part of Tens

The 5th Wave   By Rich Tennant

"Maybe next time you'll learn your negative verbs in French before having a suit made in Paris."

In this part . . .

This part is similar to one in every other *For Dummies* book. Here I include some great information in a nutshell that doesn't necessarily fit anywhere else in this book. In this part, I include two chapters with fun information that you can quickly absorb. Chapter 22 looks at ten verbs that are used the French way. Chapter 23 looks at ten verbs that are often frequently mixed-up between French and English.

Chapter 22

Ten Verbs Used the French Way

In This Chapter
▶ Distinguishing transitive from intransitive verbs
▶ Making sense of the prepositions

*I*f you've ever tried to translate something from one language to another, you probably didn't translate literally or word for word. If you did translate literally, you probably noticed something that didn't quite jive in the translation. That's because every language has a way of saying things that's unique to that language and therefore different in other languages.

French is no different. In this chapter, I help you avoid pitfalls regarding ten verbs that are used transitively in English but intransitively in French and vice versa. This means that some verbs are followed by a direct object in one language but not in the other, and some verbs take a preposition in one language but not in the other. *Transitive verbs* are followed by a direct object, whereas *intransitive verbs* aren't. (Chapter 1 gives you the complete lowdown on the differences between transitive and intransitive verbs.) This chapter looks more closely at ten common verbs that you may use in everyday conversation. (Please know that this list isn't exhaustive; I only list ten of the most common.) I start first with verbs that are transitive in French, but intransitive in English, and then move to the intransitive French verbs (and transitive English verbs).

Attendre (To Wait For)

The first French transitive verb that comes to mind is **attendre** (*to wait for*). (In English this verb is intransitive.) Think of the preposition *for* as being built into the verb itself and therefore making any other preposition unnecessary.

> **Nous attendons le train.** (*We are waiting for the train.*)
>
> **Ils attendent le professeur.** (*They are waiting for their professor.*)

Chercher (To Look For)

The verb **chercher** (*to look for*) is another verb that's transitive in French and intransitive in English. In French you say **Je cherche les clés,** which is literally *I'm looking the keys,* but in good English is *I'm looking for the keys.* The preposition *for* is built into the verb. You also use the verb **chercher** to mean *to pick up someone.* So don't panic if someone says, **Je vais chercher mes enfants à l'école.** This statement doesn't necessarily mean that *I am going to look for my children in school* in the sense that they are lost in the school — instead it means *I'm picking them up.*

Écouter (To Listen To)

Écouter (*to listen to*) is also transitive in French but intransitive in English. Notice that the following example doesn't use a preposition between the verb **écouter** and the noun, unlike in English where you use the preposition *to*.

> **Il écoute la radio.** (*He is listening to the radio.*)
>
> **Nous écoutons le president.** (*We are listening to the president.*)

Payer (To Pay)

When you go shopping, how do you pay for your purchases? How do you pay for your movie ticket or even the grocery bill? In French, the verb **payer** (*to pay*) is transitive and doesn't need a preposition (like *for*) after it like it does in English.

> **Tu paies les provisions.** (*You are paying for the groceries.*)
>
> **Nous payons les billets d'avion.** (*We are paying for the plane tickets.*)

However, don't use the verb **payer** to mean *to pay a visit to someone;* instead use the verb **rendre visite à** (see Chapter 23).

Regarder (To Look At, To Watch)

The last French transitive verb that I cover in this chapter is the verb **regarder** (*to look at, to watch*). In French, this verb is always followed by the direct object, regardless of how you translate it in English.

> **Il regarde les oiseaux.** (*He is looking at the birds.*)

Regarder also means *to watch,* and in that sense, it's transitive in both English and French.

> **Vous regardez le match.** (*You are watching the game.*)
>
> **Je regarde la télé.** (*I'm watching television.*)

Demander (To Ask)

The first intransitive French verb (but transitive English verb) that I cover is **demander** (*to ask*). With this verb and the following four verbs in this chapter, you follow the verb with the preposition **à** in French. When you ask someone a question, use the verb **demander à** followed by the person.

> **Les étudiants demandent au professeur d'expliquer la leçon.** (*The students ask the professor to explain the lesson.*)
>
> **Elle demande à ses parents si elle peut sortir.** (*She asks her parents if she can go out.*)

However, don't use the verb **demander à** when you want to ask a question; use the verb **poser** (*to put, to ask*) followed by the noun **une question** (*a question*). The person to whom you are asking the question is still indirect with this verb. The following examples clarify this construction.

> **Il pose une question.** (*He is asking a question.*)
>
> **Il pose une question au directeur.** (*He is asking a question to the director.*)

Obéir (To Obey)

You also add the preposition **à** to the verb **obéir** (*to obey*). In French, you must say to obey *to* someone, and therefore the person is the indirect object instead of the direct object. In English, the person is the direct object. The fact that you're obeying something rather than someone doesn't change the structure of the verb. You still need the preposition **à**.

> **Les enfants obéissent à leurs parents.** (*The children obey their parents.*)
>
> **Nous obéissons à la loi.** (*We obey the law.*)

Permettre (To Allow)

The same rule applies to the verb **permettre** (*to allow*). That is to say that in French, you allow *to* someone to do something, and therefore you need the preposition **à** before the noun. This verb is intransitive in French but transitive in English.

> **Le directeur permet aux employés de partir tôt.** (*The director allows the employees to leave early.*)
>
> **Mme Meneau permet à sa fille de sortir avec Mathieu.** (*Mrs. Meneau allows her daughter to go out with Mathieu.*)

Répondre (To Answer)

Another verb that you use differently in French than in English is the verb **répondre** (*to answer*). In French, you answer *to* someone as well as *to* a question.

> **Tu réponds à la question.** (*You answer the question.*)
>
> **Nous répondons à notre entraîneur.** (*We are answering our coach.*)

Téléphoner (To Telephone, To Call)

When you call someone, you actually call *to* someone in French. This meaning is conveyed by the verb **téléphoner,** followed by the preposition **à,** and then followed by either a person or a place.

> **Je téléphone à mes amis.** (*I am calling my friends.*)
>
> **Ils téléphonent à leurs parents.** (*They call their parents.*)
>
> **Nous téléphonons au bureau.** (*We're calling the office.*)

Chapter 23

Ten Most Frequently Mixed-Up Verbs

In This Chapter
▶ Deciphering nuances
▶ Recognizing false friends

rench has many ways a nonnative speaker can mix up verbs or use them incorrectly. The mix-ups are a result of these three problems:

✔ These verbs sound like or are spelled similarly to an English verb. An example is **rester.** This verb doesn't mean *to rest;* it means *to stay.*

✔ These verbs have the same meaning in English but are used differently in French. For example, the verb **visiter** means (you guessed it) *to visit,* but you can't use it to say that you're visiting friends. (Refer to "Visiting a Place or Visiting a Person" in this chapter.)

✔ Other verbs change their meanings by changing the preposition that follows them. One common example is the verb **jouer** (*to play*). It can take the preposition **à** or **de,** depending on what you're playing. (Check out "Playing a Game or Playing an Instrument" later in this chapter for more info.)

This chapter shows you how to use these verbs correctly and explains the nuances that they may entail. (Chapter 10 also looks at different types of verbs that nonnatives sometimes mix up.)

Visiting a Place or Visiting a Person

French has two different verbs that mean *to visit.* One is **visiter,** which is a regular **-er** verb conjugated just like **parler** (*to speak*) — see Chapter 2 for more on regular **-er** verbs. Use the verb **visiter** to visit places, such as cities, countries, museums, and so on.

> **Nous avons visité le Louvre l'année dernière.** (*We visited the Louvre last year.*)
>
> **Ils visiteront le Tibet au printemps.** (*They will visit Tibet in the spring.*)

To visit a person, use the verbal construction **rendre visite à,** which translates as *to pay a visit to* someone. You conjugate the verb **rendre,** which is a regular **-re** verb, and keep **visite** the way it is. Just remember to add the preposition **à** before the person or people you're visiting. The person or people to whom you're paying a visit are always the indirect object of this verb.

> **Il rend visite à ses grands-parents chaque été.** (*He visits his grandparents every summer.*)
>
> **Est-ce que tu as rendu visite à tes amis hier?** (*Did you visit your friends yesterday?*)

Spending Time or Spending Money

English doesn't have a difference between spending time or spending money because both constructions use the same verb. In French, the verb to use when you spend time doing something is **passer.**

Je passe mon temps à jardiner. (*I spend my time gardening.*)

Les enfants ont passé leur été à jouer à la plage. (*The children spent their summer playing at the beach.*)

In addition to meaning *to spend,* you also use **passer** in the construction **passer un examen,** which means *to take an exam,* such as with **Les étudiants ont passé cinq examens cette semaine** (*The students took five exams this week*). In this context, the verb doesn't actually tell you anything about whether the students passed the exam or not.

To express spending money, use the verb **dépenser.**

Elle a dépensé tout son salaire. (*She spent her entire salary.*)

Nous dépensons beaucoup d'argent au centre commercial. (*We spend a lot of money at the mall.*)

Sometimes you use the verb **dépenser** to express other things that you spend (or use), such as gas, water, or electricity.

La climatisation dépense beaucoup d'électricité. (*Air conditioning uses a lot of electricity.*)

Knowing People or Places or Knowing Something

French has two different verbs that mean *to know.* You use one for people and places, and you use the other for facts and saying that you know how to do something.

Use the verb **connaître** with people, places, and things. It expresses the idea that you're acquainted with or have a familiarity with someone or something. You need to follow this verb with a direct object because it's a transitive verb; it can't be followed by a clause or by another verb. (Check out Chapter 1 for more on transitive verbs.)

Je connais le PDG de l'entreprise. (*I know the CEO of the company.*)

Connaissez-vous l'histoire de la France? (*Do you know the history of France?*)

Nous connaissons le Quartier Latin. (*We know the Latin Quarter.*)

On the other hand, the verb **savoir** means to know facts, such as dates, names, addresses, and telephone numbers, or to know something by heart, as well as to know how to do something.

Il sait le numéro de téléphone de Céline. (*He knows Celine's telephone number.*)

Nous savons parler arabe. (*We know how to speak Arabic.*)

Je sais quand il part. (*I know when he's leaving.*)

When you want to say, *I know* or *I don't know,* you use the verb **savoir.**

Savez-vous quelle heure il est? (*Do you know what time it is?*)

Je ne sais pas. (*I don't know.*)

Playing a Game or Playing an Instrument

To play a game, a sport, or an instrument, use the verb **jouer** (*to play*), which is a regular **-er** verb (check out Chapter 2). That's not so confusing, but the preposition that follows this verb makes all the difference. Use **jouer** with the preposition **à** when playing sports or a game.

Les enfants jouent au football le samedi. (*The children play soccer on Saturdays.*)

Nous jouons aux échecs. (*We play chess.*)

When playing a musical instrument, use **jouer** with the preposition **de.**

Mes filles jouent du violon. (*My daughters play violin.*)

Il aime jouer de la batterie. (*He likes to play the drums.*)

Leaving or Leaving Something Behind

The verbs **partir, s'en aller, quitter,** and **laisser** all mean *to leave,* but you use them differently.

Partir and **s'en aller** are synonyms. When you want to say quite simply *I am leaving* or *someone or something is leaving,* use these verbs.

Je m'en vais. (*I'm leaving.*)

Il part. (*He is leaving.*)

Le train part à dix heures. (*The train leaves at 10 o'clock.*)

On the other hand, the verb **quitter** is always followed by a direct object. In other words, use this verb when you're leaving a place or a person. When **quitter** is used with people, it usually means *to abandon.*

Elle a quitté la salle. (*She left the room.*)

Il a quitté sa femme. (*He left his wife.*)

The verb **laisser** means that you're leaving something behind.

J'ai laissé mes clés dans la voiture. (*I left my keys in the car.*)

Ils laissent leurs affaires partout. (*They leave their things everywhere.*)

You also use the verb **laisser** to mean *to allow* or *to let* someone do something when it's followed by an infinitive.

Je laisse jouer les enfants. (*I let the children play.*)

Il me laisse partir. (*He's letting me leave.*)

Returning Home, Returning Something, or Just Returning

French has four verbs that mean *to return* or *to come back*. They are **retourner, rentrer, revenir,** and **rendre.** You use **retourner** for coming back to a place other than home.

Le chien retourne à son endroit favori. (*The dog returns to his favorite spot.*)

Les étudiants retournent à l'école. (*The students return to school.*)

You use the verb **revenir** (*to come back*) like the verb **retourner** (*to return*), but **revenir** implies to come back to the same place you set off from. The verbs **retourner** and **revenir** take the auxiliary **être** when used in a compound past tense like the passé composé. (See Chapter 12 for more on the passé composé.) Unlike **revenir**, **retourner** can be followed by a direct object, in which case it takes the auxiliary **avoir.**

Je reviendrai dans un quart d'heure. (*I'll be back in 15 minutes.*)

You use the verb **rentrer** to mean *to return home*. Remember that this verb, like the verbs **revenir** and **retourner**, takes the auxiliary **être** when you use it in a compound past tense like the passé composé.

Nous sommes rentrés tard hier soir. (*We came back [home] late last night.*)

Elle rentre toujours à sept heures. (*She always comes home at 7 o'clock.*)

You use **rendre** when you return something, usually a borrowed object, or when you give something back.

Il a rendu les livres à la bibliothèque. (*He returned the books to the library.*)

Le professeur rend les compositions. (*The professor is giving back the compositions.*)

Leading, Bringing, or Taking Someone

The verbs **amener, ramener, emmener,** and **remmener** are all compounds of the verb **mener** (*to lead*).

Le Maire mène le défilé. (*The Mayor is leading the parade.*)

Elle mène une vie privée. (*She leads a private life.*)

Amener means *to bring someone somewhere*, and **ramener** means *to bring someone back*.

Elle amène ses enfants à l'école. (*She brings her children to school.*)

Elle ramène ses enfants de l'école. (*She brings back her children from school.*)

Emmener means *to take someone along*, and **remmener** means *to take someone back*.

Quand nous allons en vacances, nous emmenons notre fille. (*When we go on vacation, we take our daughter along.*)

Il doit remmener sa petite amie. (*He has to take his girlfriend back.*)

Carrying, Bringing, Taking, or Taking Back Something

Apporter, rapporter, emporter, and **remporter** are compounds of **porter** (*to wear*). You can use these verbs with things. You also use the verb **porter** when you *carry something*.

Nous portons notre sac à dos. (*We are carrying our book bag.*)

Le petit chaperon rouge porte une corbeille. (*Little Red Riding Hood is carrying a basket.*)

The verb **apporter** means *to bring something,* and **rapporter** is *to bring something back.*

Je vais apporter une bouteille de vin. (*I am going to bring a bottle of wine.*)

Papa, rapporte des chocolats de Suisse. (*Dad, bring some chocolates back from Switzerland.*)

To take something along with you, use the verb **emporter.**

Nous emportons des vêtements chauds pour notre voyage en Alaska. (*We are taking warm clothes for our trip to Alaska.*)

Also, use **emporter** when you *take out* or *carry out* food.

Ce restaurant a des plats délicieux à emporter. (*This restaurant has delicious meals to/for takeout.*)

Remporter means *to take back* or *to take away.*

Remportez le bifteck, ce n'est pas assez cuit. (*Take back the steak; it's not cooked enough.*)

Les étudiants remportent leurs cahiers à la fin du semestre. (*The students take back their notebooks at the end of the semester.*)

Thinking or Thinking About

In French, the verb **penser** (*to think*) is a regular **-er** verb. However, you can follow this verb with either the preposition **à** or the preposition **de.** How do you choose between these two prepositions? Well, if you want to say that you're *thinking about someone or something,* use the preposition **à.**

Il pense à ses enfants. (*He's thinking of/about his children.*)

Nous pensons à notre avenir. (*We're thinking about our future.*)

You use **penser de** to ask the question *What do you think about someone or something?*

Qu'est-ce que tu penses de ton patron? (*What do you think of your boss?*)

Que pensent-ils du film? (*What do they think about the film?*)

Don't use the preposition **de** to answer these questions. Instead, use **penser que** in your response.

> **Qu'est-ce que tu penses de ton patron?** (*What do you think of your boss?*)
>
> You answer: **Je pense qu'il est gentil.** (*I think he is nice.*)

Waiting or Attending

French has many false friends, or **faux amis.** These false friends are words that may look the same as a word in English but have a different meaning. This is the case with the verbs **attendre** and **assister à.** Keep in mind that **attendre** doesn't mean *to attend* and **assister à** doesn't mean *to assist.* In fact, **assister à** means *to attend.* Don't forget to use the preposition **à** after this verb.

> **Nous assisterons à la conference.** (*We will attend the lecture/conference.*)
>
> **Ils assistent au match.** (*They are attending the game.*)

Attendre means *to wait for* and is a transitive verb in French that's followed by a direct object. (Refer to Chapter 1 for more on transitive verbs.)

> **Elle attend ses amies.** (*She's waiting for her friends.*)
>
> **J'attends les résultats.** (*I'm waiting for the results.*)

Part VII
Appendixes

The 5th Wave — By Rich Tennant

©RICHTENNANT

"...and remember, no more French tongue twisters until you know the language better."

In this part . . .

This part includes three appendixes, two of which are very helpful glossaries: Appendix A is a French-to-English verb glossary where I list all the French verbs that I use in this book (and a few bonus ones) along with their English translations, and Appendix B is an English-to-French glossary that lists the verbs first by the English followed by a French translation. Appendix C may be one of the most helpful pieces in this book because it helps you keep irregular verbs in order.

Appendix A
French-to-English Verb Glossary

....

Have you encountered a French verb, but aren't sure of its translation? Not to worry. Just use this glossary to find its English meaning. This glossary doesn't contain every single French verb, but it does include all the French verbs I use in this book and a few more bonus ones. I place an asterisk beside the French verb to alert you that it's an irregular verb. (Check out Appendix C to see how to conjugate the irregular verbs.) All the regular verbs are conjugated the same way, depending on whether the verb is an **-er, -ir,** or **-re** verb.

accueillir*: *to welcome, to greet*

accuser: *to accuse*

acheter: *to buy*

admettre*: *to admit*

admirer: *to admire*

adorer: *to adore*

agacer: *to annoy, to irritate*

agir: *to act*

s'agir de: *to be a question of, to be about*

aimer: *to like, to love*

aller*: *to go*

amener: *to bring someone*

s'amuser: *to have fun*

annoncer: *to announce, to declare*

apercevoir*: *to perceive, to notice*

apparaître*: *to appear*

appartenir*: *to belong to*

appeler: *to call*

s'appeler: *to be named*

apporter: *to bring something*

apprendre*: *to learn*

arranger: *to arrange*

s'arrêter: *to stop oneself*

arriver: *to arrive*

assister à: *to attend*

attacher: *to attach*

attendre: *to wait for*

avancer: *to advance*

avoir*: *to have*

se baigner: *to bathe*

balancer: *to swing*

balayer: *to sweep*

bâtir: *to build*

bavarder: *to chat, to talk*

bercer: *to rock, to cradle*

blesser: *to hurt, to wound*

boire*: *to drink*

bouger: *to move*

se brosser: *to brush*

bronzer: *to tan*

cacher: *to hide*

célébrer: *to celebrate*

changer: *to change*

chanter: *to sing*

chercher: *to look for*

choisir: *to choose*

se coiffer: *to do one's hair*

commencer: *to begin*

commettre*: *to commit*

comparer: *to compare*

comprendre*: *to understand*

compromettre*: *to compromise*

concevoir*: *to conceive*

conduire*: *to drive*

congeler: *to freeze*

connaître*: *to know*

conseiller: *to advise*

consentir*: *to consent*

construire*: *to construct, to build*

contenir*: *to contain*

continuer: *to continue*

contredire*: *to contradict*

corriger: *to correct*

se coucher: *to go to bed*

couper: *to cut*

couvrir*: *to cover*

craindre*: *to fear*

croire*: *to believe*

cueillir*: *to pick, to gather*

cuire*: *to cook*

danser: *to dance*

se débrouiller: *to manage*

déceler: *to detect, to reveal*

décevoir*: *to disappoint*

décider: *to decide*

décourager: *to discourage*

découvrir*: *to discover*

décrire*: *to describe*

dédicacer: *to sign, to autograph*

défendre: *to defend*

défendre de: *to forbid*

demander: *to ask*

se demander: *to wonder*

déménager: *to move, to change residence*

dénoncer: *to denounce*

se dépêcher: *to hurry*

déplacer: *to displace*

déranger: *to bother, to disturb*

descendre: *to go down, to take down*

désirer: *to desire, to want*

détester: *to hate*

devenir*: *to become*

devoir*: *to have to, to must, to owe*

dire*: *to say*

disparaître*: *to disappear*

disputer: *to argue*

divorcer: *to get a divorce*

donner: *to give*

dormir*: *to sleep*

écouter: *to listen*

écrire*: *to write*

effacer: *to erase*

effrayer: *to frighten, to scare*

élire*: *to elect*

embrasser: *to kiss, to embrace*

emmener: *to take someone along*

employer: *to use*

emporter: *to take something along*

s'en aller*: *to leave*

encourager: *to encourage*

s'endormir*: *to fall asleep*

s'énerver: *to become irritated*

ennuyer: *to bother*

s'ennuyer: *to be bored*

enrager: *to be furious, to be in a rage*

enseigner: *to teach*

entendre: *to hear*

s'entendre: *to get along*

entreprendre*: *to undertake*

entrer: *to enter*

entrevoir*: *to catch a glimpse of, to make out*

envoyer: *to send*

épeler: *to spell*

espérer: *to hope*

essayer: *to try*

essuyer: *to wipe*

établir: *to establish*

être*: *to be*

étudier: *to study*

exagérer: *to exaggerate*

s'excuser: *to excuse oneself*

exiger: *to require, to demand*

faire*: *to do, to make*

se fiancer: *to be/get engaged*

finir: *to finish*

fondre: *to melt*

forcer: *to force, to compel*

geler: *to freeze*

glacer: *to chill, to glaze*

grandir: *to grow (up)*

grossir: *to gain weight*

guérir: *to cure, to heal*

s'habiller: *to get dressed*

habiter: *to live (somewhere), to reside*

hésiter: *to hesitate*

infliger: *to inflict, to impose*

influencer: *to influence*

s' inquiéter: *to be worried*

interdire*: *to forbid*

inviter: *to invite*

jeter: *to throw*

jouer: *to play*

juger: *to judge*

laisser: *to allow, to let, to leave something/someone*

(se) laver: *to wash*

lever: *to raise, to lift*

se lever: *to get up*

lire*: *to read*

loger: *to accommodate, to lodge*

maigrir: *to lose weight*

manger: *to eat*

se maquiller: *to put makeup on*

marcher: *to walk*

mélanger: *to mix*

menacer: *to threaten*

mener: *to lead*

mentir: *to lie*

mettre*: *to put, to place*

se mettre à*: *to begin*

monter: *to climb, to go up, to get in*

nager: *to swim*

nettoyer: *to clean*

nuire*: *to be harmful, to harm*

obéir à: *to obey*

obliger: *to oblige, to compel*

obtenir*: *to obtain*

offrir*: *to offer*

oublier: *to forget*

ouvrir*: *to open*

pâlir: *to turn pale*

paraître*: *to appear*

parler: *to speak*

partager: *to share*

partir*: *to leave*

passer: *to spend, to pass*

payer: *to pay*

se peigner: *to comb one's hair*

peler: *to peel*

pendre: *to hang*

penser: *to think*

percer: *to pierce*

perdre: *to lose, to waste*

peser: *to weigh*

pincer: *to pinch*

placer: *to place*

plonger: *to dive*

polir: *to polish*

porter: *to wear, to carry*

pouvoir*: *to be able to*

prédire*: *to predict*

préférer: *to prefer*

prendre*: *to take*

préparer: *to prepare*

présenter: *to present, to introduce*

prévoir*: *to foresee, to anticipate*

prolonger: *to prolong*

se promener: *to take a walk, to stroll*

promettre*: *to promise*

prononcer: *to pronounce*

proposer: *to propose*

proscrire*: *to banish, to prohibit*

protéger: *to protect*

punir: *to punish*

quitter: *to leave, to abandon*

ramener: *to bring someone back*

ranger: *to put in order, to arrange*

se rappeler: *to remember*

rapporter: *to bring something back*

se raser: *to shave*

ravager: *to devastate, to ravage*

réagir: *to react*

recevoir*: *to receive*

recommencer: *to start again*

reconnaître*: *to recognize*

recouvrer*: *to recover*

récrire*: *to rewrite*

rédiger: *to draft, to write*

redire*: *to repeat*

réfléchir à: *to reflect, to think*

refuser: *to refuse*

regarder: *to watch*

rejeter: *to reject*

réjouir: *to rejoice, to delight*

relire*: *to reread*

remettre*: *to put back*

remmener: *to take someone back*

remplacer: *to replace*

remplir: *to fill*

remporter: *to take back, to take away*

rencontrer: *to meet*

rendre: *to give back, to return*

se rendre compte de: *to realize*

rendre visite à quelqu'un: *to pay a visit to someone (to visit someone)*

renforcer: *to reinforce*

renoncer: *to give up, to renounce*

rentrer: *to come back home*

repartir*: *to leave again*

répéter: *to repeat*

répondre à: *to answer*

se reposer: *to rest*

reprendre*: *to take (up) again, to continue*

ressentir*: *to feel*

retenir*: *to retain*

réunir: *to unite, to gather, to assemble*

réussir à: *to succeed*

se réveiller: *to wake up*

revenir*: *to come back*

rêver: *to dream*

revoir*: *to see again*

rire*: *to laugh*

rougir: *to blush*

savoir*: *to know*

sentir*: *to feel, to smell*

servir*: *to serve*

songer (à): *to dream, to think over*

sortir*: *to go out*

souffrir*: *to suffer*

soulager: *to relieve*

soumettre*: *to subject, to subjugate*

sourire*: *to smile*

se souvenir de*: *to remember*

suggérer: *to suggest*

surprendre*: *to surprise*

téléphoner: *to call*

tenir*: *to hold*

tomber: *to fall*

tondre: *to mow*

tracer: *to draw, to trace*

trahir: *to betray*

transmettre*: *to transmit*

travailler: *to work*

trouver: *to find*

tutoyer: *to address someone as "tu"*

unir: *to unite*

vendre: *to sell*

venger: *to avenge*

venir*: *to come*

vieillir: *to grow old*

visiter: *to visit (a place)*

voir*: *to see*

vouloir*: *to want*

vouvoyer: *to address someone as "vous"*

voyager: *to travel*

Appendix B

English-to-French Verb Glossary

• •

*H*ave you been talking away in French only to come to a complete halt because you're not quite sure of the French verb? This glossary can help. Just look up the English verb for the French translation. Voilà! (I add an asterisk after the French verb to help you identify the irregular verbs; you can then check out Appendix C on how to conjugate the irregular verb.)

to accommodate, to lodge: **loger**

to accuse: **accuser**

to act: **agir**

to address someone as "tu": **tutoyer**

to address someone as "vous": **vouvoyer**

to admire: **admirer**

to admit: **admettre***

to adore: **adorer**

to advance: **avancer**

to advise: **conseiller**

to allow, to let, to leave something/ someone: **laisser**

to announce, to declare: **annoncer**

to annoy, to irritate: **agacer**

to answer: **répondre à**

to appear, to seem: **apparaître***

to appear: **paraître***

to argue: **disputer**

to arrange: **arranger**

to arrive: **arriver**

to ask: **demander**

to attach: **attacher**

to attend: **assister à**

to avenge: **venger**

to banish, to prohibit: **proscrire***

to bathe: **se baigner**

to be: **être***

to be a question of, to be about: **s'agir de**

to be able to: **pouvoir***

to be bored: **s'ennuyer**

to be engaged: **se fiancer**

to be furious, to be in a rage: **enrager**

to be harmful, to harm: **nuire***

to be named: **s'appeler**

to be worried: **s' inquiéter**

to become: **devenir***

to become irritated: **s'énerver**

to begin: **commencer**

to begin: **se mettre à***

to believe: **croire***

to belong to: **appartenir***

to betray: **trahir**

to blush: **rougir**

to bother: **ennuyer**

to bother, to disturb: **déranger**

to bring someone: **amener**

to bring someone back: **ramener**

to bring something: **apporter**

to bring something back: **rapporter**

to brush: **se brosser**

to build: **bâtir**

to buy: **acheter**

to call: **appeler**

to call: **téléphoner**

to catch a glimpse of, to make out: **entrevoir***

to celebrate: **célébrer**

to change: **changer**

to chat, to talk: **bavarder**

to chill, to glaze: **glacer**

to choose: **choisir**

to clean: **nettoyer**

to climb, to go up, to get in: **monter**

to comb one's hair: **se peigner**

to come: **venir***

to come back: **revenir***

to come back home: **rentrer**

to commit: **commettre***

to compare: **comparer**

to compromise: **compromettre***

to conceive: **concevoir***

to consent: **consentir***

to construct, to build: **construire***

to contain: **contenir***

to continue: **continuer**

to contradict: **contredire***

to cook: **cuire***

to correct: **corriger**

to cover: **couvrir***

to cure, to heal: **guérir**

to cut: **couper**

to cut oneself: **se couper**

to dance: **danser**

to decide: **décider**

to defend: **défendre**

to denounce: **dénoncer**

to describe: **décrire***

to desire, to want: **désirer**

to detect, to reveal: **déceler**

to devastate, to ravage: **ravager**

to disappear: **disparaître***

to disappoint: **décevoir***

to discourage: **décourager**

to discover: **découvrir***

to displace: **déplacer**

to dive: **plonger**

to do, to make: **faire***

to do one's hair: **se coiffer**

to draft, to write: **rédiger**

to draw, to trace: **tracer**

to dream: **rêver**

to dream, to think over: **songer (à)**

to drink: **boire***

to drive: **conduire***

to eat: **manger**

to elect: **élire***

to encourage: **encourager**

to enter: **entrer**

to erase: **effacer**

to establish: **établir**

to exaggerate: **exagérer**

to excuse oneself: **s'excuser**

to fall: **tomber**

to fall asleep: **s'endormir***

to fear: **craindre***

to feel: **ressentir***

to feel, to smell: **sentir***

to feel: **se sentir***

to fill: **remplir**

to find: **trouver**

to finish: **finir**

to forbid: **défendre de**

to forbid: **interdire***

to force, to compel: **forcer**

to foresee, to anticipate: **prévoir***

to forget: **oublier**

to freeze: **congeler**

to freeze: **geler**

to frighten, to scare: **effrayer**

to gain weight: **grossir**

to get a divorce: **divorcer**

to get along: **s'entendre**

to get dressed: **s'habiller**

to get up: **se lever**

to give: **donner**

to give back, to return: **rendre**

to give up, to renounce: **renoncer**

to go: **aller***

to go down, to take down: **descendre**

to go out: **sortir***

to go to bed: **se coucher**

to grow (up): **grandir**

to grow old: **vieillir**

to hang: **pendre**

to hate: **détester**

to have: **avoir***

to have fun: **s'amuser**

to have to, to must, to owe: **devoir***

to hear: **entendre**

to hesitate: **hésiter**

to hide: **cacher**

to hold: **tenir***

to hope: **espérer**

to hurry: **se dépêcher**

to hurt, to wound: **blesser**

to inflict, to impose: **infliger**

to influence: **influencer**

to invite: **inviter**

to judge: **juger**

to kiss, to embrace: **embrasser**

to know: **connaître***

to know: **savoir***

to laugh: **rire***

to lead: **mener**

to learn: **apprendre***

to leave: **partir***

to leave, to abandon: **quitter**

to leave: **s'en aller***

to leave again: **repartir***

to lie: **mentir***

to like, to love: **aimer**

to listen: **écouter**

to live (somewhere), to reside: **habiter**

to look for: **chercher**

to lose weight: **maigrir**

to lose, to waste: **perdre**

to manage: **se débrouiller**

to meet: **rencontrer**

to melt: **fondre**

to mix: **mélanger**

to move: **bouger**

to move, to change residence: **déménager**

to mow: **tondre**

to notice: **s'apercevoir de***

to obey: **obéir à**

to oblige someone to do something, to force: **obliger**

to obtain: **obtenir**

to offer: **offrir***

to open: **ouvrir***

to pay: **payer**

to pay a visit to someone (to visit someone): **rendre visite à quelqu'un**

to peel: **peler**

to perceive, to notice: **apercevoir***

to pick, to gather: **cueillir***

to pierce: **percer**

to pinch: **pincer**

to place: **placer**

to play: **jouer**

to polish: **polir**

to predict: **prédire***

to prefer: **préférer**

to prepare: **préparer**

to present, to introduce: **présenter**

to prolong: **prolonger**

to promise: **promettre***

to pronounce: **prononcer**

to propose: **proposer**

to protect: **protéger**

to punish: **punir**

to put, to place: **mettre***

to put back: **remettre***

to put in order, to arrange: **ranger**

to put on makeup: **se maquiller**

to raise, to lift: **lever**

to react: **réagir**

to read: **lire***

to realize: **se rendre compte de**

to receive: **recevoir***

to recover: **recouvrer***

to reflect, to think: **réfléchir à**

to refuse: **refuser**

to reinforce: **renforcer**

to reject: **rejeter**

to rejoice, to delight: **réjouir**

to relieve: **soulager**

to remember: **se rappeler**

to remember: **se souvenir* de**

to repeat, to say again: **redire***

to repeat: **répéter**

to replace: **remplacer**

to require, to demand: **exiger**

to reread: **relire***

to rest: **se reposer**

to retain: **retenir***

to rewrite: **récrire***

to rock, to cradle: **bercer**

to say: **dire***

to see: **voir***

to see again: **revoir***

to sell: **vendre**

to send: **envoyer**

to serve: **servir***

to share: **partager**

to shave: **se raser**

to sign, to autograph: **dédicacer**

to sing: **chanter**

to sleep: **dormir***

to smile: **sourire***

to speak: **parler**

to spell: **épeler**

to spend, to pass: **passer**

to start again: **recommencer**

to stop oneself: **s'arrêter**

to study: **étudier**

to subject, to subjugate: **soumettre***

to succeed: **réussir à**

to suffer: **souffrir***

to suggest: **suggérer**

to surprise: **surprendre***

to sweep: **balayer**

to swim: **nager**

to swing: **balancer**

to take: **prendre***

to take back, to take away: **remporter**

to take someone along: **emmener**

to take someone back: **remmener**

to take something along: **emporter**

to take (up) again, to continue: **reprendre***

to take a walk, to stroll: **se promener**

to tan: **bronzer**

to teach: **enseigner**

to think: **penser**

to threaten: **menacer**

to throw: **jeter**

to transmit: **transmettre***

to travel: **voyager**

to try: **essayer**

to turn pale: **pâlir**

to understand: **comprendre***

to undertake: **entreprendre***

to unite: **unir**

to unite, to gather, to assemble: **réunir**

to use: **employer**

to visit (a place): **visiter**

to wait for: **attendre**

to wake up: **se réveiller**

to walk: **marcher**

to want: **vouloir***

to wash: **(se) laver**

to watch: **regarder**

to wear, to carry: **porter**

to weigh: **peser**

to welcome, to greet: **accueillir***

to wipe: **essuyer**

to wonder: **se demander**

to work: **travailler**

to write: **écrire***

Appendix C
Conjugating Common Irregular Verbs

• •

This appendix contains the most common irregular French verbs. Just remember the six pronouns (**je, tu, il/elle/on, nous, vous,** and **ils/elles**) and voila! You can use any verb in its correct form.

Acheter (to buy)

Present Participle: achetant; **Imperative:** achète, achetons, achetez

Present Indicative: achète, achètes, achète, achetons, achetez, achètent

Passé Composé: ai acheté, as acheté, a acheté, avons acheté, avez acheté, ont acheté

Imperfect: achetais, achetais, achetait, achetions, achetiez, achetaient

Pluperfect: avais acheté, avais acheté, avait acheté, avions acheté, aviez acheté, avaient acheté

Future: achèterai, achèteras, achètera, achèterons, achèterez, achèteront

Fut. Perfect: aurai acheté, auras acheté, aura acheté, aurons acheté, aurez acheté, auront acheté

Conditional: achèterais, achèterais, achèterait, achèterions, achèteriez, achèteraient

Past Cond.: aurais acheté, aurais acheté, aurait acheté, aurions acheté, auriez acheté, auraient acheté

Subjunctive: achète, achètes, achète, achetions, achetiez, achètent

Past Subj.: aie acheté, aies acheté, ait acheté, ayons acheté, ayez acheté, aient acheté

Verbs conjugated like **acheter** include **congeler** (*to freeze*), **déceler** (*to detect*), **geler** (*to freeze*), **lever** (*to raise*), **se lever** (*to get up*), **mener** (*to lead*) and all its compounds, and **peler** (*to peel*).

Aller (to go)

Present Participle: allant; **Imperative:** va, allons, allez

Present Indicative: vais, vas, va, allons, allez, vont

Passé Composé: suis allé(e), es allé(e), est allé(e), sommes allés(es), êtes allé(e)(s)(es), sont allés(es)

Imperfect: allais, allais, allait, allions, alliez, allaient

Pluperfect: étais allé(e), étais allé(e), était allé(e), étions allés(es), étiez allé(e)(s)(es), étaient allés(es)

Future: irai, iras, ira, irons, irez, iront

Fut. Perfect: serai allé(e), seras allé(e), sera allé(e), serons allés(es), serez allé(e)(s)(es), seront allés(es)

Conditional: irais, irais, irait, irions, iriez, iraient

Past Cond.: serais allé(e), serais allé(e), serait allé(e), serions allés(es), seriez allé(e)(s)(es), seraient allés(es)

Subjunctive: aille, ailles, aille, allions, alliez, aillent

Past Subj.: sois allé(e), sois allé(e), soit allé(e), soyons allés(es), vous soyez allé(e)(s)(es), soient allés (es)

Appeler (to call)

Present Participle: appelant; **Imperative:** appelle, appelons, appelez

Present Indicative: appelle, appelles, appelle, appelons, appelez, appellent

Passé Composé: ai appelé, as appelé, a appelé, avons appelé, avez appelé, ont appelé

Imperfect: appelais, appelais, appelait, appelions, appeliez, appelaient

Pluperfect: avais appelé, avais appelé, avait appelé, avions appelé, aviez appelé, avaient appelé

Future: appellerai, appelleras, appellera, appellerons, appellerez, appelleront

Fut. Perfect: aurai appelé, auras appelé, aura appelé, aurons appelé, aurez appelé, auront appelé

Conditional: appellerais, appellerais, appellerait, appellerions, appelleriez, appelleraient

Past Cond.: aurais appelé, aurais appelé, aurait appelé, aurions appelé, auriez appelé, auraient appelé

Subjunctive: appelle, appelles, appelle, appelions, appeliez, appellent

Past Subj.: aie appelé, aies appelé, ait appelé, ayons appelé, ayez appelé, aient appelé

Verbs conjugated like **appeler** include **épeler** (*to spell*), **jeter** (*to throw*), **(se) rappeler** (*to remember*), and **rejeter** (*to reject, to throw back*). For **jeter** and **rejeter,** double the **tt** where you double the **ll** in **appeler.**

Avoir (to have)

Present Participle: ayant; **Imperative:** aie, ayons, ayez

Present Indicative: ai, as, a, avons, avez, ont

Passé Composé: ai eu, as eu, a eu, avons eu, avez eu, ont eu

Imperfect: avais, avais, avait, avions, aviez, avaient

Pluperfect: avais eu, avais eu, avait eu, avions eu, aviez eu, avaient eu

Future: aurai, auras, aura, aurons, aurez, auront

Fut. Perfect: aurai eu, auras eu, aura eu, aurons eu, aurez eu, auront eu

Conditional: aurais, aurais, aurait, aurions, auriez, auraient

Past Cond.: aurais eu, aurais eu, aurait eu, aurions eu, auriez eu, auraient eu

Subjunctive: aie, aies, ait, ayons, ayez, aient

Past Subj.: aie eu, aies eu, ait eu, ayons eu, ayez eu, aient eu

Boire (to drink)

Present Participle: buvant; **Imperative:** bois, buvons, buvez

Present Indicative: bois, bois, boit, buvons, buvez, boivent

Passé Composé: ai bu, as bu, a bu, avons bu, avez bu, ont bu

Imperfect: buvais, buvais, buvait, buvions, buviez, buvaient

Pluperfect: avais bu, avais bu, avait bu, avions bu, aviez bu, avaient bu

Future: boirai, boiras, boira, boirons, boirez, boiront

Fut. Perfect: aurai bu, auras bu, aura bu, aurons bu, aurez bu, auront bu

Conditional: boirais, boirais, boirait, boirions, boiriez, boiraient

Past Cond.: aurais bu, aurais bu, aurait bu, aurions bu, auriez bu, auraient bu

Subjunctive: boive, boives, boive, buvions, buviez, boivent

Past Subj.: aie bu, aies bu, ait bu, ayons bu, ayez bu, aient bu

Commencer (to begin)

Present Participle: commençant; **Imperative:** commence, commençons, commencez

Present Indicative: commence, commences, commence, commençons, commencez, commencent

Passé Composé: ai commencé, as commencé, a commencé, avons commencé, avez commencé, ont commencé

Imperfect: commençais, commençais, commençait, commencions, commenciez, commençaient

Pluperfect: avais commencé, avais commencé, avait commencé, avions commencé, aviez commencé, avaient commencé

Future: commencerai, commenceras, commencera, commencerons, commencerez, commenceront

Fut. Perfect: aurai commencé, auras commencé, aura commencé, aurons commencé, aurez commencé, auront commencé

Conditional: commencerais, commencerais, commencerait, commencerions, commenceriez, commenceraient

Past Cond.: aurais commencé, aurais commencé, aurait commencé, aurions commencé, auriez commencé, auraient commencé

Subjunctive: commence, commences, commence, commencions, commenciez, commencent

Past Subj.: aie commencé, aies commencé, ait commencé, ayons commencé, ayez commencé, aient commencé

Verbs conjugated like **commencer** include **agacer** (*to irritate*), **annoncer** (*to announce*), **avancer** (*to advance*), **balancer** (*to swing*), **bercer** (*to cradle*), **dédicacer** (*to sign, to autograph*), **dénoncer** (*to denounce*), **déplacer** (*to transfer, to move*), **divorcer** (*to get divorced*), **effacer** (*to erase*), **(se) fiancer** (*to get engaged*), **forcer** (*to force*), **glacer** (*to freeze, to chill*), **influencer** (*to influence*), **menacer** (*to threaten*), **percer** (*to pierce*), **pincer** (*to pinch*), **placer** (*to place*), **prononcer** (*to pronounce*), **recommencer** (*to start again, to resume*), **remplacer** (*to replace*), **renforcer** (*to reinforce*), **renoncer** (*to give up*), and **tracer** (*to trace*).

Conduire (to drive)

Present Participle: conduisant; **Imperative:** conduis, conduisons, conduisez

Present Indicative: conduis, conduis, conduit, conduisons, conduisez, conduisent

Passé Composé: ai conduit, as conduit, a conduit, avons conduit, avez conduit, ont conduit

Imperfect: conduisais, conduisais, conduisait, conduisions, conduisiez, conduisaient

Pluperfect: avais conduit, avais conduit, avait conduit, avions conduit, aviez conduit, avaient conduit

Future: conduirai, conduiras, conduira, conduirons, conduirez, conduiront

Fut. Perfect: aurai conduit, auras conduit, aura conduit, aurons conduit, aurez conduit, auront conduit

Conditional: conduirais, conduirais, conduirait, conduirions, conduiriez, conduiraient

Past Cond.: aurais conduit, aurais conduit, aurait conduit, aurions conduit, auriez conduit, auraient conduit

Subjunctive: conduise, conduises, conduise, conduisions, conduisiez, conduisent

Past Subj.: aie conduit, aies conduit, ait conduit, ayons conduit, ayez conduit, aient conduit

Verbs conjugated like **conduire** include **construire** (*to build, to construct*), **cuire** (*to cook*), and **nuire** (*to harm*).

Connaître (to know)

Present Participle: connaissant; **Imperative:** connais, connaissons, connaissez

Present Indicative: connais, connais, connaît, connaissons, connaissez, connaissent

Passé Composé: ai connu, as connu, a connu, avons connu, avez connu, ont connu

Imperfect: connaissais, connaissais, connaissait, connaissions, connaissiez, connaissaient

Pluperfect: avais connu, avais connu, avait connu, avions connu, aviez connu, avaient connu

Future: connaîtrai, connaîtras, connaîtra, connaîtrons, connaîtrez, connaîtront

Fut. Perfect: aurai connu, auras connu, aura connu, aurons connu, aurez connu, auront connu

Conditional: connaîtrais, connaîtrais, connaîtrait, connaîtrions, connaîtriez, connaîtraient

Past Cond.: aurais connu, aurais connu, aurait connu, aurions connu, auriez connu, auraient connu

Subjunctive: connaisse, connaisses, connaisse, connaissions, connaissiez, connaissent

Past Subj.: aie connu, aies connu, ait connu, ayons connu, ayez connu, aient connu

Verbs conjugated like **connaître** include **apparaître** (*to appear, to seem*), **disparaître** (*to disappear*), **paraître** (*to seem, to appear*), and **reconnaître** (*to recognize*).

Craindre (to fear)
Present Participle: craignant; **Imperative:** crains, craignons, craignez

Present Indicative: crains, crains, craint, craignons, craignez, craignent

Passé Composé: ai craint, as craint, a craint, avons craint, avez craint, ont craint

Imperfect: craignais, craignais, craignait, craignions, craigniez, craignaient

Pluperfect: avais craint, avais craint, avait craint, avions craint, aviez craint, avaient craint

Future: craindrai, craindras, craindra, craindrons, craindrez, craindront

Fut. Perfect: aurai craint, auras craint, aura craint, aurons craint, aurez craint, auront craint

Conditional: craindrais, craindrais, craindrait, craindrions, craindriez, craindraient

Past Cond.: aurais craint, aurais craint, aurait craint, aurions craint, auriez craint, auraient craint

Subjunctive: craigne, craignes, craigne, craignions, craigniez, craignent

Past Subj.: aie craint, aies craint, ait craint, ayons craint, ayez craint, aient craint

Croire (to believe)
Present Participle: croyant; **Imperative:** crois, croyons, croyez

Present Indicative: crois, crois, croit, croyons, croyez, croient

Passé Composé: ai cru, as cru, a cru, avons cru, avez cru, ont cru

Imperfect: croyais, croyais, croyait, croyions, croyiez, croyaient

Pluperfect: avais cru, avais cru, avait cru, avions cru, aviez cru, avaient cru

Future: croirai, croiras, croira, croirons, croirez, croiront

Fut. Perfect: aurai cru, auras cru, aura cru, aurons cru, aurez cru, auront cru

Conditional: croirais, croirais, croirait, croirions, croiriez, croiraient

Past Cond.: aurais cru, aurais cru, aurait cru, aurions cru, auriez cru, auraient cru

Subjunctive: croie, croies, croie, croyions, croyiez, croient

Past Subj.: aie cru, aies cru, ait cru, ayons cru, ayez cru, aient cru

Devoir (to have to, must)

Present Participle: devant; **Imperative:** dois, devons, devez

Present Indicative: dois, dois, doit, devons, devez, doivent

Passé Composé: ai dû, as dû, a dû, avons dû, avez dû, ont dû

Imperfect: devais, devais, devait, devions, deviez, devaient

Pluperfect: avais dû, avais dû, avait dû, avions dû, aviez dû, avaient dû

Future: devrai, devras, devra, devrons, devrez, devront

Fut. Perfect: aurai dû, auras dû, aura dû, aurons dû, aurez dû, auront dû

Conditional: devrais, devrais, devrait, devrions, devriez, devraient

Past Cond.: aurais dû, aurais dû, aurait dû, aurions dû, auriez dû, auraient dû

Subjunctive: doive, doives, doive, devions, deviez, doivent

Past Subj.: aie dû, aies dû, ait dû, ayons dû, ayez dû, aient dû

Dire (to say)

Present Participle: disant; **Imperative:** dis, disons, dites

Present Indicative: dis, dis, dit, disons, dites, disent

Passé Composé: ai dit, as dit, a dit, avons dit, avez dit, ont dit

Imperfect: disais, disais, disait, disions, disiez, disaient

Pluperfect: avais dit, avais dit, avait dit, avions dit, aviez dit, avaient dit

Future: dirai, diras, dira, dirons, direz, diront

Fut. Perfect: aurai dit, auras dit, aura dit, aurons dit, aurez dit, auront dit

Conditional: dirais, dirais, dirait, dirions, diriez, diraient

Past Cond.: aurais dit, aurais dit, aurait dit, aurions dit, auriez dit, auraient dit

Subjunctive: dise, dises, dise, disions, disiez, disent

Past Subj.: aie dit, aies dit, ait dit, ayons dit, ayez dit, aient dit

Verbs conjugated like **dire** include **contredire*** (*to contradict*), **interdire*** (*to forbid*), **prédire*** (*to predict*), and **redire** (*to repeat*). *The **vous** form of the present indicative and the imperative ends in **-disez**. For example, **vous contredisez, vous interdisez,** and **vous prédisez.**

Écrire (to write)

Present Participle: écrivant; **Imperative:** écris, écrivons, écrivez

Present Indicative: écris, écris, écrit, écrivons, écrivez, écrivent

Passé Composé: ai écrit, as écrit, a écrit, avons écrit, avez écrit, ont écrit

Imperfect: écrivais, écrivais, écrivait, écrivions, écriviez, écrivaient

Pluperfect: avais écrit, avais écrit, avait écrit, avions écrit, aviez écrit, avaient écrit

Future: écrirai, écriras, écrira, écrirons, écrirez, écriront

Fut. Perfect: aurai écrit, auras écrit, aura écrit, aurons écrit, aurez écrit, auront écrit

Conditional: écrirais, écrirais, écrirait, écririons, écririez, écriraient

Past Cond.: aurais écrit, aurais écrit, aurait écrit, aurions écrit, auriez écrit, auraient écrit

Subjunctive: écrive, écrives, écrive, écrivions, écriviez, écrivent

Past Subj.: aie écrit, aies écrit, ait écrit, ayons écrit, ayez écrit, aient écrit

Verbs conjugated like **écrire** include **décrire** (*to discribe*), **prescrire** (*to prescribe*), **proscrire** (*to banish, to prohibit*), and **récrire** (*to rewrite*).

Espérer (to hope)

Present Participle: espérant; **Imperative:** espère, espérons, espérez

Present Indicative: espère, espères, espère, espérons, espérez, espèrent

Passé Composé: ai espéré, as espéré, a espéré, avons espéré, avez espéré, ont espéré

Imperfect: espérais, espérais, espérait, espérions, espériez, espéraient

Pluperfect: avais espéré, avais espéré, avait espéré, avions espéré, aviez espéré, avaient espéré

Future: espérerai, espéreras, espérera, espérerons, espérerez, espéreront

Fut. Perfect: aurai espéré, auras espéré, aura espéré, aurons espéré, aurez espéré, auront espéré

Conditional: espérerais, espérerais, espérerait, espérerions, espéreriez, espéreraient

Past Cond.: aurais espéré, aurais espéré, aurait espéré, aurions espéré, auriez espéré, auraient espéré

Subjunctive: espère, espères, espère, espérions, espériez, espèrent

Past Subj.: aie espéré, aies espéré, ait espéré, ayons espéré, ayez espéré, aient espéré

Verbs that are conjugated like **espérer** include **célébrer** (*to celebrate*), **exagérer** (*to exaggerate*), **(s') inquiéter** (*to worry*), **préférer** (*to prefer*), **protéger** (*to protect*), **répéter** (*to repeat*), and **suggérer** (*to suggest*). *Note:* **Espérer, préférer,** and **répéter** don't have a stem change in the future or conditional, but the rest of these verbs do. For example, the future and conditional of **célébrer** is **célèbrerai(s).**

Essayer (to try)

Present Participle: essayant; **Imperative:** essaie, essayons, essayez

Present Indicative: essaie, essaies, essaie, essayons, essayez, essaient

Passé Composé: ai essayé, as essayé, a essayé, avons essayé, avez essayé, ont essayé

Imperfect: essayais, essayais, essayait, essayions, essayiez, essayaient

Pluperfect: avais essayé, avais essayé, avait essayé, avions essayé, aviez essayé, avaient essayé

Future: essaierai, essaieras, essaiera, essaierons, essaierez, essaieront

Fut. Perfect: aurai essayé, auras essayé, aura essayé, aurons essayé, aurez essayé, auront essayé

Conditional: essaierais, essaierais, essaierait, essaierions, essaieriez, essaieraient

Past Cond.: aurais essayé, aurais essayé, aurait essayé, aurions essayé, auriez essayé, auraient essayé

Subjunctive: essaie, essaies, essaie, essayions, essayiez, essaient

Past Subj.: aie essayé, aies essayé, ait essayé, ayons essayé, ayez essayé, aient essayé

Verbs conjugated like **essayer** include **balayer** (*to sweep*), **effrayer** (*to frighten*), **employer** (*to use*), **ennuyer** (*to bother*), **(s') ennuyer** (*to be bored*), **envoyer*** (*to send*), **essuyer** (*to wipe*), **nettoyer** (*to clean*), **payer** (*to pay*), **tutoyer** (*to address someone in the **tu** form*), and **vouvoyer** (*to address someone in the **vous** form*). *The verb **envoyer** in the future and conditional stem changes to **enverr-**.

Être (to be)

Present Participle: étant; **Imperative:** sois, soyons, soyez

Present Indicative: suis, es, est, sommes, êtes, sont

Passé Composé: ai été, as été, a été, avons été, avez été, ont été

Imperfect: étais, étais, était, étions, étiez, étaient

Pluperfect: avais été, avais été, avait été, avions été, aviez été, avaient été

Future: serai, seras, sera, serons, serez, seront

Fut. Perfect: aurai été, auras été, aura été, aurons été, aurez été, auront été

Conditional: serais, serais, serait, serions, seriez, seraient

Past Cond.: aurais été, aurais été, aurait été, aurions été, auriez été, auraient été

Subjunctive: sois, sois, soit, soyons, soyez, soient

Past Subj.: aie été, aies été, ait été, ayons été, ayez été, aient été

Faire (to do, to make)

Present Participle: faisant; **Imperative:** fais, faisons, faites

Present Indicative: fais, fais, fait, faisons, faites, font

Passé Composé: ai fait, as fait, a fait, avons fait, avez fait, ont fait

Imperfect: faisais, faisais, faisait, faisions, faisiez, faisaient

Pluperfect: avais fait, avais fait, avait fait, avions fait, aviez fait, avaient fait

Future: ferai, feras, fera, ferons, ferez, feront

Fut. Perfect: aurai fait, auras fait, aura fait, aurons fait, aurez fait, auront fait

Conditional: ferais, ferais, ferait, ferions, feriez, feraient

Past Cond.: aurais fait, aurais fait, aurait fait, aurions fait, auriez fait, auraient fait

Subjunctive: fasse, fasses, fasse, fassions, fassiez, fassent

Past Subj.: aie fait, aies fait, ait fait, ayons fait, ayez fait, aient fait

Lire (to read)

Present Participle: lisant; **Imperative:** lis, lisons, lisez

Present Indicative: lis, lis, lit, lisons, lisez, lisent

Passé Composé: ai lu, as lu, a lu, avons lu, avez lu, ont lu

Imperfect: lisais, lisais, lisait, lisions, lisiez, lisaient

Pluperfect: avais lu, avais lu, avait lu, avions lu, aviez lu, avaient lu

Future: lirai, liras, lira, lirons, lirez, liront

Fut. Perfect: aurai lu, auras lu, aura lu, aurons lu, aurez lu, auront lu

Conditional: lirais, lirais, lirait, lirions, liriez, liraient

Past Cond.: aurais lu, aurais lu, aurait lu, aurions lu, auriez lu, auraient lu

Subjunctive: lise, lises, lise, lisions, lisiez, lisent

Past Subj.: aie lu, aies lu, ait lu, ayons lu, ayez lu, aient lu

Verbs conjugated like **lire** include **élire** (*to elect*) and **relire** (*to reread*).

Mettre (to put, to put on, to place)

Present Participle: mettant; **Imperative:** mets, mettons, mettez

Present Indicative: mets, mets, met, mettons, mettez, mettent

Passé Composé: ai mis, as mis, a mis, avons mis, avez mis, ont mis

Imperfect: mettais, mettais, mettait, mettions, mettiez, mettaient

Pluperfect: avais mis, avais mis, avait mis, avions mis, aviez mis, avaient mis

Future: mettrai, mettras, mettra, mettrons, mettrez, mettront

Fut. Perfect: aurai mis, auras mis, aura mis, aurons mis, aurez mis, auront mis

Conditional: mettrais, mettrais, mettrait, mettrions, mettriez, mettraient

Past Cond.: aurais mis, aurais mis, aurait mis, aurions mis, auriez mis, auraient mis

Subjunctive: mette, mettes, mette, mettions, mettiez, mettent

Past Subj.: aie mis, aies mis, ait mis, ayons mis, ayez mis, aient mis

Verbs conjugated like **mettre** include **admettre** (*to admit*), **commettre** (*to commit*), **compromettre** (*to compromise*), **promettre** (*to promise*), **remettre** (*to put something on again, to put something back*), **soumettre** (*to submit*), and **transmettre** (*to transmit*).

Ouvrir (to open)

Present Participle: ouvrant; **Imperative:** ouvre, ouvrons, ouvrez

Present Indicative: ouvre, ouvres, ouvre, ouvrons, ouvrez, ouvrent

Passé Composé: ai ouvert, as ouvert, a ouvert, avons ouvert, avez ouvert, ont ouvert

Imperfect: ouvrais, ouvrais, ouvrait, ouvrions, ouvriez, ouvraient

Pluperfect: avais ouvert, avais ouvert, avait ouvert, avions ouvert, aviez ouvert, avaient ouvert

Future: ouvrirai, ouvriras, ouvrira, ouvrirons, ouvrirez, ouvriront

Fut. Perfect: aurai ouvert, auras ouvert, aura ouvert, aurons ouvert, aurez ouvert, auront ouvert

Conditional: ouvrirais, ouvrirais, ouvrirait, ouvririons, ouvririez, ouvriraient

Past Cond.: aurais ouvert, aurais ouvert, aurait ouvert, aurions ouvert, auriez ouvert, auraient ouvert

Subjunctive: ouvre, ouvres, ouvre, ouvrions, ouvriez, ouvrent

Past Subj.: aie ouvert, aies ouvert, ait ouvert, ayons ouvert, ayez ouvert, aient ouvert

Verbs conjugated like **ouvrir** include **accueillir** (*to welcome*), **couvrir** (*to cover*), **cueillir** (*to pick, to gather*), **découvrir** (*to discover*), **offrir** (*to offer*), **recouvrer** (*to recover*), and **souffrir** (*to suffer*).

Partir (to leave)

Present Participle: partant; **Imperative:** pars, partons, partez

Present Indicative: pars, pars, part, partons, partez, partent

Passé Composé: suis parti(e), es parti(e), est parti(e), sommes partis(es), êtes parti(s)(e)(es), sont partis(es)

Imperfect: partais, partais, partait, partions, partiez, partaient

Pluperfect: étais parti(e), étais parti(e), était parti(e), étions partis(es), étiez parti(s)(e)(es), étaient partis(es)

Future: partirai, partiras, partira, partirons, partirez, partiront

Fut. Perfect: serai parti(e), seras parti(e), sera parti(e), serons partis(es), serez parti(s)(e)(es), seront partis(es)

Conditional: partirais, partirais, partirait, partirions, partiriez, partiraient

Past Cond.: serais parti(e), serais parti(e), serait parti(e), serions partis(es), seriez parti(s)(e)(es), seraient partis(es)

Subjunctive: parte, partes, parte, partions, partiez, partent

Past Subj.: sois parti(e), sois parti(e), soit parti(e), soyons partis(es), soyez parti(s)(e)(es), soient partis(es)

Verbs conjugated like **partir** include **consentir*** (*to consent*), **dormir*** (*to sleep*), **s'endormir** (*to fall asleep*), **mentir*** (*to lie*), **repartir** (*to leave again*), **ressentir*** (*to feel*), **se sentir** (*to feel, as in well or unwell*), **sentir*** (*to smell, to feel, to taste*), **servir*** (*to serve*), and **sortir** (*to go out*). *These verbs are conjugated with **avoir.**

Pouvoir (to be able to)
Present Participle: pouvant; **Imperative:** No imperative form

Present: peux, peux, peut, pouvons, pouvez, peuvent

Passé Composé: ai pu, as pu, a pu, avons pu, avez pu, ont pu

Imperfect: pouvais, pouvais, pouvait, pouvions, pouviez, pouvaient

Pluperfect: avais pu, avais pu, avait pu, avions pu, aviez pu, avaient pu

Future: pourrai, pourras, pourra, pourrons, pourrez, pourront

Fut. Perfect: aurai pu, auras pu, aura pu, aurons pu, aurez pu, auront pu

Conditional: pourrais, pourrais, pourrait, pourrions, pourriez, pourraient

Past Cond.: aurais pu, aurais pu, aurait pu, aurions pu, auriez pu, auraient pu

Subjunctive: puisse, puisses, puisse, puissions, puissiez, puissent

Past Subj.: aie pu, aies pu, ait pu, ayons pu, ayez pu, aient pu

Prendre (to take)
Present Participle: prenant; **Imperative:** prends, prenons, prenez

Present Indicative: prends, prends, prend, prenons, prenez, prennent

Passé Composé: ai pris, as pris, a pris, avons pris, avez pris, ont pris

Imperfect: prenais, prenais, prenait, prenions, preniez, prenaient

Pluperfect: avais pris, avais pris, avait pris, avions pris, aviez pris, avaient pris

Future: prendrai, prendras, prendra, prendrons, prendrez, prendront

Fut. Perfect: aurai pris, auras pris, aura pris, aurons pris, aurez pris, auront pris

Conditional: prendrais, prendrais, prendrait, prendrions, prendriez, prendraient

Past Cond.: aurais pris, aurais pris, aurait pris, aurions pris, auriez pris, auraient pris

Subjunctive: prenne, prennes, prenne, prenions, preniez, prennent

Past Subj.: aie pris, aies pris, ait pris, ayons pris, ayez pris, aient pris

Verbs conjugated like **prendre** include **apprendre** (*to learn*), **comprendre** (*to understand*), **entreprendre** (*to undertake*), **reprendre** (*to recapture*), and **surprendre** (*to surprise*).

Recevoir (to receive)
Present Participle: recevant; **Imperative:** reçois, recevons, recevez

Present Indicative: reçois, reçois, reçoit, recevons, recevez, reçoivent

Passé Composé: ai reçu, as reçu, a reçu, avons reçu, avez reçu, ont reçu

Imperfect: recevais, recevais, recevait, recevions, receviez, recevaient

Pluperfect: avais reçu, avais reçu, avait reçu, avions reçu, aviez reçu, avaient reçu

Future: recevrai, recevras, recevra, recevrons, recevrez, recevront

Fut. Perfect: aurai reçu, auras reçu, aura reçu, aurons reçu, aurez reçu, auront reçu

Conditional: recevrais, recevrais, recevrait, recevrions, recevriez, recevraient

Past Cond.: aurais reçu, aurais reçu, aurait reçu, aurions reçu, auriez reçu, auraient reçu

Subjunctive: reçoive, reçoives, reçoive, recevions, receviez, reçoivent

Past Subj.: aie reçu, aies reçu, ait reçu, ayons reçu, ayez reçu, aient reçu

Verbs conjugated like **recevoir** include **apercevoir** (*to perceive, to notice*), **concevoir** (*to conceive*), and **décevoir** (*to disappoint*).

Rire (to laugh)
Present Participle: riant; **Imperative:** ris, rions, riez

Present Indicative: ris, ris, rit, rions, riez, rient

Passé Composé: ai ri, as ri, a ri, avons ri, avez ri, ont ri

Imperfect: riais, riais, riait, riions, riiez, riaient

Pluperfect: avais ri, avais ri, avait ri, avions ri, aviez ri, avaient ri

Future: rirai, riras, rira, rirons, rirez, riront

Fut. Perfect: aurai ri, auras ri, aura ri, aurons ri, aurez ri, auront ri

Conditional: rirais, rirais, rirait, ririons, ririez, riraient

Past Cond.: aurais ri, aurais ri, aurait ri, aurions ri, auriez ri, auraient ri

Subjunctive: rie, ries, rie, riions, riiez, rient

Past Subj.: aie ri, aies ri, ait ri, ayons ri, ayez ri, aient ri

Verbs conjugated like **rire** include **sourire** (*to smile*).

Savoir (to know)

Present Participle: sachant; **Imperative:** sache, sachons, sachez

Present Indicative: sais, sais, sait, savons, savez, savent

Passé Composé: ai su, as su, a su, avons su, avez su, ont su

Imperfect: savais, savais, savait, savions, saviez, savaient

Pluperfect: avais su, avais su, avait su, avions su, aviez su, avaient su

Future: saurai, sauras, saura, saurons, saurez, sauront

Fut. Perfect: aurai su, auras su, aura su, aurons su, aurez su, auront su

Conditional: saurais, saurais, saurait, saurions, sauriez, sauraient

Past Cond.: aurais su, aurais su, aurait su, aurions su, auriez su, auraient su

Subjunctive: sache, saches, sache, sachions, sachiez, sachent

Past Subj.: aie su, aies su, ait su, ayons su, ayez su, aient su

Venir (to come)

Present Participle: venant; **Imperative:** viens, venons, venez

Present Indicative: viens, viens, vient, venons, venez, viennent

Passé Composé: suis venu(e), es venu(e), est venu(e), sommes venus(es), êtes venu(s)(e)(es), ils/elles sont venus(es)

Imperfect: venais, venais, venait, venions, veniez, venaient

Pluperfect: étais venu(e), étais venu(e), était venu(e), étions venus(es), étiez venu(s)(e)(es), étaient venus(es)

Future: viendrai, viendras, viendra, viendrons, viendrez, viendront

Fut. Perfect: serai venu(e), seras venu(e), sera venu(e), serons venus(es), serez venu(s)(e)(es), seront venus(es)

Conditional: viendrais, viendrais, viendrait, viendrions, viendriez, viendraient

Past Cond.: serais venu(e), serais venu(e), serait venu(e), serions venus(es), seriez venu(s)(e)(es), seraient venus(es)

Subjunctive: vienne, viennes, vienne, venions, veniez, viennent

Past Subj.: sois venu(e), sois venu(e), soit venu(e), soyons venus(es), soyez venu(s)(e)(es), soient venus(es)

Verbs conjugated like **venir** include **convenir** (*to be suitable*), **devenir** (*to become*), **intervenir** (*to intervene*), **parvenir** (*to reach, to manage*), **revenir** (*to come back*), **se souvenir** (*to remember*), and **survenir** (*to occur, to arise*).

Voir (to see)

Present Participle: voyant; **Imperative:** vois, voyons, voyez

Present Indicative: vois, vois, voit, voyons, voyez, voient

Passé Composé: ai vu, as vu, a vu, avons vu, avez vu, ont vu

Imperfect: voyais, voyais, voyait, voyions, voyiez, voyaient

Pluperfect: avais vu, avais vu, avait vu, avions vu, aviez vu, avaient vu

Future: verrai, verras, verra, verrons, verrez, verront

Fut. Perfect: aurai vu, auras vu, aura vu, aurons vu, aurez vu, auront vu

Conditional: verrais, verrais, verrait, verrions, verriez, verraient

Past Cond.: aurais vu, aurais vu, aurait vu, aurions vu, auriez vu, auraient vu

Subjunctive: voie, voies, voie, voyions, voyiez, voient

Past Subj.: aie vu, aies vu, ait vu, ayons vu, ayez vu, aient vu

Verbs conjugated like **voir** include **entrevoir** (*to catch a glimpse of*), **prévoir** (*to foresee*), and **revoir** (*to see again*).

Vouloir (to want)

Present Participle: voulant; **Imperative:** veuille, veuillons, veuillez

Present Indicative: veux, veux, veut, voulons, voulez, veulent

Passé Composé: ai voulu, as voulu, a voulu, avons voulu, avez voulu, ont voulu

Imperfect: voulais, voulais, voulait, voulions, vouliez, voulaient

Pluperfect: avais voulu, avais voulu, avait voulu, avions voulu, aviez voulu, avaient voulu

Future: voudrai, voudras, voudra, voudrons, voudrez, voudront

Fut. Perfect: aurai voulu, auras voulu, aura voulu, aurons voulu, aurez voulu, auront voulu

Conditional: voudrais, voudrais, voudrait, voudrions, voudriez, voudraient

Past Cond.: aurais voulu, aurais voulu, aurait voulu, aurions voulu, auriez voulu, auraient voulu

Subjunctive: veuille, veuilles, veuille, voulions, vouliez, veuillent

Past Subj.: aie voulu, aies voulu, ait voulu, ayons voulu, ayez voulu, aient voulu

Index

• A •

à (preposition), 10, 104
acheter (to buy), 33, 269
adjectives, present participle as, 70
adverbs, modifying actions with, 23–24
aller à (to go to), 103–104, 269–270
aller (to go), 12, 44, 101, 105–106, 219
amener (to bring someone somewhere), 252
answering questions, 79–86, 202
appeler (to call), 270
apporter (to bring something), 253
arriver (to arrive), 184
articles, 63, 104
assister à (to attend), 253–254
attending, 254
attendre (to wait for), 91, 245, 254
auxiliary verbs, 11, 72–73, 133. *See also* avoir (to have); être (to be)
avoir (to have)
  complete list of conjugations, 270–271
  expressions formed with, 113–115
  forming passé composé, 133–134, 139, 144, 146
  forming past conditional, 201, 202
  forming past subjunctive, 237, 238
  future perfect, 184
  imperative, 93
  imperfect, 148
  passé simple, 165
  past participle, 135
  present, 44
  present participle, 70, 73
  present subjunctive, 220

• B •

boire (to drink), 55, 165, 215, 271
boot verbs, 215–217
bringing someone versus bringing something, 252–253

• C •

carrying, 253
-cer endings, 31–32, 125
chercher (to look for), 245
commands, forming
  as imperative mood, 12
  irregular verbs, 92–94
  negative, 94–95
  pronominal verbs, 95–96
  regular verbs, 89–91
commencer (to begin), 31, 125, 271–272
compound tenses, 13
conditional mood, 12, 191–197
conduire (to drive), 272
conjugations. *See* present tense
connaître (to know people, places, things), 109, 110, 250, 272–273
could have/would have (past conditional tense), 201–206
could/would (present conditional tense), 191–197
craindre (to fear), 56, 273
croire (to believe), 56, 157, 216, 273–274

• D •

de (preposition), 10, 102–103, 104
demander (to ask), 246–247
dépenser (to spend money), 250
devoir (to have to, must), 12, 46, 157, 217, 274
dire (to say), 54, 166, 274

• E •

e (unaccented), 32–33
é (e with accent aigu), 34, 134
écouter (to listen to), 246
écrire (to write), 54, 275
elle, elles (she, it, they), 14, 80
emmener (to take someone along), 252
emporter (to take something along, to take out food), 253
en (some, any, from there, of them), 98
en (to, while, by, upon, etc.), 71
-er verb conjugations. *See also* parler (to speak)
  passé composé, 134
  passé simple, 164
  present, 18–20
espérer (to hope), 34, 275
essayer (to try), 36, 217, 276
est-ce que?, 79
-eter and -eler endings, as spelling-change verbs, 35
être en train de, 129
être (to be)
  complete list of conjugations, 276
  future perfect, 184
  imperative, 93
  imperfect, 121, 126, 148
  passé composé, 140–142
  passé simple, 165
  past conditional, 201, 202
  past subjunctive, 237, 238
  present, 44
  present participle, 70, 73
  present subjunctive, 220
étudier (to study), 125, 202, 213

• F •

faire (to do, to make), 12, 44, 115–117, 219, 277
falloir (to have to), 157
faux amis (misleadingly similar verbs), 254
finir (to finish)
  future, 174
  future perfect, 184
  imperative, 90
  imperfect, 122
  passé composé, 134
  passé simple, 164
  present, 20
  present conditional, 192
  present subjunctive, 212
future perfect tense, 183–188
future tense
  expressions used with, 179–180
  forming, 173–178
  immediate, 101–102
  variations from English usage, 178–179

• G •

geographical locations' gender, 106
-ger endings, 29–30, 125
gerunds, 12, 71–72

• H •

habitual actions. *See* imperfect tense
helping verbs, 11, 12, 45–46
hypothetical situations, 12, 130, 191, 196–197

• I •

idiomatic pronominal verbs, 65–67
il est. . . (it is. . .), 11
il faut. . . (it is. . .), 11
il, ils (he, it, they), 14, 80
imperative mood, 12. *See also* commands, forming
imperfect tense. *See also* past tense
  common expressions, 127
  compared to passé composé, 153–159
  definition, 121
  in hypothetical sentences, 203, 204
  irregular verbs, 123–126
  regular verbs, 121–123
  using, 126–130
impersonal verbs, 11
indicative mood, 12
indirect discourse, 197
infinitive mood, 12, 83–84, 85
infinitives
  endings for, 17
  immediate future tense, 101–102
  immediate past tense, 102
  negative, 85–86
interrupted actions, 129
intransitive verbs, 8–9, 245, 246–247
inversion of subject and verb (interrogatory), 79–83
-ir verb conjugations. *See also* finir (to finish)
  irregular -er-like forms, 49–50
  irregular "pseudo" forms, 47–48

irregular stems, 50–51
  passé composé, 134
  passé simple, 164
  present, 20–21
irregular verbs. *See also specific tenses; specific verbs*
  commonly used, 43–44
  definition, 8
  future, 177–178
  imperative, 92–94
  miscellaneous, 55–57
  passé composé, 135–138
  passé simple, 164–167
  present conditional, 194–195
  present subjunctive, 218–220
  useful groupings, 47–55
it is (il est and il faut), 11

• J •

je (I), 13
jeter (to throw), 35
jouer (to play), 111–112, 251

• K •

knowing, 250–251

• L •

la (her/it), 97
laisser (to leave alone, to leave something behind, or to allow), 12, 251
laver (to wash something or someone), 62
le (him/it), 97
leading, 252
leaving, 251
les (them, to them), 97
leur (to them), 97
linking verbs, 11
lire (to read), 54, 92, 277
lui (to him/her), 97
"ly" words. *See* adverbs

• M •

manger (to eat), 30, 125
me (me, to me), 97
mener (to lead), 252
mettre (to put, to place), 53, 277–278

• N •

ne . . . pas, placement of, 83–84, 85–86, 102, 186, 202
negative
  future perfect, 185
  of infinitives, 85–86
  by inversion, 85
  passé composé, 147–148
  past conditional, 202
  responding in, 83–84
n'est-ce pas?, 79
nouns, gerunds and participles, 70, 71
nous (we, us, to us), 90, 97

• O •

obéir (to obey), 247
on (one), 14, 80
orders, requests, directives. *See* commands, forming
ouvrir (to open), 49, 278

• P •

parler (to speak)
  future, 174
  imperative, 90
  imperfect, 122
  passé antérieur, 168
  passé composé, 134
  passé simple, 164
  present, 18
  present conditional, 192
  present subjunctive, 212
participles, as adjectives, 12
partir (to leave)
  complete list of conjugations, 278–279
  examples, 251
  passé antérieur, 168
  passé composé, 142
  past conditional, 202
  past subjunctive, 238
  present, 48
passé antérieur, 167–168
passé composé
  agreement of past participle, 138–140, 142
  compared to imperfect, 153–159
  forming, 133–138
  forming with either avoir or être, 146–147

forming with **être**, 140–142
forming with pronominal
	verbs, 143–145
interrogatorial inversion, 82
making negative, 147–148
when to use, 133
passé simple, 163–167
passer (to spend time doing...
	or to take an exam), 250
past conditional tense, 201–206
past participle
	agreement with object,
		138–140
	forming, 133–137
	forming passé simple from,
		164–166
	for past conditional, 201–202
past subjunctive tense, 237–240
past tense. *See also* imperfect
		tense; passé composé
	immediate, 102–103
	passé antérieur, 167–168
	passé simple, 163–167
	past conditional, 201–206
	pluperfect, 133, 148, 148–149
payer (to pay), 246
penser (to think of, to think
		about), 253–254
perfect subjunctive tense, 237
permettre (to allow), 247
personal mood verbs, 12
playing games versus
		instruments, 251
pluperfect tense, 133, 148,
		148–149, 203, 204
porter (to wear, to carry
		something), 253
pouvoir (to be able to), 12, 46,
		157, 219, 279
prendre (to take), 52, 92, 215,
		279–280
prepositions
	articles with, 10, 104
	with **avoir** (to have), 114
	with **faire** (to do, to make),
		115–117
	with **jouer** (to play), 111–112
	used for going and coming, 106
present conditional tense,
		191–197
present participle, 69–71, 72–73
present subjunctive tense
	compared to past subjunctive,
		239–240
	considering indefinite,
		doubtful, or subjective
		antecedents, 231–232

criteria for using, 223
expressing condition, time,
		concession, and
		consequence, 229–231
expressing doubt or
		uncertainty, 227–228
expressing emotion or
		judgment, 225–227
expressing opinion,
		necessity, and possibility,
		228–229
expressing will, wish,
		preference, and command,
		224–225
idiomatic expressions and
		commands, 232–233
irregular verbs, 218–220
regular irregular verbs,
		213–214
regular verbs, 211–213
stem change verbs, 215–217
present tense
	-er verb conjugations, 18–20
	in hypothetical sentences,
		203, 204
	-ir verb conjugations, 20–21
	-re verb conjugations, 21–23
	varieties of meaning, 17
pronominal verbs
	definition, 8, 61
	idiomatic, 65–67
	immediate future, 101
	in immediate past tense,
		102–103
	imperative, 95–96
	imperfect, 122
	interrogatorial inversion,
		81–82
	matching subject, 72–73
	passé composé, 143–145
	past subjunctive, 237, 238
	placement of **ne . . . pas**,
		83–84, 95
	reciprocal, 64–65
	reflexive, 61–63
pronouns, 13, 96–97, 97,
		138–139, 143, 144–145

• **Q** •

questions, asking and
		answering, 79–86, 202
quitter (to leave a place or
		person), 251

• **R** •

ramener (to bring someone
		back), 252
rapporter (to bring something
		back), 253
-re verb conjugations. *See also*
		vendre (to sell)
	irregular forms, 51–52, 54–55
	passé composé, 134
	passé simple, 164
	present, 21–23
recevoir (to receive),
		56, 216, 280
reciprocal pronominal verbs,
		64–65
reciprocal verbs, 8
reflexive pronominal verbs,
		61–63
reflexive pronouns, 61–62
reflexive verbs, 8
regarder (to look at, to watch),
		246
regret, missed opportunity,
		expressing, 201, 203
regular verbs. *See also specific
		tenses; specific verbs*
	definition, 7
	future, 173–174
	gerunds, 71–72
	imperative, 89–91
	passé simple, 164
	past participle, 73–74
	present, 17–25
	present conditional, 191–194
	present participle, 69–70
	present subjunctive, 211–213,
		213–214
remmener (to take someone
		back), 252
remporter (to take back or to
		take away), 253
rendre (to return something),
		252
rendre visite à (to pay a
		visit to), 249
rentrer (to return home), 252
répondre (to answer), 247
requests, directives, orders.
		See commands, forming
retourner (to return), 252
returning home, returning
		something, 252
revenir (to come back), 252
rire (to laugh), 280–281

• S •

s' and se reflexive verbs, 61–63
savoir (to know facts, how to
    do something), 281
  examples, 250
  imperative, 93
  imperfect versus passé
    composé, 157
  present, 110
  present participle, 70
  present subjunctive, 219
se coucher (to go to bed), 143
se laver (to wash oneself),
    62, 143–144
se lever (to get up), 95, 202, 238
se promener (to take a walk/
    a stroll), 122
se réveiller (to wake up), 185
second person pronouns, 13
semi-auxiliary verbs, 12
sentences, forming
  with helping verbs plus
    infinitives, 46–47
  with subject, verb, and
    adverb, 24–25, 38–39
s'habiller (to dress oneself/
    to get dressed), 62, 95
si (if)
  with imperfect, 130, 196–197,
    203, 204
  for past conditional, 203–206
  with pluperfect, 148, 203, 204
  with present, 203, 204
  for present conditional,
    196–197
simultaneity, expressing, 129
spelling-change verbs
  -cer endings, 31–32
  definition, 7, 29
  e as mute or silent, 32–33
  é in second to last
    syllable, 34
  -eter and -eler endings, 35
  future, 175–176
  -ger endings, 29–30, 125

present conditional, 193–194
singular and plural, 13
when to use, 13
-yer endings, 36–37, 193, 217
spending time versus money,
    250
stem change verbs, present
    subjunctive, 215–217
subject-verb inversion
    (interrogatory), 79–83
subjunctive mood. *See also*
    present subjunctive tense
  definition, 12
  past subjunctive tense,
    237–240
suggestions and wishes,
    expressing, 130, 191,
    195–196

• T •

taking someone versus taking
    (back) something, 252–253
te (you, to you), 97
téléphoner (to telephone,
    to call), 247
tenses. *See also specific tenses*
  simple and compound, 13
  thinking or thinking about,
    253–254
third person pronouns, 13
transitive verbs, 8–9, 245,
    245–246
tu (familiar you), 90

• V •

vendre (to sell)
  future, 174
  imperfect, 122
  passé composé, 134
  passé simple, 164
  present, 22
  present conditional, 192
  present subjunctive, 212

venir de (to come back from),
    104
venir (to come), 281–282
  immediate future tense,
    102, 105–106
  immediate past tense, 102
  passé simple, 167
  present, 50
  present subjunctive, 216
verbs. *See also* irregular verbs
  classifying, 8–11
  ten most frequently
    mistranslated,
    249–254
  ten most frequently misused
    as transitive or intransitive,
    245–247
  transitive and intransitive,
    8–9
  types, 7–8
verbs, English-to-French
    glossary, 263–268
verbs, French-to-English
    glossary, 257–262
visiting places versus persons,
    249
voir (to see), 56, 238, 282
vouloir (to want, to want to),
    12, 46, 93, 157, 219, 282
vous (formal you, to you),
    90, 97
vowels, separating with t, 80

• W •

waiting for, 254
wishes and suggestions,
    expressing, 130, 191,
    195–196

• Y •

y (there, in it), 98
-yer endings, 36–37, 193, 217

BUSINESS, CAREERS & PERSONAL FINANCE

0-7645-5307-0

0-7645-5331-3 *†

Also available:

📖 Accounting For Dummies †
0-7645-5314-3

📖 Business Plans Kit For Dummies †
0-7645-5365-8

📖 Cover Letters For Dummies
0-7645-5224-4

📖 Frugal Living For Dummies
0-7645-5403-4

📖 Leadership For Dummies
0-7645-5176-0

📖 Managing For Dummies
0-7645-1771-6

📖 Marketing For Dummies
0-7645-5600-2

📖 Personal Finance For Dummies *
0-7645-2590-5

📖 Project Management For Dummies
0-7645-5283-X

📖 Resumes For Dummies †
0-7645-5471-9

📖 Selling For Dummies
0-7645-5363-1

📖 Small Business Kit For Dummies *†
0-7645-5093-4

HOME & BUSINESS COMPUTER BASICS

0-7645-4074-2

0-7645-3758-X

Also available:

📖 ACT! 6 For Dummies
0-7645-2645-6

📖 iLife '04 All-in-One Desk Reference
For Dummies
0-7645-7347-0

📖 iPAQ For Dummies
0-7645-6769-1

📖 Mac OS X Panther Timesaving
Techniques For Dummies
0-7645-5812-9

📖 Macs For Dummies
0-7645-5656-8

📖 Microsoft Money 2004 For Dummies
0-7645-4195-1

📖 Office 2003 All-in-One Desk Reference
For Dummies
0-7645-3883-7

📖 Outlook 2003 For Dummies
0-7645-3759-8

📖 PCs For Dummies
0-7645-4074-2

📖 TiVo For Dummies
0-7645-6923-6

📖 Upgrading and Fixing PCs For Dummies
0-7645-1665-5

📖 Windows XP Timesaving Techniques
For Dummies
0-7645-3748-2

FOOD, HOME, GARDEN, HOBBIES, MUSIC & PETS

0-7645-5295-3

0-7645-5232-5

Also available:

📖 Bass Guitar For Dummies
0-7645-2487-9

📖 Diabetes Cookbook For Dummies
0-7645-5230-9

📖 Gardening For Dummies *
0-7645-5130-2

📖 Guitar For Dummies
0-7645-5106-X

📖 Holiday Decorating For Dummies
0-7645-2570-0

📖 Home Improvement All-in-One
For Dummies
0-7645-5680-0

📖 Knitting For Dummies
0-7645-5395-X

📖 Piano For Dummies
0-7645-5105-1

📖 Puppies For Dummies
0-7645-5255-4

📖 Scrapbooking For Dummies
0-7645-7208-3

📖 Senior Dogs For Dummies
0-7645-5818-8

📖 Singing For Dummies
0-7645-2475-5

📖 30-Minute Meals For Dummies
0-7645-2589-1

INTERNET & DIGITAL MEDIA

0-7645-1664-7

0-7645-6924-4

Also available:

📖 2005 Online Shopping Directory
For Dummies
0-7645-7495-7

📖 CD & DVD Recording For Dummies
0-7645-5956-7

📖 eBay For Dummies
0-7645-5654-1

📖 Fighting Spam For Dummies
0-7645-5965-6

📖 Genealogy Online For Dummies
0-7645-5964-8

📖 Google For Dummies
0-7645-4420-9

📖 Home Recording For Musicians
For Dummies
0-7645-1634-5

📖 The Internet For Dummies
0-7645-4173-0

📖 iPod & iTunes For Dummies
0-7645-7772-7

📖 Preventing Identity Theft For Dummies
0-7645-7336-5

📖 Pro Tools All-in-One Desk Reference
For Dummies
0-7645-5714-9

📖 Roxio Easy Media Creator For Dummies
0-7645-7131-1

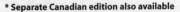

* Separate Canadian edition also available
† Separate U.K. edition also available

SPORTS, FITNESS, PARENTING, RELIGION & SPIRITUALITY

0-7645-5146-9

0-7645-5418-2

Also available:
- Adoption For Dummies
  0-7645-5488-3
- Basketball For Dummies
  0-7645-5248-1
- The Bible For Dummies
  0-7645-5296-1
- Buddhism For Dummies
  0-7645-5359-3
- Catholicism For Dummies
  0-7645-5391-7
- Hockey For Dummies
  0-7645-5228-7

- Judaism For Dummies
  0-7645-5299-6
- Martial Arts For Dummies
  0-7645-5358-5
- Pilates For Dummies
  0-7645-5397-6
- Religion For Dummies
  0-7645-5264-3
- Teaching Kids to Read For Dummies
  0-7645-4043-2
- Weight Training For Dummies
  0-7645-5168-X
- Yoga For Dummies
  0-7645-5117-5

TRAVEL

0-7645-5438-7

0-7645-5453-0

Also available:
- Alaska For Dummies
  0-7645-1761-9
- Arizona For Dummies
  0-7645-6938-4
- Cancún and the Yucatán For Dummies
  0-7645-2437-2
- Cruise Vacations For Dummies
  0-7645-6941-4
- Europe For Dummies
  0-7645-5456-5
- Ireland For Dummies
  0-7645-5455-7

- Las Vegas For Dummies
  0-7645-5448-4
- London For Dummies
  0-7645-4277-X
- New York City For Dummies
  0-7645-6945-7
- Paris For Dummies
  0-7645-5494-8
- RV Vacations For Dummies
  0-7645-5443-3
- Walt Disney World & Orlando For Dummies
  0-7645-6943-0

GRAPHICS, DESIGN & WEB DEVELOPMENT

0-7645-4345-8

0-7645-5589-8

Also available:
- Adobe Acrobat 6 PDF For Dummies
  0-7645-3760-1
- Building a Web Site For Dummies
  0-7645-7144-3
- Dreamweaver MX 2004 For Dummies
  0-7645-4342-3
- FrontPage 2003 For Dummies
  0-7645-3882-9
- HTML 4 For Dummies
  0-7645-1995-6
- Illustrator cs For Dummies
  0-7645-4084-X

- Macromedia Flash MX 2004 For Dummies
  0-7645-4358-X
- Photoshop 7 All-in-One Desk Reference
  For Dummies
  0-7645-1667-1
- Photoshop cs Timesaving Techniques
  For Dummies
  0-7645-6782-9
- PHP 5 For Dummies
  0-7645-4166-8
- PowerPoint 2003 For Dummies
  0-7645-3908-6
- QuarkXPress 6 For Dummies
  0-7645-2593-X

NETWORKING, SECURITY, PROGRAMMING & DATABASES

0-7645-6852-3

0-7645-5784-X

Also available:
- A+ Certification For Dummies
  0-7645-4187-0
- Access 2003 All-in-One Desk Reference
  For Dummies
  0-7645-3988-4
- Beginning Programming For Dummies
  0-7645-4997-9
- C For Dummies
  0-7645-7068-4
- Firewalls For Dummies
  0-7645-4048-3
- Home Networking For Dummies
  0-7645-42796

- Network Security For Dummies
  0-7645-1679-5
- Networking For Dummies
  0-7645-1677-9
- TCP/IP For Dummies
  0-7645-1760-0
- VBA For Dummies
  0-7645-3989-2
- Wireless All In-One Desk Reference
  For Dummies
  0-7645-7496-5
- Wireless Home Networking For Dummies
  0-7645-3910-8

HEALTH & SELF-HELP

0-7645-6820-5 *†

0-7645-2566-2

Also available:

- Alzheimer's For Dummies
  0-7645-3899-3
- Asthma For Dummies
  0-7645-4233-8
- Controlling Cholesterol For Dummies
  0-7645-5440-9
- Depression For Dummies
  0-7645-3900-0
- Dieting For Dummies
  0-7645-4149-8
- Fertility For Dummies
  0-7645-2549-2
- Fibromyalgia For Dummies
  0-7645-5441-7

- Improving Your Memory For Dummies
  0-7645-5435-2
- Pregnancy For Dummies †
  0-7645-4483-7
- Quitting Smoking For Dummies
  0-7645-2629-4
- Relationships For Dummies
  0-7645-5384-4
- Thyroid For Dummies
  0-7645-5385-2

EDUCATION, HISTORY, REFERENCE & TEST PREPARATION

0-7645-5194-9

0-7645-4186-2

Also available:

- Algebra For Dummies
  0-7645-5325-9
- British History For Dummies
  0-7645-7021-8
- Calculus For Dummies
  0-7645-2498-4
- English Grammar For Dummies
  0-7645-5322-4
- Forensics For Dummies
  0-7645-5580-4
- The GMAT For Dummies
  0-7645-5251-1
- Inglés Para Dummies
  0-7645-5427-1

- Italian For Dummies
  0-7645-5196-5
- Latin For Dummies
  0-7645-5431-X
- Lewis & Clark For Dummies
  0-7645-2545-X
- Research Papers For Dummies
  0-7645-5426-3
- The SAT I For Dummies
  0-7645-7193-1
- Science Fair Projects For Dummies
  0-7645-5460-3
- U.S. History For Dummies
  0-7645-5249-X

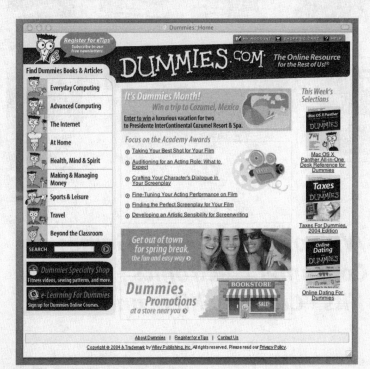

Get smart @ dummies.com®

- **Find a full list of Dummies titles**
- **Look into loads of FREE on-site articles**
- **Sign up for FREE eTips e-mailed to you weekly**
- **See what other products carry the Dummies name**
- **Shop directly from the Dummies bookstore**
- **Enter to win new prizes every month!**

* Separate Canadian edition also available
† Separate U.K. edition also available

Available wherever books are sold. For more information or to order direct: U.S. customers visit www.dummies.com or call 1-877-762-2974.
U.K. customers visit www.wileyeurope.com or call 0800 243407. Canadian customers visit www.wiley.ca or call 1-800-567-4797.